The ICT Handbook
for Primary Teachers

The ICT Handbook for Primary Teachers will help all those involved in primary education, whether in training, teaching or leadership roles, to develop the ICT knowledge, understanding and skills required to enhance children's learning in the classroom.

Covering theory and practise this essential handbook explores and outlines the usefulness of ICT in a range of primary contexts, and advice is offered on assessing whether ICT is preferable to other approaches for 'enhancing learning'. With additional online resources providing activities, multimedia resources and further reading, the book covers:

- statutory requirements for using ICT in the curriculum at all levels
- using ICT in core curriculum subjects and in cross-curricular contexts, referring to key PNS framework objectives
- advice on incorporating a range of ICT resources into children's learning
- different models of e-learning (handheld devices, interactive whiteboards, the Internet)
- how ICT can be used to help pupils with special educational needs
- using ICT for planning, delivery, assessment and recording.

This book is an indispensible guide to ICT for students on PGCE, BEd and undergraduate teaching courses, along with practising teachers, SENCOs, ICT coordinators and school leaders.

David Hall is senior lecturer in Education and ICT at University College Birmingham, he runs the website www.primaryict.org.uk and offers training courses to schools in ICT.

The ICT Handbook
for Primary Teachers

A guide for students and professionals

David Hall

Routledge
Taylor & Francis Group

LONDON AND NEW YORK

This edition published 2010
by Routledge
2 Park Square, Milton Park, Abingdon, Oxon OX14 4RN

Simultaneously published in the USA and Canada
by Routledge
270 Madison Avenue, New York, NY 10016

Routledge is an imprint of the Taylor & Francis Group, an informa business

© 2010 David Hall

Typeset in Bembo by
HWA Text and Data Management, London
Printed and bound in Great Britain by
The MPG Books Group

British Library Cataloguing in Publication Data
A catalogue record for this book is available from the British Library

Library of Congress Cataloging-in-Publication Data
Hall, David.
  The ICT handbook for primary teachers : a guide for students and professionals / David Hall.
    p. cm.
  Includes bibliographical references.
  1. Computer-assisted instruction – Great Britain.   2. Information technology – Study and
  teaching (Elementary) – Great Britain.   3. Elementary school teaching – Great Britain –
  Computer network resources.   I. Title.
  LB1028.5.H3135 2010
  371.33´4--dc22   2009025346

ISBN10: 0-415-55808-5 (hbk)
ISBN10: 0-415-55809-3 (pbk)
ISBN10: 0-203-86293-7 (ebk)

ISBN13: 978-0-415-55808-2 (hbk)
ISBN13: 978-0-415-55809-9 (pbk)
ISBN13: 978-0-203-86293-3 (ebk)

Contents

Acknowledgements

The author would like to thank all the people who contributed to the content of this book and in particular:

Alison Carter – Longwill School for the Deaf, Birmingham
Bharti Sisodia – Braidwood School for the Deaf, Birmingham
FutureLab (www.futurelab.org.uk)
Joanne Walker – Solihull Inclusion Support Service (Sensory Team)
Newland St. John's Primary School
Net Media Education (www.netmediaeducation.com)
Shaldon Primary School
Tameside Authority (www.teachingandlearningtameside.net/ict)

Feedback

As the reader of this book, *you* are the most important critic and commentator. Your opinion is extremely valuable no matter what it happens to be. In order to continually improve this book in future revisions, please let the author know what you have found interesting and how the content can be improved.
Send an email to: office@primaryict.org.uk.

Permissions and copyright notices

1

Introduction

Aim of the book

Technology is a key factor in everyday life, yet many opportunities for its use in children's education and wider social development are often missed.

In his 2008 review of the primary curriculum, Sir Jim Rose reported that, despite the increased emphasis and spending on technology in schools, the benefits are still not fully realised. As one teacher reported, 'ICT is not working hard enough to support learning or to help us manage the curriculum'. Rose recommends that ICT be given increased priority because it has 'the unique capacity and potential for developing and enlivening all domains of learning' (Rose, 2008: 43).

This book supports the view of Jim Rose and aims to help you to develop the ICT knowledge, understanding and skills required to enhance the teaching and learning of children and the administration and management in primary schools (and the foundation stage).

A promotion of the use of technology within learning environments can only be successful if practitioners in the field have a clear idea of its benefits and are confident in its use. These are the issues which this book aims to address. The book is informed by contemporary issues, best practice in schools and the latest government initiatives.

By the end of the book you will be better positioned to:

- recognise the statutory requirements for using ICT in the National Curriculum and the early years foundation stage;

- understand the many ways in which ICT can enhance children's learning in all curriculum subjects;

- incorporate a range of ICT resources (software, hardware and the Internet) into children's learning activities;

- identify a number of approaches ('models') to e-learning;

- appreciate the diversity of available ICT resources and assistive technology that can be used to support children with special educational needs (SEN);

- provide opportunities for extended learning using a learning platform;

- make effective use of ICT in the planning, delivery, assessment and recording of learning;

- effectively manage and lead the improvement of a school's ICT capability (and achieve the Becta ICT Mark).

Who is this book for?

The book is built around the notion that successful implementation of ICT in a school depends upon the identification, management and operation of a number of key processes. It also maintains that success depends not only on good leadership but also on the involvement of all stakeholders – teachers, teaching assistants, pupils, subject heads, technicians, SENCO, ICT coordinators and the head/deputy head teacher. There is therefore something in the book for all practitioners in primary schools and the early years foundation stage. It is also suitable for trainee teachers on primary PGCE, BEd and SCITT programmes, students of Education, ICT, Early Years and Early Childhood Studies degrees and local authority ICT advisers.

What does the book cover?

The development of ICT in UK schools

Offers a short, historical perspective on the use of ICT in schools since the early 1970s in terms of the resources deployed and associated developments in the school curriculum.

ICT in the National Curriculum

Examines the National Curriculum for ICT in terms of the knowledge, skills and understanding which should be gained in primary school and the attainment targets against which these are measured. This chapter presents some initial ideas for ICT activities and resources, relating them to the National Curriculum and to the QCA schemes of work.

Using ICT to enhance literacy, numeracy and science

Two chapters that deal with the many ways in which ICT resources, used in carefully planned activities, can enhance children's learning in the core National Curriculum subjects. Emphasis is placed on the achievement of desired learning outcomes rather than simply the motivational effect of technology. The reader will be invited to participate in a variety of activities (via the author's website), carefully reflecting on each. The aim is to ascertain when and why ICT-based activities might be comparable, or indeed preferable, to conventional approaches.

ICT in non-core subjects

Follows on from the core subjects and, aside from considering the importance of ICT in each discrete subject, it introduces the notion of a cross-curricular approach to teaching, learning and assessing. In this chapter the emphasis switches toward the 'reader as researcher' and promotes an exploratory approach to the discovery of appropriate ICT 'tools' to use in other areas of the curriculum.

Models of e-learning

Case studies in primary schools throughout the UK reveal distinct differences in the preferred approach to the use of ICT in the delivery and facilitation of learning. This chapter compares and contrasts these 'models' of e-learning and seeks to expose the strengths and weaknesses of each. It also looks at the government's e-strategy for deploying learning platforms and learning spaces.

ICT and special educational needs

Investigates strategies for using ICT to support learners with a wide range of learning needs, including: communication and interaction; cognition and learning; behavioural, emotional and social difficulties; sensory, physical and medical; physical disabilities; English as an additional language (EAL); and gifted and talented (G&T).

ICT management and leadership

Leadership is a crucial component in the effective procurement and application of ICT in schools. This chapter provides knowledge and skills for those with educational management roles and ICT responsibilities. It will help them to make informed decisions about the purchasing and implementation of ICT resources and activities and will consider a range of methods which will help in using ICT effectively in strategic planning, management, and leadership at all levels.

ICT resources

Outlines a process for identifying, selecting and managing software, hardware and web-based resources (including individual and aggregate purchasing). It also addresses the need to properly evaluate ICT resources before using them with children and before committing to buy. A range of possible suppliers is identified and, in addition, the potential for using open source software is explored.

How does this book compare to others?

There are of course other books on the topic of ICT though many have a much narrower focus and lack the practical detail offered in this 'essential' handbook. It is a well illustrated publication which offers:

■ a broad yet detailed coverage of all the important ICT issues;
■ an unusual balance between practical advice and academic rigour;
■ access to lots of resources in electronic format;
■ listings of important publications and suppliers.

Supplementary materials

The book is supported with a number of activities, some of which require supplementary materials. These are available from the PrimaryICT website at www.primaryict.org.uk/roict.htm.

 Activity

The activities, which include sample ICT resources, readings, presentations, videos, and audio excerpts, are highlighted by this laptop icon.

The activities are optional but offer you the opportunity to explore some of the issues in more detail.

ICT training

Readers who wish to take the next step and undertake some simple training, at their own pace and at very low cost are invited to check out the online programme of short e-courses at www.primaryict.org.uk.

Hyperlinks

Throughout the book you will find a number of hyperlinks to useful websites. Whilst the future stability of these links cannot be guaranteed, it is better that they are included rather than omitted.

You can usually find your way to the intended information via the root of the site if the full path doesn't work.

A final thought before you begin the book

Imagine that the head of your primary school has provided you with a sum of money to spend on ICT equipment which is to be used to support the whole curriculum. The amount is limited and you certainly can't afford everything that you would like. What would you purchase and what justification could you provide? Would you consider free software? How would you go about teaching ICT and embedding it into the curriculum? You might like to consider these questions whilst reading the book and, by the end, you should have most of the answers. Read on ...

2

The development of
ICT in UK schools

A brief history of computing in schools

As long ago as the early 1970s, educational researchers could appreciate that the system of didactic teaching was about to undergo a transformation. The notion that most learning is the result of teaching was, even then, an illusion. The reasons for this are many but the advent and steady development of technology has certainly played a major part.

Many teachers once feared that there was a danger of the machine replacing them in the classroom. It is hardly surprising that they have been ambivalent about these devices; but the mood is ever-changing and the current model of computing in schools is one of the computer and other ICT resources as tools, rather than as teaching systems, enhancing learning rather than leading it.

The first computer terminals appeared in schools in 1970 in the guise of mini-computers. However, these were very much the preserve of administrators. By 1982 most primary schools had at least one primitive computer for the purpose of educating children (usually the BBC B model). During that decade, computing began to permeate into the curriculum in some schools under the heading of Curriculum Science.

Personal computers (PCs), in the desktop format with which we are now familiar, were available in the mid-1980s though they were prohibitively costly (£2000-£3000 each), suffered from a lack of available software and ran using pre-Windows operating systems which were not particularly user friendly.

When the National Curriculum was introduced in 1988, technology was included as a subject in its own right. It wasn't until the mid-1990s however that the subject made any real impact and 1994/95 marked an important milestone – the introduction of the Windows 95 operating system and the formation of the World Wide Web Consortium (W3C). It was around this time that the PC was marketed to the public and began its real journey as an educational tool both in school and at home.

In 1997 the cost of computing was already falling steadily and the projection was that it would continue to do so. The prospect of realising the potential benefits of information and communication technology (ICT) became a reality and the government announced plans to encourage its widespread use by equipping schools with modern ICT facilities, creating a National Grid for Learning (NGfL) and providing organised training for teachers.

One year later the British Educational Communications and Technology Agency (Becta) was formed as an agency of the Department for Education and Skills (DfES). It is the government's lead partner in the strategic development and delivery of its e-strategy for schools and oversees the procurement of all ICT equipment. Becta is one of a number of key websites which this book recommends as a provider of information and advice (www.becta.org.uk).

At the turn of the century, ICT became a National Curriculum subject both as a discrete topic and as a means of supporting and enhancing learning across all subjects (including the newly introduced national literacy and numeracy strategies). The government also established Regional Broadband Consortia (RBC) which are consortia of local authorities that procure cost-effective broadband connectivity for schools in England. There are 10 RBCs covering 139 of the 150 local authorities (11 authorities have opted out of the scheme). All of the RBCs and some of the 'opt-out' authorities are interconnected via the SuperJANET backbone.

The first decade of the new millennium has witnessed significant development in all aspects of ICT. The range of available resources has increased exponentially whilst the incurred costs have fallen commensurately. Realistic funding has provided the opportunity for the government to realise its aims; equipping schools with networked computing and Internet connectivity, training staff and providing many initiatives and projects to help schools to become 'e-enabled'. The government has invested £5billion in schools' ICT since 1997, with another £837million earmarked over the three-year period 2009-2011 (via the Harnessing Technology Grant and other funds). Therefore, progress looks set to continue.

Where are we now (autumn 2009)?

Today, in many schools, the computer and many other ICT resources can be found in abundance. They are providing learners, teachers, administrators and management with an effective set of tools to improve the preparation and delivery of the curriculum, to enhance learning processes, to enable and empower pupils, to extend learning beyond the classroom, to reach disaffected learners, to enable communication between stakeholders and to manage information.

Becta has led many initiatives and commissioned several reports over the past decade including Impact2 and Impact 2007, the ICT Test Bed Project, the New Opportunities Fund (NOF) training, the Laptops for Teachers Scheme, the Interactive Whiteboard Project, the Becta Self Review Framework (and ICT Mark), Learning Platforms and more. Its most recent is the Harnessing Technology Strategy. Launched in 2005, it set out a system-wide approach to the application of ICT in education, skills and children's services. Becta has reviewed the strategy each year since and the 2008 report reveals a mixed picture.

Primary schools are developing well and 28 per cent are said to be 'e-enabled' which means that they are making full and effective use of a range of technologies which are capable of bringing about improvement to all aspects of the school. These include learning, teaching, inclusion, administration, leadership, information management, communication, pupil attainment, extended learning and working practice. However, whilst this is encouraging, the take up is rather slow and whilst most schools appear to show an interest in ICT, there are many that are still ambivalent or indeed quite indifferent.

The use of ICT in learning and teaching is increasing steadily and the vast majority of learners have good access to technology both at school and at home. Figures (Becta 2008h) for primary schools show that they have, on average:

- 37 computers each – that's approximately 1 computer for every 6.25 children (better than the DCSF baseline of 1:8);

- 95% have interactive whiteboards;

- 91% have a network in place;

- 99% are connected to the Internet;

- 78% have a broadband connection;

- over 1000 schools have been awarded the Becta ICT Mark (and many more are in the process of obtaining it).

 Activity

You might compare these figures with your own school (and other schools you know). If they differ, is there a justifiable reason?
If they do compare then you may have the technology you need in place. If not then steps may be needed to evaluate your position and bring about the necessary change in order to best advantage your staff and pupils in the future. This book should help you to do this.

Sharing of resources is becoming more popular. Many teachers access learning materials and activities on the Internet and share them freely within their own schools. As the use of learning platforms grows, the potential to share resources between schools will increase too.

In assessment, ICT is used mostly for recording and subsequent reporting rather than as a component part of the assessment process itself. Some schools make use of software which incorporates assessment and others make effective use of interactive response systems. There is still scope however for using technology for online assessments, electronic submission of work and e-portfolios. Learning platforms will undoubtedly help in this respect.

Despite the aim of the Department for Children, Schools and Families (DCSF) that schools should implement a learning platform by spring 2008, ICT coordinators report that only one-fifth of primary schools have actually achieved this. However, it is early days and it would seem inevitable that, in time, the aim will be met because:

- the many advantages of learning platforms will eventually become apparent;

- children that use technology to support learning at home stand a better chance of doing well at school (Next Generation Learning, 2009).

- a majority of parents use computers with their children at home and they would like more involvement in their children's education and up to date information on their progress;

- local authorities are generally offering strong support.

There is clear evidence that technology can play a role in the inclusion of disaffected learners and there are plentiful examples of initiatives which motivate such pupils to learn (e.g. making use of popular handheld technologies and gaming devices).

E-safety has become a national priority and, whilst the benefits of the Internet are widely acknowledged, there is now an increased emphasis on keeping children safe online.

Summary

Schools, teachers and learners have changed much over a relatively short period of time and the job of classroom practitioners is vastly different from 20 years ago. Computers and other ICT resources are becoming established as generic tools for learning which have relevance across the entire curriculum. Newly qualified teachers and many of their experienced colleagues now accept ICT as an integral part of their professional life and understand how to use ICT effectively both in lessons and in their general working practice. The development of ICT looks set to continue though, as the Becta Harnessing Technology Review 2008 reports, there is a long way to go and there are still many areas for concern including:

- pockets of limited adoption of ICT in general and 'a long tail of primary schools with limited provision and use';

- use of learning platforms is still at an early stage and only a minority of them are linked to central management information systems;

- those without access to technology are most likely to come from deprived backgrounds and those whose first language is not English;

- schools' capacity for online reporting to parents (to foster better relationships between schools and parents) is currently very poor;

- primary schools are generally receiving a technology service that is far from reliable and professional;

- limitations in most schools' infrastructure to support mobile and remote access to the network are a major concern;

- a high percentage of practitioners are still reporting that they 'rarely or never' use technology.

Becta (2008h)

For those who rarely or never use ICT then there may be a number of reasons:

- insufficient resources or limited access to resources;
- disinterest (or fear) and lack of ICT skills by some teachers;
- lack of ICT skills by pupils;
- the 'digital divide';
- the notion that using ICT is in some way 'cheating';

- ICT challenges traditional pedagogy (in some subjects more than others) which is itself resistant to change.

In addition, reluctant teachers that concede to using ICT tend to fit it into their existing teaching style rather than modifying their style to suit.

It may be that this book will help to overcome some of these barriers.

 Activity

Finally, if you are not already familiar with Becta then you might visit the website (www.becta.org.uk) and familiarise yourself with the information and advice it provides (follow the Schools link).

The Becta site is a valuable commodity and, whilst it is not the sole provider of information and advice, it is a good place to keep yourself updated on current initiatives.

3

ICT in the National Curriculum

Introduction

Information and communication technology (ICT) prepares pupils to participate in a rapidly changing world in which work and other activities are increasingly transformed by access to varied and developing technology. Pupils use ICT tools to find, explore, analyse, exchange and present information responsibly, creatively and with discrimination. They learn how to employ ICT to enable rapid access to ideas and experiences from a wide range of people, communities and cultures. Increased capability in the use of ICT promotes initiative and independent learning, with pupils being able to make informed judgements about when and where to use ICT to best effect, and to consider its implications for home and work both now and in the future. This chapter covers the requirements of ICT in the National Curriculum and offers you the opportunity to explore key websites.

The release of this book coincides with the approval of a new primary curriculum (following a comprehensive independent review by Sir Jim Rose). The curriculum, which is less prescriptive and more flexible, will be introduced into schools from September 2011. It will change from the existing core and non-core subjects to six 'areas of learning' where traditional subjects are more closely integrated (this is a similar approach to the Early Years Foundation Stage curriculum and will therefore promote a smoother transition into primary school).

The new curriculum recognises the importance of ICT and raises its priority alongside literacy and numeracy. Rose further emphasises the need to teach essential ICT skills and provide ample opportunities for children to use and apply them across the curriculum (Rose, 2008). The information and guidance in this book will apply equally to both the existing and the new curriculum (albeit that some aspects of the Key Stage 3 curriculum may be brought forward to Key Stage 2 in due course).

 Activity

If you would like more information you can access a copy of the full Report by Sir Jim Rose on the Primary ICT website (www.primaryict.org.uk/roict.htm).

Accessing the curriculum

In addition to printed versions, the National Curriculum is available online from the Qualifications and Curriculum Authority (QCA) website (http://curriculum.qca.org.uk). This in itself is good use of ICT because the curriculum is shown 'in action' (using video case studies of effective practice), information can be accessed and linked in a variety of ways and useful resources can be easily downloaded.

Pupils' ICT entitlement

- All pupils have an entitlement to develop skills in ICT.
- In addition, pupils can expect to use ICT in school to enhance their learning across the curriculum.

ICT in the curriculum

- In the Foundation Stage (birth to 5), it is recommended that children find out about and identify the uses of everyday technology and use ICT and programmable toys to support their learning.
- At KS1 and KS2, ICT is predominantly taught and applied across the curriculum though some aspects can be taught as a discrete subject.
- It is statutory to use ICT in all subjects at KS2 (with the exception of physical education).
- It is statutory to use ICT in core subjects only at KS1 (for non-core subjects, teachers should use their discretion).

Knowledge, skills and understanding

During Key Stage 1, pupils explore ICT and learn to use it confidently and with purpose to achieve specific outcomes. They start to use ICT to develop their ideas and record their creative work. They become familiar with hardware and software. During Key Stage 2 pupils use a wider range of ICT tools and information sources to support their work in other subjects. They develop their research skills and decide what information is appropriate for their work. They begin to question the plausibility and quality of information. They learn how to amend their work and present it in a way that suits its audience.

In both stages this is achieved by four elements of knowledge, skills and understanding:

1. Finding things out from a variety of sources, selecting and synthesising the information to meet their needs and developing an ability to question its accuracy, bias and plausibility.

2. Developing their ideas using ICT tools to amend and refine their work and enhance its quality and accuracy.

3. Exchanging and sharing information, both directly and through electronic media.

4. Reviewing, modifying and evaluating their work, reflecting critically on its quality, as it progresses.

QCA (2008a: 1)

The complexity of each of these four aspects increases with each key stage.

Attainment targets

Competence in ICT is assessed using attainment targets (levels 1 to 8 and exceptional performance).

■ Children work within levels 1–3 at Key Stage 1 (and should attain at least level 2 by the end of the key stage).

■ Children work within levels 2–5 at Key Stage 2 (and should attain at least level 4 by the end of the key stage).

 Activity

Visit the National Curriculum website at http://curriculum.qca.org.uk and familiarise yourself with the information it provides.

Follow the links: Key Stages 1 & 2 > Subjects > ICT and examine the knowledge, skills and understanding (KSU) for KS1 and KS2. How do they compare?

They each have the same four aspects though the level of complexity increases at KS2. For example, KS1 children will gather information from a variety of sources which have been identified by the teacher, whereas KS2 children will be expected to decide for themselves where they might find the information they need.

 Activity

Think about the ICT resources and the types of activity which children might carry out in order to satisfy the knowledge skills and understanding. For example, in what way might Year 2 children gather and store information, alter the information they have gathered, and present this information effectively.

There are lots of possible activities and you'll come across plenty in this book. One example would be for the teacher to prepare a short piece from a familiar story (e.g. Goldilocks) as a text file in MSWord – with errors in it. Children would access the file from the school learning platform and save it into their own workspace. They would then correct the passage (less able children might be given an error-free version in print form for comparison). Finally, they add their own name, save it and print out the finished story. This activity could follow on from reading the story from a book or talking CD-ROM.

Activity

Return to the National Curriculum website and examine the attainment targets. How would you modify the above activity such that it would be suitable for a child working toward attainment level 4?

You could start by highlighting the essential differences between attainment levels 2 and 4 (KS1 and KS2). Children might find a passage of a story themselves (perhaps from the Internet). The text could be formatted using a variety of features (include a picture perhaps). Finally, the work could be shared with others by emailing.

If you have a reception class, then most of the principles which relate to KS1 and KS2 will also hold for the Foundation Stage. You need not adopt the same structured approach as may be required for the National Curriculum but you can nevertheless plan suitable activities which use ICT to enhance learning. Many of these will be of a role play nature.

As you will soon discover, ICT is about much more than just computers.

 Activity

Link to the Primary ICT site (www.primaryict.org.uk/roict.htm) and consult the statutory framework for the Early Years. Determine what the recommendations are for the use of ICT in the foundation stage.

You should find that ICT is given only a brief mention under the early learning goal 'Knowledge and Understanding of the World (KUW)'. Here, children are required to 'Find out about and identify the uses of everyday technology and use information and communication technology and programmable toys to support their learning'. However, ICT is not restricted to KUW and can easily be applied to all six areas of learning.

You will find many useful documents relating to the early years on the DfES Standards site at http://nationalstrategies.standards.dcsf.gov.uk/earlyyears.

Schemes of work

The DfES Standards website provides schemes of work for schools – they are not statutory but can provide useful ideas or whole activities. You may find that current schemes of work are, to some extent, dated because they don't entirely reflect advances in technology. However, they are a good starting point for developing lesson plans.

The ideas for the Goldilocks activity came from DfES schemes of work.

Activity

Visit the DfES Standards website and examine the ICT schemes of work for years 1 to 6. (www.standards.dfes.gov.uk/schemes2/it/?view=get). Make a note of the principles involved, the resources used and the types of activity in which children might be engaged. Are children in your school engaged in such activities? Are you familiar with these principles and resources yourself?

It may be that you are not entirely comfortable with retrieving, storing, manipulating and presenting information yourself. You may not have experienced some of the software in the schemes of work (e.g. presentation software, spreadsheet and database).

Whilst this may appear daunting, there is no need to feel overly concerned. You (and your pupils) need only be familiar with the basic features of these packages. If you require help, you will find it in our Creative ICT Help Sheets (available from the Primary ICT website at www.primaryict.org.uk/roict.htm).

ICT resources

The Primary and Foundation Stages are encouraged to use a wide range of resources. The range includes: lower-case keyboards, infant mice, large monitors for whole-class activities, colour printers, speakers, headphones, microphones, scanners, digital cameras (with movie facility), digital microscopes, overlay keyboards, talking word processors with a word bank facility, paint programs, data-handling packages, presentation programs, drag-and-drop software, a range of CD-ROMs, floor robots, remote control toys, video recorders, radios, tape recorders, CD players, DVD players, video cameras, music keyboards, photocopiers, laminators, calculators, toy and real telephones, mobile phones, cookers, microwaves, fridges, toasters, toy cash registers, swipe cards, typewriters and other play equipment that model ICT appliances.

This list is far from exhaustive but does highlight the fact that ICT is much more than computers and software. You might think of it in terms of the equation: $ICT \neq PC$

 Activity

Link to the Primary ICT site (www.primaryict.org.uk/roict.htm) and watch the Primary ICT video and/or the Foundation ICT video (depending on your preference).

These videos are taken from a box set of CD-ROMs entitled 'Learning and Teaching using ICT: Example materials from Foundation Stage to Year 6'. They have been produced to help primary schools make better use of ICT. You may be able to obtain a free copy by contacting the DCSF: dcsf@prolog.uk.com or telephoning 0845 6022260.

This chapter has outlined the ICT knowledge, skills and understanding that primary school and Foundation Stage children need to acquire. It has also offered a glimpse of some of the ICT resources available. The following chapters will examine how these resources, and many others, can be used to support children's learning across the curriculum.

4

Using ICT to enhance English

Introduction

The next three chapters will introduce ideas for using ICT effectively in learning and teaching within and across all National Curriculum subjects. References to the requirements for teaching the National Curriculum are taken from the QCA (2008a) and these are aligned with the Primary Framework for Literacy (DfES Standards, 2008). We begin with English.

There are plenty of activities in this chapter to whet your appetite.

ICT or not ICT?

Before you introduce technology into the learning or teaching of any lesson, in any subject, it is essential that you consider whether or not ICT should be used at all. Don't just use it for the sake of it, ask yourself the following questions. Does ICT:

- facilitate teaching or learning that could not be achieved by traditional methods (e.g. the interactivity provided by an interactive whiteboard, the ease of editing and formatting work using a word processor or the ability to record and recall learning events using a digital camera);

- make it easier, quicker or more enjoyable to accomplish a task;

- improve the quality of work;

- provide a welcome alternative approach to learning;

- enable learners;

- provide motivation;

- help to achieve the desired learning outcome(s)?

Providing that ICT is not the predominant method, it is not overused and it is used effectively then a positive response to any of the above may be a good reason to include it.

The list above is by no means exhaustive; there are other criteria which you might like to consider. For each of the sample activities in this book you can decide for yourself whether ICT is used appropriately.

Whilst there is much evidence of the potential effectiveness of ICT as a tool for learning, not everyone subscribes to this notion. There are those who rightly raise pedagogical, technical or health and safety concerns about ICT. In the end, only you can decide.

English curriculum

If you are not familiar with the curriculum for English there are three useful websites with which you should become familiar:

1. The National Curriculum for English (from the QCA) http://curriculum.qca.org.uk/key-stages-1-and-2/subjects/index.aspx.

2. The Primary National Strategy (from the DCSF Standards Site) http://nationalstrategies.standards.dcsf.gov.uk/primary/primary.

3. The Early Years Foundation Stage (from the DfES standards website) www.standards.dfes.gov.uk/eyfs.

English is organised under the language skills of speaking, listening, reading and writing. Children are taught to:

- speak clearly with diction (using standard English), listen with understanding and participate in discussions;

- read increasingly demanding texts (using a repertoire of reading strategies), analysing and evaluating for information as required;

- develop skills in meaningful writing.

ICT in English can help children to:

- talk, read and write for a purpose;

- organise and present information in a variety of forms;

- identify key characteristics and features of text;

- develop an understanding of language.

It also helps children to explore language by allowing them to:

- compose, present, read and transform texts;

- explore information.

The emphasis is on working at word, sentence and text level:

- *Word level* would include listening to single words, linking them to associated pictures, phonic and word recognition programs, spelling programs and the use of spell-check and thesaurus features of word processors (with caution).

- *Sentence level* would test ability in punctuation and grammar.

- *Text level* would include writing and editing own text, reading and interrogating other people's text and cloze (fill in the blank) exercises.

When using ICT, all of the above will also develop fine motor control through the use of mouse and keyboard.

ICT resources and activities for literacy

Talking stories (CD-ROMs and websites)

These utilise colourful pictures, animation and sound to stimulate the senses – words are highlighted as they are spoken. They are often interactive, allowing parts of the picture to be clicked in order to provide further animation and sounds.

A wide variety are available (e.g. Ridiculous Rhymes, Naughty Stories, 2Simple Stories (with links to EAL), and Cbeebies Storycircle (BBC)).

Many originate in the UK and have English speaking voices (you should be cautious of those with American accents and synthetic voices).

Figure 4.1 Talking book

In primary schools and nurseries, talking stories are often projected onto a large screen which enables teacher-led group activities in reading and speaking. With the aid of an interactive whiteboard (IWB), the activities can become even more interactive. There is more information on the IWB in Chapter 7.

 Activity

Link to the Cbeebies website (www.bbc.co.uk/cbeebies/storycircle) and explore some of the stories. Decide whether these have educational value.

You may find that some are better than others. It depends of course on what we mean by educational value. It helps if they are fun and motivating but it is important that they contribute to the achievement of some desired learning outcomes.

 Activity

Now explore the Internet and see if you can find any other useful sites with talking stories. You may also come across examples of CD-ROMs.

There are many sites to be found and you might begin compiling a list (a start has been made for you in Appendix 2). However, you should always fully evaluate websites (and other ICT resources) before using them with children. You will be offered some advice about evaluating resources in Chapter 10.

Using word processors to write

Software can be categorised as 'content rich' or 'content free'. Talking Story CD-ROMs are an example of the former – the content already exists (and most likely can't be modified). Content rich packages have the advantage of offering pre-existing, high-quality materials which potentially save teachers a great deal of work. They do however suffer from several disadvantages – they most often don't give you 'exactly' what you want, they may not help to achieve specified learning goals, they can provide the wrong sort of motivation and, of course, they come at a cost.

Content free packages, as the name implies, are blank canvasses inside which children can use their creative talents in a variety of ways. They can also be used by teachers to create simple activities for children to follow. These packages often exist as part of a larger suite of programs, sometimes known as 'software toolkits'.

A word processor is a prime example of a content free package. Children will use word processors as one method of presenting their work but they can also be used for a number of useful literacy activities such as creating and editing text (perhaps using prepared word banks), converting text from one form to another (e.g. a narrative to a play), cloze exercises, and labelling and classifying.

MS Word is an obvious choice because it is freely available in all schools and is very much the standard word processor. However, young children will benefit from a child-friendly package such as TextEase CT or the 2Simple range. Many word processors for primary and Foundation Stage now incorporate a talking facility to aid spelling development. But beware of synthetic voices and American accents.

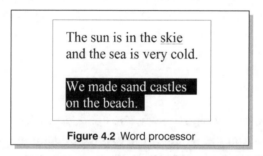

The sun is in the skie
and the sea is very cold.

We made sand castles
on the beach.

Figure 4.2 Word processor

The choice of word processing activities should match the curriculum and might include: writing about oneself, writing a letter, writing a story or rhyme, writing about a character in a story, etc.

Children can also practise computer skills such as mouse control, keyboard skills, formatting and manipulating text, and saving and printing work.

It may prove useful to begin writing by introducing a paper keyboard with upper-case characters and getting children to colour the important function keys (Spacebar, Shift, Delete, Backspace and Enter) and writing the lower-case letters alongside each upper case equivalent.

Figure 4.3 A paper keyboard

 Activity

Download the paper keyboard (paper_keyboard.doc) and paper keyboard ideas (keyboard_ideas.doc) from the Primary ICT site and try out some activities for yourself.

There are many other useful activities that you can devise using a paper keyboard. Perhaps you can think of some.

 Activity

Another useful activity is editing text. Here, children recognise that ICT lets them correct and improve their work – either as they are working or at a later date. They can also practise formatting.

Use MS Word to create the following text (with deliberate errors) and present to children as an on-screen activity. If you are unsure how to do this, consult the Creative ICT Help Sheets on the Primary ICT site.

Using a printed, error-free version, children can make the necessary corrections to the on-screen version, saving and printing their work if required (don't allow spell-checkers at this stage). More able children can do this without the printed copy.

The Gingerbread Boy

One day a litle old wuman made a boy out of jinger bread and the boy came to life and ran away and evryone chast him. A sli fox saw him by the river and the fox trikked the boy into climing up onto his back. Hafway acros the river the fox tost the boy into the air and opened his jaws and SNAP the jinger bread boy was gon.

Children are taught to present text to different audiences for different purposes. It is possible to change a piece of text designed for one audience to make it suitable for another. For example, a short story involving two or three characters is written as a 'narrative'. This can be changed to a presentation by transferring it to a set of slides or to a 'play' with speaking parts for each of the characters.

Narrative	Play	
The teacher entered the classroom and said, "Good morning children". The class didn't respond except for a quiet voice in the corner who replied, "So what's good about it then?". It was Sharon.	**Teacher:**	"Good morning children".
	Sharon:	"So what's good about it then?".

Finally, here are a number of possible writing activities you can offer your class:

- begin a story, children write the end;
- read a short story and children draw a picture about it;
- children practise writing their name;
- children add labels to a picture;
- children join letters to the correct picture;
- children reply to an email from Goldilocks;
- children build a story using a word/picture bank that you have created;
- children match picture and word cards that you have created and laminated.

Cloze exercises

Several software packages (e.g. Cloze Pro and 2Simple Developing Tray) provide cloze exercises. Children fill in the gaps in the text produced by the program. It tests knowledge of language use and reading comprehension. Words may be chosen from a bank and the word chosen for each gap will be the most appropriate one that fits the sentence and paragraph in both grammar and meaning.

Activity

Use MS Word to create the following cloze passage. The word bank is optional. For best effect, make use of MS Word's 'forms' toolbar. If you are unsure how to do this, consult the Creative ICT Help Sheets on the Primary ICT site.

My Cat

My _ _ _ is called Molly. She is black. She has got a long _ _ _ _ that she swishes when she is cross. She uses her _ _ _ _ _ _ to wash herself. When she's hungry she makes a _ _ _ _ sound.

cat   meow   tongue   tail

Labelling and classifying

Labelling and classifying is one of the requirements of the national literacy strategy. Software packages exist for this purpose but it is often best for the teacher to design an activity using a simple word-processing or graphics package (e.g. MS Word, TextEase, Publisher or 2Simple Science Simulation). This can include posters and collages.

Activity

The activity below has been created in MS Word. It makes use of the forms toolbar and uses drop-down boxes to offer word choice to children.

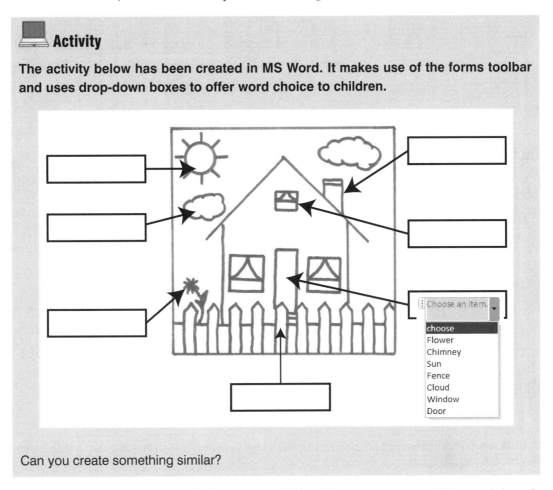

Can you create something similar?

MS Word is an obvious choice for designing activities. However, younger children will benefit from a simpler package such as TextEase.

Activity

Can you label the picture?

foot
head
hand
arm

This is a drag-and-drop labelling activity using TextEase Studio CT. TextEase is more conducive to this type of design than MS Word and is a child-friendly software toolkit

You are encouraged you to try out TextEase (you can obtain a 30-day trial package from the downloads page at www. textease.com).

Dictionaries and encyclopaedias

There are several dictionary and encyclopaedia packages on CD-ROM and on the Internet. Some of the many examples are:

On CD-ROM	Internet
Children's Dictionary (by Websters)	www.dictionary.com
Concise Oxford English Dictionary	www.yourdictionary.com
Big Bus – Animal Dictionary	www.pdictionary.com
Encarta	www.encarta.msn.com

The Internet offerings now tend to take precedence because they are free, much more comprehensive and continually updated.

Communicating

ICT surely comes into its own when used for communicating. Children can:

- present their work (e.g. create a slide show using presentation software such as MS PowerPoint or TextEase Presenter);

- publish information (e.g. design a poster using desktop publishing software such as MS Publisher or TextEase);

- use email and the Internet for a variety of purposes – we will look at these in more detail in a later section.

Paper-based activities

The computer can be used to produce a number of activities in paper format (e.g. printed and laminated word and picture sets, colouring sheets, number puzzles etc). These not only provide an alternative method for those who learn better off-line but they also provide a good contingency plan just in case your ICT equipment decides to fail you! You can also find many prepared activities on the Internet (see the list of websites in Appendix 2).

Digital cameras

There are many hardware devices, aside from a PC and its peripherals, which can support literacy (e.g. speaking and writing toys, listening centres and electronic dictionaries). Perhaps the most versatile is the digital camera. They are easy and fun to use and, armed with a camera, children will have the opportunity to use their imagination and be creative and innovative.

They are capable of capturing and permanently storing images of children's own learning experiences which allows for consolidation and reflection at any time in the future. Images can be presented in a variety of ways including wall displays, presentations, teacher-created activities, written work (especially stories), web pages, blogs and printed and laminated activities. Images of actual objects are an excellent way to create resources and to aid language and number work.

> There are great benefits in being able to capture images from the child's actual environment to aid language recognition, to create a link between the text and the concept, and to help rerun specific teaching experiences.
>
> (DCSF, 2008a)

Digital cameras are relatively cheap and are also available in robust, child friendly versions for as little as £20 (e.g. the Digital Blue collection of still and moving cameras: www.digitalblue. org.uk).

Note: Some schools are particularly cautious about taking photos of their children. If you are going to use pictures of children, be sure that you don't infringe your school policy and you have permission from a parent or guardian.

 Activity

Link to the Primary ICT site, and watch the Literacy Video:

- Is the digital camera an effective resource here?
- Could you achieve the same learning outcomes without it?
- Is it motivating for children – does it enable them?
- What are the advantages of using a digital camera?
- What are the disadvantages?

Hopefully your advantages will outweigh the disadvantages. The teacher and children in the video have certainly used a camera effectively and in a motivating way. The ability to gather pictorial information and recall it whenever it is needed provides for a speedy and clear point of discussion. Cameras are relatively cheap and simple to use. Indeed, as with many other ICT resources, you can allow children to explore and experiment rather than providing formal tuition on the camera.

Software toolkits

The most effective (and cost-effective) way to develop a child's ICT capability is by using a good 'software toolkit' (a suite of software packages, mostly content free).

Typical toolkits will include: word processor, spreadsheet, database (including branching database), graphics package, desktop publishing, turtle (LOGO), presentation software, Internet browser and email editor.

Toolkits allow teachers to devise activities (for use on-screen or off) and allow children to use their creative talents in a variety of ways.

Examples include: MS Word, TextEase Studio CT, Tizzy's First Tools, 2Simple, and BlackCat SuperTools. Perhaps the most versatile, child-friendly and age-independent is TextEase.

 Activity

If you'd like to preview TextEase, access the TextEase website (www.textease.com) and view the video demos.

 Activity

Link to the Primary ICT site, and try out the zoo activity.

You will need TextEase installed on your computer. If you don't own the program, download a 30-day trial package from www.textease.com.

This is a simple activity but one which utilises a range of features including sound (and sound recording), images and word banks.

An information page has been provided for the teacher which outlines the activity and lists the desired learning outcomes. This is always good practice.

The zoo activity could have been designed using an alternative content free package such as MS Word, MS PowerPoint or Clicker 5.

Content rich software

There's a whole host of content rich software packages on the market. Some are excellent and others are not. No particular recommendations here – you can explore some of the retailers' websites yourself (e.g. Granada, Sherston, Semerc, Curriculum Online, RM, Widgit, Cricksoft, and more – see Appendix 3).

It's important that you evaluate software before using it with children and before committing to purchase. This is covered in Chapter 10.

Podcasting

Audio recording is nothing new in education and yet podcasting has given it a whole new meaning. Many primary schools have ventured into this area and whole school podcasting is now a popular activity.

A podcast is an audio recording of an event which is made available as one or more episodes, each contained in an audio file (usually mp3 or wav). It can be played on a PC, PDA, mp3 player and other mobile devices.

The term podcast is derived from 'iPod broadcast' (for iPod read mp3 player). Podcasts as individual files are now accompanied by the wider application of multiple files, each containing an 'episode' of a learning unit. They can be downloaded manually or automatically via RSS feeds.

 Activity

Link to the Primary ICT site, and listen to the two podcasts. In what ways do you think podcasts can benefit the teaching of literacy?

There are many potential benefits for both teachers and pupils including: the convenience of listening anywhere, anytime; useful for children who miss lessons (e.g. due to illness); a new approach to homework (e.g. audio notes to reinforce learning); concentration on speaking and listening skills; and an opportunity for children to exploit their creative talents. You will find more on podcasting (and vidcasting) in Chapter 7.

Phonics

The Rose report (DfES, 2006) recommended that early reading instruction must include synthetic phonics. Whilst contentious, synthetic phonics is certainly a contemporary issue in literacy and part of the new Primary National Strategy.

Commercial content rich phonics software includes:

- *Jolly Phonics* – a complete foundation programme of reading and writing for children aged 3 to 6. It uses the synthetic phonics method of teaching the letter sounds in a way that is fun and multi-sensory. Children learn how to use the letter sounds to read and write words (visit www.jollylearning.co.uk for more information).

- *Big Cat Phonics* – delivers all criteria in the DfES *Independent Review of Teaching of Early Reading* (visit www.collinseducation.com for more information).

- *Handheld Phonics* – is a powerful synthetic phonics software package for teachers and parents. The software works on a PC or laptop, an interactive whiteboard and also on PDAs and Sony PSPs (visit www.syntheticphonics.co.uk for more information).

You may find that, however good the phonics program, it doesn't entirely fit the bill for one reason or another. In this case you may wish to develop some supplementary resources yourself. In the following activity you will examine a self-made activity which has been created in MS PowerPoint.

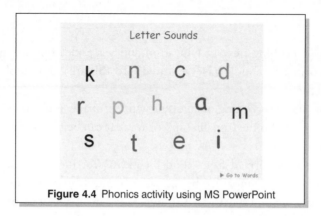

Figure 4.4 Phonics activity using MS PowerPoint

 Activity

Link to the Primary ICT site and try out the CVC slide show. It allows children to practice letter sounds (from sets 1 to 5 of the DCSF Letters and Sounds programme) and then introduces a number of CVC words incorporating the practised letters.

If you think the CVC slide show is a useful resource, you will find more on the Teacher Resource Exchange (TRE) website. You may wish to explore these resources (www.tre. ngfl.gov.uk).

You can adapt the TRE resources to suit your own learning objectives or you might like to create your own PowerPoint resources from scratch.

Digital pens

Digital pens (and digital paper) allow conventional writing and drawings to be captured and uploaded to a computer. They incorporate a miniature video camera which captures the pen strokes and, when uploaded, reproduces them faithfully on screen. Some pens also provide audio capture which is time-aligned with the text. They provide a handy way to capture notes and sketches when away from the computer and pupils can create their own illustrations rather than depend on clipart.

5

Using ICT to enhance maths and science

Introduction

Mathematics and science have been deliberately combined in this chapter because many of the available ICT resources and types of activity are common to both.

In mathematics, children deal essentially with number, shape, space and measurement. This includes:

- counting;
- calculating (using the four number operations);
- reasoning;
- exploring shape;
- taking measurements;
- creating diagrams and charts;
- presenting results.

They develop their knowledge and understanding through practical activity, exploration and discussion (using mathematical language).

In science, the programme of study deals with:

- scientific enquiry;
- life processes and living things;
- physical processes.

These include: animals, plants and organisms; materials and their properties; physical phenomena related to electricity; force and motion; light and sound; energy resources and energy transfer; and physical quantities.

ICT in mathematics and in science is good for a great many things.

Picture...

- a lesson on the Sun brought to life by an Internet link displayed on a large screen that shows the fiery ball rotating, fountains of fire spurting from the inferno below;

- how much easier it is to follow a photosynthesis investigation when the results are displayed in real time from a data-logger on the [interactive] whiteboard for comment, annotation and examination;

- taking a digital microscope and laptop outside with a group of nursery children to take a movie of woodlice in their natural habitat to be shown back in the playroom alongside the children's work and ideas.

The advent of durable, simple-to-use equipment makes this a reality.

Learning and Teaching Scotland (2008: 1)

ICT resources and activities for maths and science

An imaginary project?

There are many ways in which ICT can be used to support your lessons, but is the following project taking things a little too far?

 Activity

Look at the following science project:

The teacher launches the experiment and provides background information using an **interactive whiteboard** and **smart notebook**. Some **images** and **data** from previous work are used to refresh the topic. The **notebook file** is saved and uploaded onto the school's **learning platform** using a **wifi** link so that pupils can access it from home. Pupils undertake the experiment using **data-logging** equipment and take **digital photos** and a **video** as work progresses. On completion, pupils discuss the results with another school using **web cams** and **video conferencing software**.

Pupils go home and reflect on their experiment, sharing and exchanging ideas with other pupils via **email** and a threaded **discussion board**. They write up the experiment using **word processing software**, incorporating **images** and references from the **Internet** and from **CD-ROMs** on the school **intranet**. A summary is uploaded to their personal **e-portfolio** or **weblog**. They also carry out an analysis of the results and incorporate graphs with the help of a **spreadsheet**.

The completed report is **emailed** to the teacher or posted into the **digital drop box** on the school's **virtual learning environment (VLE)**. The teacher marks the work **electronically** and sends individual feedback via the **drop box**.

This is a comprehensive project incorporating a number of resources. Do you think this is realistic or simply imaginary?

Most activities don't incorporate such an extensive range of ICT resources even though it is quite possible. Perhaps this is an exaggeration by one of those teachers who we may class as an 'enthusiast'.

We aren't all enthusiasts and we don't necessarily have the time or the inclination to mimic an activity such as this. However, we should consider making appropriate use of some ICT resources in our maths and science lessons.

Activity

Imagine you are delivering a maths or science lesson. What are the general salient features of ICT resources which might influence you to include them in your activities? There are of course many features including uniqueness, speed, accuracy, capacity, automaticity, interactivity, dexterity, capability, quality, communication, multimedia, enjoyment, motivation … and more!

Floor robots

Programmable floor robots are extremely useful in mathematics for activities involving estimation, angles and direction, shape, spatial awareness, instructions, and control and investigation. In addition to number work, robots facilitate group work, design and technology, and road safety.

They also cover some of the ICT requirements of the Foundation Stage which specifies that children should use ICT and programmable toys to support their learning.

These devices have evolved over recent years and the original robots (Roamer and Pixie) are now accompanied by many lightweight, low power models including the BeeBot, Ladybird and iBug. There are also several software versions which will allow you to simulate the actions of the robots on-screen. Examples include Turtle and BeeBot Simulation.

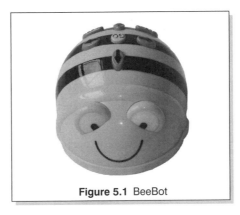

Figure 5.1 BeeBot

You will of course need access to floor robots in order to try them out. As a taster, why not have a go using a software version?

You will first need to download the BeeBot 14 day trial demo software from: www.tts–group.co.uk/Product.aspx?cref=TTSPR780717#Demo.

Activity

Link to the Primary ICT site and try out the BeeBot Hoops activity (the BeeBot has been programmed to find its way through the hoops and back to the start).

Experiment with the software and the BeeBot commands. Now design a simple activity for your pupils.

You could use the shapes mat and program the BeeBot to visit all circles in turn (and perhaps in order of size). You might link the activity to English by, for example, using the 'alphabet' mat and programming the BeeBot to spell out simple words.

You might also consider providing some instruction and familiarisation exercises. However some children may prefer to experiment and find out how the software works for themselves.

It isn't necessary (and it's virtually impossible) for classroom practitioners to know everything about the operation of all their ICT resources so you shouldn't be concerned if you are not wholly conversant with the software. In fact, children will only be too delighted to enlighten you themselves!

You should specify learning outcomes for the activity as you would in any other lesson.

Digital microscopes

The microscope is an invaluable tool in science. It provides a unique function and allows pupils to become engaged in the hands-on learning process supported and facilitated by many current teachers. Unfortunately, conventional apparatus lacks versatility and can often make an activity dull.

This is where the digital microscope comes into its own. Simple to use, portable and robust, it has a variety of purposeful uses. Magnified items are displayed on-screen and, when projected onto a large screen (or interactive whiteboard), enhance a lesson because they can be viewed by the whole class. Images (still or moving) can be permanently captured and then used to support written work. A good example is the QX5 digital microscope produced by Digital Blue.

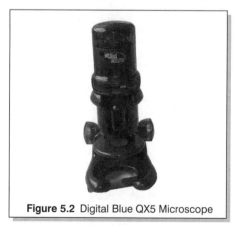

Figure 5.2 Digital Blue QX5 Microscope

Activity

Link to the Primary ICT site and watch the first part of the Digital Blue Microscope video (courtesy of Teachers TV*). How might you use a digital microscope in your own teaching?

There are many experiments you can conduct from exploring 'minibeasts' to examining your own hair. For a comprehensive activity on the structure of flowers, link to Learning and Teaching Scotland at www.ltscotland.org.uk/sharingpractice/i/flowerstructure/introduction. asp.

* Funded by the DCSF, Teachers TV (www.teachers.tv) is a web-based service for schools with programmes (videos) covering all curriculum subjects across the 4 key stages. Programmes can be viewed online or downloaded and played on Windows Media Player.

Digital cameras

The digital camera was introduced in Chapter 4. However, it is such an important resource that it is included again in this section.

You might begin by teaching the whole class how to take pictures with a camera – though many children will prefer to work it out for themselves.

There are lots of ideas for using a digital camera in mathematics. For example, children find groups of objects in the school or classroom which correspond with a given number (e.g. 3 buttons on a coat, 5 crayons, 2 books). The pictures can be imported into MS PowerPoint (or printed out) to create a number book.

There are many cameras on the market and most claim to be robust enough for use by children. These cameras offer an astounding range of features for as little as £80 and, whilst you can certainly buy cheaper, the features of a camera increase almost exponentially with price.

If you want to play safe and purchase a camera designed specifically for children then try the Digital Blue Camera or the tough plastic camera by Fisher Price. There are fewer features but they cost only £20 – £30.

Figure 5.3 Digital Blue Camers

Activity

Link to the Primary ICT site and try out the Number Book activity. Is this better than a book off the shelf?

The book is interactive and is supported with voice-overs (created by the children). It could be developed to include other multimedia. Children will take pride in something that they have created themselves. They can reflect on their actual experiences and relate the contents of the book directly to objects in the school or classroom.

Unlike printed materials, the finished product can easily be made available to the whole school via the learning platform and displayed on Interactive Whiteboards for whole class work.

Control

Computer control allows children to create and manipulate models of real life situations. They do this by programming a sequence of events which will take place over a period of time. For example, they can control a set of traffic lights, operate a burglar alarm system, control a plant irrigation system and move a vehicle forwards and backwards. In general, any system which includes output devices (such as lamps, motors, buzzers and bells) and input devices (such as sensors for light, sound or temperature) can be controlled.

Programming can be child friendly and will use relatively simple instructions or flowcharts.

The National Curriculum at KS2 is quite specific about including control in children's learning. In particular, children should be taught:

- how to create, test, improve and refine sequences of instructions to make things happen and to monitor events and respond to them [for example, monitoring changes in temperature, detecting light levels and turning on a light];

- how mechanisms can be used to make things move in different ways, using a range of equipment including an ICT control program.

QCA (2008a: 1)

The QCA schemes of work also refer to opportunities for using ICT in monitoring and control.

Activity

Examine the following flow chart. Can you work out what it is controlling?

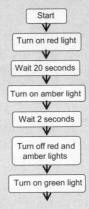

```
        Start
          ↓
  Turn on red light
          ↓
   Wait 20 seconds
          ↓
 Turn on amber light
          ↓
    Wait 2 seconds
          ↓
  Turn off red and
    amber lights
          ↓
  Turn on green light
          ↓
```

Well you probably recognise this as part of the sequence for a standard set of traffic lights. KS2 children will not find this particularly difficult and will be proud of their efforts when they see it controlling a set of lights (either a miniature model or an onscreen simulation).

You may first wish to take the class to see a real set of traffic lights (or a pelican crossing) and get them to record how they work and the sequencing of lights. They can then convert their records into an actual control sequence.

Once children are confident with creating his simple model they could elaborate by including a push button control of a pedestrian crossing.

There are lots of control kits available. For KS1/KS2 there is 2Simple's software 2Control NXT (www.2simple.com) which works in conjunction with Lego Mindstorms NXT hardware.

For KS2 you might try the Economatics Control Station (www.economatics–education. co.uk).

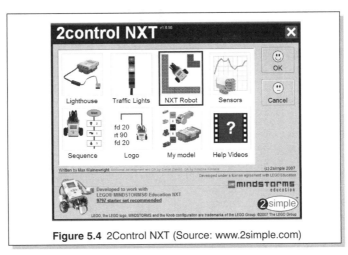

Figure 5.4 2Control NXT (Source: www.2simple.com)

You can download a demo of the Economatics Control Station from their website at www. economatics–education.co.uk/downloads/product_demos.htm.

Data logging

Data–logging is the collection of readings from sensors over a period of time. There are many types of sensor but most primary schools keep it simple and use sensors for measuring temperature, light and sound (most data-logging devices will have these three sensors built in).

Data collected can be displayed as charts and graphs or on a continually updated number display.

The sensors may be used as part of scientific experiments which require the gathering of data and they are often used in conjunction with control equipment to control simple systems such as the temperature in a fish tank.

Data–logging equipment will normally be connected to a PC whilst data collection is taking place. However, when information needs to be collected over a long period of time (e.g. weather data), the equipment can be used remotely and the data transferred to a PC later.

Typical data–logging activities include:

- monitoring the temperature in the classroom;

- measuring traffic noise outside the school;

- testing heat insulation and cooling effects (e.g. melting ice); and

- keeping weather records.

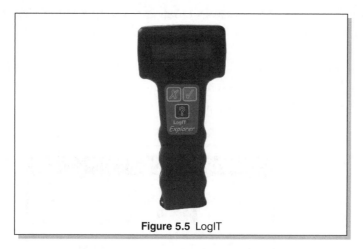

Figure 5.5 LogIT

Activity

Link to the Primary ICT site and access the files DataLoggingInfo and DataLoggingActivities. These should present you with some ideas which link to the QCA schemes of work for science: 1F Sound and hearing; 2B Habitat; 3F Light and shadows; 4C Keeping warm; 4D Solids, liquids and how they can be separated; 4F Circuits and conductors; 5D Changing state; 5F Changing sounds (i) – transmission; 5F Changing sounds (ii) – muffling; and 6G Changing circuits.

These are simple yet comprehensive activities which fit in well with the National Curriculum objectives for science. You can do some of these activities without data-logging equipment (e.g. you can use a thermometer to measure temperature) but loggers are relatively inexpensive and can be left alone for periods of time, taking readings without manual intervention.

Simulation

Simulations allow children to safely explore concepts which would be difficult or perhaps impossible without ICT. Pupils can experience processes which may be too slow, too fast, too dangerous or too expensive to do in school. For example, learning about electricity, exploring space travel and changes in the populations of micro-organisms in different conditions.

 Activity

Link to the BBC website – try the Light and Dark simulation www.bbc.co.uk/schools/scienceclips/ages/5_6/light_dark.shtml (for Years 1 and 2). How does this compare to the real thing?

There is, of course, no substitute for real life situations. However, an experiment such as this would be difficult to set up in school and might prove to be quite dangerous too! In addition, free simulations such as this are easily repeatable.

Simulation packages include: LiveWire; Junior Simulation Insight; 2Simple Science; and BBC Science Clips (www.bbc.co.uk/schools/scienceclips).

Content rich software

Content rich software is professionally made and pupils benefit from its interactivity and effective use of multimedia. It is 'ready to use' and may save you the burden of preparing ICT resources yourself. It does however come at a price and you may spend some time finding cost-effective products which satisfy the objectives of the curriculum. You might explore some of the many retailer websites for ideas – see Appendix 3.

It's important that you evaluate the software before using it with children and before committing to purchase. More on evaluation in Chapter 10.

Content free software

There are many content rich software titles on the market, some better than others. But it is often the case that, however good the packages, they don't entirely meet your needs. They may not be specific enough for the intended learning outcomes, they may be too complicated or they may not provide for differentiated learning.

If this is the case then you should consider developing simple activities yourself using content free software such as MS Office, Smart Notebook and TextEase. If you need help then consult the Creative ICT help sheets on the Primary ICT website.

Designing activities can of course place great demands on your time and, before starting to create a new project, you might try out some of the existing resources which can be downloaded freely from the Internet. In most cases you are at liberty to adapt them to suit your own needs and this may be better than starting from scratch.

 Activity

Link to the following websites and try out some of the free resources.

- Primary Resources: www.primaryresources.co.uk
- Numeracy World: www.numeracyworld.com
- Teacher Resource Exchange (TRE): www.tre.ngfl.gov.uk
- Coxhoe Primary School: www.coxhoe.durham.sch.uk/Curriculum/Curriculum.htm
- Primary Games: www.primarygames.co.uk
- BBC Schools: www.bbc.co.uk/schools
- Cbeebies: www.bbc.co.uk/cbeebies
- Science Teaching Ideas: www.teachingideas.co.uk/science/contents.htm
- Channel 4 Learning: www.channel4learning.com
- CrickWeb: www.crickweb.co.uk
- Primary Interactive: www.primaryinteractive.co.uk
- Naace: Primary Classroom Activities: www.mape.org.uk/activities/index.htm

There are many other sources of activities to be found on the Internet. Try searching (using Google or Yahoo) to see what you can find. It also pays to search for 'Primary Schools' and 'Grids for Learning' as these are good sources too.

Spreadsheets

Spreadsheets are an essential element of the primary curriculum and feature in the knowledge, skills and understanding for ICT (see the QCA scheme of work units 5d and 6b).

Children are expected to enter data (numbers and text), to use simple rules and formulae to calculate totals, and to create associated graphs and charts. They will be expected to apply spreadsheets to simple mathematical and scientific models, answering 'what if …?' questions.

The very thought of spreadsheets fill some of us with trepidation! However, we need to be able to support our pupils and it need not be a major issue if you keep it simple.

Here's an example of some excellent spreadsheet work from Year 5 pupils in a primary school. The pupils had to organise a café, working out the difference between the buying and the selling price of typical items.

Item	Price	Sold	Income	Costs	Profit
Coffee	1.75	12	21	8	42.75
Tea	1.5	15	22.5	4.5	43.5
Soup	2.5	8	20	10	40.5
Sandwich	3.8	11	41.8	17	73.6
Cake	2.1	25	52.5	21	100.6
Buscuit	0.8	13	10.4	3.2	27.4
				Grand Total	328.4

Figure 5.6 Café spreadsheet

Is this complicated? Well no, it's just arithmetic performed using an advanced calculator! Of course the spreadsheet is capable of much more including the creation of graphs and charts.

In the following activity, TextEase is used to create a simple, child (and teacher) friendly calculator to add two numbers together. You will need TextEase to view it. If you don't own a copy you can download a trial version from www.textease.com.

Examples of spreadsheet packages include Number Magic, TextEase and MS Excel.

 Activity

Link to the Primary ICT site and access the Add to 10 activity. Does this have the appearance of a spreadsheet?

Simple changes have been made to convert the spreadsheet from its usual matrix of numbered rows and columns to a more user friendly format. TextEase allows the use of colour and moveable text boxes to enhance the activity. Children can experiment to find all combinations of numbers that add to 10.

Databases (including branching databases)

Flat file databases

A database is used whenever there is a need to store and manipulate information. As with spreadsheets, database is a component part of the primary curriculum (see the QCA scheme of work units 3c and 4c).

Standard database packages, such as MS Access, tend to appear as 'flat' two-dimensional tables.

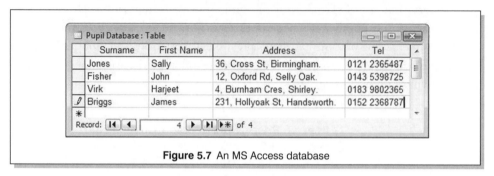

Figure 5.7 An MS Access database

It is perhaps best to introduce the concept of database by first comparing computer-based versions with paper-based systems (e.g. index cards). Children can then be introduced to the files, records and fields which make up an electronic database. They will use the database to enter and sort data, carry out simple searches, answer simple questions and produce bar charts.

The following database may have more appeal to younger children. Here they enter data and illustrations of 'minibeasts' into a TextEase database.

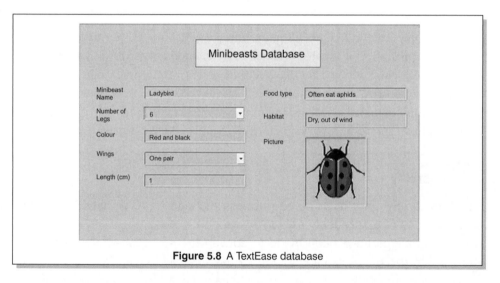

Figure 5.8 A TextEase database

Try the activity for yourself (you will need TextEase to view it. If you don't own a copy you can download a trial version from www.textease.com).

Activity

Link to the Primary ICT site and access the Minibeasts Database activity. How might this link to other activities?
The possibilities are probably endless! Here's just one:
  Children might observe and collect minibeasts from the school grounds. They could examine them using a digital microscope, documenting facts and creating images. Further research may be carried out using the Internet. The information and images gathered can then be entered into the database (which can be created by the teacher or by capable pupils).

Children can apply database applications to handle and present information in other areas of the curriculum such as geography, science, design and technology, and history. They can also be used to produce graphs, charts and pictograms.

Branching databases
Another useful application is the branching database. These are used for children to learn to sort and classify information by using 'yes/no' questions to separate a set of objects into two sub-sets. For example, they can apply this concept to classify plants and animals in science.

The following database tests a child's ability to recognise the order of numbers in the range 1 to 10. The child is given a number on a flash card and the speaking program asks a series of yes/no questions in order to identify the number.

Examples of database packages include 2Investigate, TextEase, FlexiTREE and MS Access.

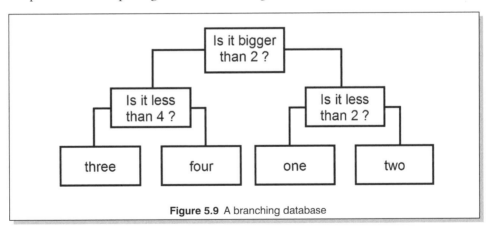

Figure 5.9 A branching database

Activity

Link to the Primary ICT site and access the Number Branch activity. How might you use this database to classify other types of information?
You could identify animals by using yes/no questions to successively differentiate between flying and non-flying, swimming and non-swimming, two legs and four legs and so on.

TextEase will guide you verbally through the process and you can use sets of numbers, words or pictures.

The latest version of TextEase (TextEase CT) has a reasonable British speech engine, unlike its predecessor which had a rather disconcerting synthetic American accent.

Calculators

There would appear to be a lack of agreement about the consequences of calculator use in the primary classroom.

Some would profess that it reduces number facility and enables children to 'cheat at sums'. They believe that it is only used because it is a requirement of the National Curriculum and is used in Standard Assessment Tests (SATs).

Others recognise the potential of calculators in that they have an inbuilt structure of the place value system, the use of signs and symbols and mathematical ideas such as decimal notation and negative numbers.

The jury may still be out, however, as with any ICT resource, the calculator will only ever be used by those who value it as a learning tool. If you are unsure, and want to decide for yourself, then try out some of the activities on the Primary ICT website.

 Activity

Link to the Primary ICT site and try out the Calculator Activities. How do you feel about primary school children using the calculator?

Programming

You have seen the benefits of programmable robots and their on-screen versions (such as the Turtle). Here we take a brief look at programming in its own right.

Programming was introduced into children's education by the eminent mathematician Seymour Papert who developed the LOGO language in the 1960s. It has very few instructions to learn and is based on making an object (turtle) on the screen move according to the instructions given by children. The language teaches some basic operations which are used in any programming language; in particular the useful 'repeat' operation.

Some teachers are far from convinced that programming is an essential skill for children. However, controlling a turtle promotes development in some areas of mathematics and provides a systematic approach to problem solving or to the achievement of routine tasks.

There are several children's programming languages and programming packages available such as Logo, BASIC, Scratch and Phrogram. You can obtain a free copy of LOGO from Softronix at www.softronix.com/logo.html.

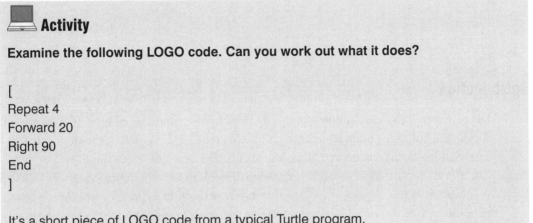

Activity

Examine the following LOGO code. Can you work out what it does?

```
[
Repeat 4
Forward 20
Right 90
End
]
```

It's a short piece of LOGO code from a typical Turtle program.

The turtle moves forward 20 units and then turns 90° to the right. These two instructions are repeated 4 times to form a square.

Extending these instructions can make this simple language quite powerful.

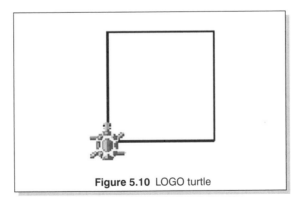

Figure 5.10 LOGO turtle

6

Using ICT in non-core subjects

Introduction

Having covered the core subjects you may now have some ideas of how ICT can be used to support and enhance children's learning. This chapter examines each of the non-core subjects in somewhat less detail but, nevertheless, offers a number of useful ideas and links.

ICT is such a vast subject area that it is often difficult to know where to start when deliberating over its possible use in any particular subject. Whatever your approach, you should try to avoid the tendency to choose ICT resources and then decide where they might fit into the curriculum. Your strategy ought to be quite the reverse – first identify the learning objectives and outcomes and then choose ICT resources which will help to achieve those objectives.

Online access to the curriculum will help to identify learning objectives for your chosen subject. There are many available sources including: the National Curriculum Online (http://curriculum.qca.org.uk) and the QCA/DfES Schemes of Work (www.standards.dfes.gov.uk/schemes3). You should visit these from time to time in order to keep abreast of developments and to ensure that your own practice remains in keeping with statutory requirements. However, for most teachers, a pragmatic approach is called for. There is little point in reinventing the wheel if effective learning activities already exist (albeit you should seek to continually evaluate and improve your offerings).

Some activities will include ICT resources (if deemed appropriate) and some will not. Remember, it's no different to choosing resources in general. Along with books, pencils and paper, paints and crayons, blackboards, flip charts and role play equipment, ICT is just another option to consider.

ICT is sometimes considered as one single 'entity' and, as such, it is too easy to completely include or completely dismiss it. It should be split into its many component parts with due consideration being given to each part.

Aside from the activities already used in your own school (and hopefully contained within a resource guide) there are plenty of ideas floating around the Internet. You can carry out a search but some of the best places to visit are:

■ National Curriculum in Action (on the QCA website) – offering:

  ☐ the statutory requirements for using ICT at each key stage;

☐ general and specific ways in which ICT can help pupils (including plenty of real life examples);

☐ a listing of some of the possible hardware and software for each subject.

■ databases of resources such as Teacher Resource Exchange (TRE), Teachers Evaluating Educational Multimedia (TEEM), ICTeachers, TeacherNet and the DfES Standards Site.

■ other schools which freely and selflessly allow access to ICT resources via their own school website (e.g. Coxhoe Primary School).

The web addresses for all these sites are listed in Appendix 2. Alternatively, you could take a traditional activity and design its ICT equivalent using a content free package.

Art and design

The National Curriculum for art and design expects primary school children to: explore ideas; make observations; select and record visual and other information; investigate materials and processes; try out tools and techniques (including painting and drawing); make images and artefacts; adapt, improve and develop their work; and acquire knowledge of the work of artists, craftspeople and designers.

ICT has much to offer including: reducing the costs of resources; speeding up processes; allowing experimentation and risk taking without penalty; introducing new media; helping to combine the sensory experiences of sound, image and movement; offering new ways to present and communicate work; and providing ready access to a wealth of information on the Internet.

Word processors and content free packages

Most word processors and content free packages include features for the creation of simple drawings and shapes (e.g. MS Word, TextEase, Publisher, PowerPoint and the Smart Notebook). They also allow images to be inserted including clipart and pictures which children have taken themselves using a digital camera.

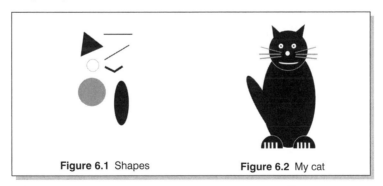

Figure 6.1 Shapes   **Figure 6.2** My cat

Here, shapes and freehand drawing from MS Word's drawing toolbar have been used by KS1 pupils. They are exploring shape and colour to create 'my cat'.

Whilst satisfying some of the knowledge requirements of art and design, they are also able to practice many useful ICT skills including mouse control, copy and paste, and grouping.

 Activity

Link to the Primary ICT site and access the My Cat activity. Can you piece together a cat using the drawing toolbar?
If you are not familiar with the drawing toolbar in MS Word, refer to the Creative ICT Help Sheets. MS Word is not the ideal art package but you can produce quite sophisticated drawings if you put your mind to it.

Paint packages

Paint packages are designed with drawing and painting in mind. Most packages are quite simple to use and there are plenty to choose from. You might try 2Paint A Picture, TextEase Paint, BlackCat Primary Schoolbox, Dazzle, FacePaint, Revelation Natural Art, Adobe Photoshop and Microsoft Paint.

Microsoft Paint comes free with the Windows operating system. You'll find it by accessing Start → Programs → Accessories.

 Activity

Link to the Primary ICT site and try out the two MS Paint activities: Using Paint 1 and Using Paint 2.
This activity is courtesy of Teaching Ideas: www.teachingideas.co.uk

Resources

Useful resources for art and design include:

■ graphics tablets (e.g. Art Pad) which are better options than a mouse when drawing, writing, sketching, colouring and picture editing;

■ digital cameras, video cameras, scanners and editing software for the capture and editing of images;

■ printers.

Activity ideas

1. Year 1 children take photos of themselves using a digital camera. The pictures are inserted into a paint package and the children paint their own Halloween faces over the top.

Figure 6.3 Face paint activity

2. Year 4 pupils investigate pattern and symmetry. They use the available shapes in a paint package as simple building blocks. Using copy, paste and grouping they gradually create a number of patterned squares which are reflected in the horizontal and vertical axes of symmetry provided by the package.

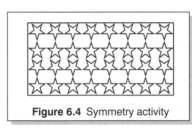

Figure 6.4 Symmetry activity

3. Year 3 children use paint software to create their own online art gallery, displaying their own imitations of a famous artist. The paintings are displayed using presentation software (e.g. PowerPoint), photo album software (e.g. Adobe Photoshop) or the Windows Picture and Fax viewer. Finally, they use a word processor to write about the artist.

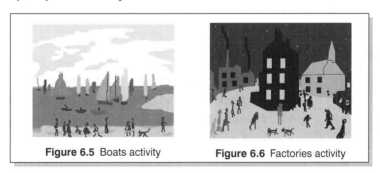

Figure 6.5 Boats activity   **Figure 6.6** Factories activity

Design and technology

In Key Stage 1 children will use tools to join and combine materials and produce quality products. They will use pictures, words, labelled sketches and models to describe, in simple terms, what they want to do and to communicate the details of their designs to others. In Key Stage 2, children will produce step-by-step plans and work from them to create products with some accuracy, paying attention to quality of finish and to function. They are able to check their work as it develops identifying what is working well and what could be improved. Finally, they will test and evaluate their products.

ICT allows children to be creative and can be used to: examine manufacturing processes; use appropriate software packages to design and accurately manufacture products; and use the Internet and CD-ROMs to investigate materials. It dovetails nicely with the ICT curriculum for 'developing ideas and making things happen'.

ICT can also allow children to simulate and model ideas and to control and program electrical and mechanical designs. However simulation and control were outlined in Chapter 5 so they won't be covered again here.

Design and manufacture

Children can be expected to create designs for simple two- and three-dimensional products such as a photo frame, packaging for a product, house plans and elevations, clothing, models and vehicles. More often than not, a simple paint or drawing package will suffice. Should you wish to use something more elaborate then try one of the following: 2Design; Junior CAD; Primary CAD; Design Tools; FlexiCAD; or CAD CAM … and don't forget the digital camera.

Web-based materials

There are many web-based resources which can be used to support children's learning in design and technology. Becta provide a useful guide.

 Activity

Link to the Primary ICT site and try out some of the web based resources in the Becta D&T Guide. One of the better resources in the guide can be found at Flying Pig (www. flying-pig.co.uk/mechanisms/pages/pulley.html).

Resources

Useful resources for design and technology include:

- scanners
- colour inkjet printers
- interactive whiteboards
- digital cameras.

Activity ideas

1. Year 3 children design packaging for a set of 6 paint pots. The dimensions are calculated and a drawing package is used to create a template. The template is printed out on card which is cut and glued to form a box.

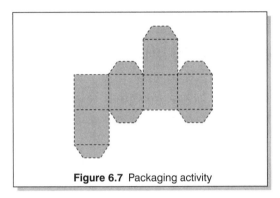

Figure 6.7 Packaging activity

Why is it good to use ICT here? Well, if the first attempt doesn't work, the template can be quickly modified – not so easy if it were done with pencil and paper from the outset!

2. Year 5 pupils are tasked with creating a low-fat menu for the school café. They search the Internet for information on food composition, recommended daily intakes and menu suggestions. A spreadsheet is used to calculate percentage values for carbohydrates, fat and protein and to check that each menu option satisfies the daily nutritional requirements.

	Protein	Fat	Carbs
Chicken (200g)	70	0	0
Salad (50g)	Trace	0	3.5
Tomato	0	0.2	1.5

Figure 6.8 Nutrition activity

3. An interactive whiteboard is used with a class of Year 6 children who are required to investigate motors and gear mechanisms which are used to operate fairground rides. They identify the mechanisms involved and work out how they are joined together. The interactive whiteboard allows easy linking to prepared animations and to a number of information websites.

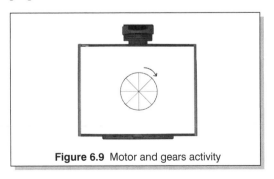

Figure 6.9 Motor and gears activity

Activity

Link to the Primary ICT site and watch the video on Fairground Rides.

Geography

In geography, children use geographical enquiry to gain an appreciation of:

- physical features (e.g. rivers, the weather), human features (e.g. buildings, railways) and the way in which things are arranged (e.g. trends in weather during the year, the way that streets are arranged in a locality, the layout of hedgerows in a farming landscape);

- processes which cause change (e.g. building of new houses, changing the look of the landscape, erosion of a river bank);

- places/geographical areas (e.g. villages, cities, districts, countries);

- physical and human environments (e.g. deserts, rivers, streets, cities);

- people (e.g. communities, the world as a global community, the rights and responsibilities of citizens within communities).

ICT can be used in a number of ways:

- Maps and route planners are available in electronic form which allow the scale to be changed to suit the depth of enquiry. Images can be captured and presented in a variety of forms.

- There are lots of secondary sources of textual and pictorial information on CD-ROM and the Internet.

- Digital cameras can provide permanent records of important features, landmarks, people and places.

- Completed work can be stored, manipulated and presented in many different ways.

- Data-logging equipment can be used to investigate 'micro-climates' around the school.

- An automatic weather station can be used for weather and climate investigations.

Resources

Useful resources for geography include:

- data-logging equipment
- automatic weather stations
- digital cameras
- CD-ROM maps and information sources including: All about Weather and Seasons; DK Become a British Isles Explorer / DK Become a World Explorer; Eye2eye Britain Panoramic; Living Library; Oxford Infant Atlas; Rivers; and Worldwise Interactive 3D Atlas.

Activity ideas

1. Year 2 children explore their local area in search of landmarks. They download a map from the Internet and copy it into a publishing package. Equipped with a print-out of the map and a digital camera they go for a walk and capture images of the library, local shop, school etc. On return to the school the images are superimposed onto the map which is printed out and placed on the classroom wall.

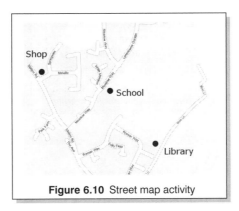

Figure 6.10 Street map activity

2. Year 3 children establish the population of countries around the world using the Internet. The results are presented in a bar chart with a suitable scale and are also added to a database which the children gradually develop as a source of information about countries around the world.

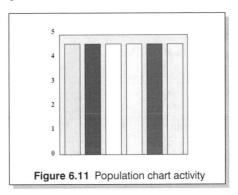

Figure 6.11 Population chart activity

3. Year 6 children carry out a survey to find out about pupils' habits (hobbies, food etc). They use a word processor to devise a questionnaire which is uploaded to the school website. Pupils download and complete the questionnaire, emailing a copy back to the class teacher. Y6 children transfer the information into a spreadsheet, analyse it and present a summary of the results on the school website.

```
My hobbies are:

Sport
Painting
Writing
Reading
Gardening
Building models
Needlework
Playing an instrument
Other
```

Figure 6.12 Hobbies activity

History

The five main aspects of history are: chronological understanding; knowledge and understanding of events, people and changes in the past; historical interpretation; historical enquiry; and organisation and communication. Children will gain factual knowledge and understanding of the main events and people during historical periods of the past in Britain and the wider world and place events within a chronological framework.

It is more difficult to identify specific ICT resources for history. The most useful will probably be information sources such as websites (particularly those hosted by major libraries, galleries and other public institutions) and CD-ROMs.

Resources

Useful resources for history include:

- Internet connection
- history CD-ROMs including: My World of Geography & History, Roman Britain, Victorian Britain, Vikings and Ancient Egypt
- a means of recording fieldwork such as a laptop computer or palm top computer (PDA), a digital camera, a camcorder and a digital voice recorder (mp3/mp4)
- data-handling software (e.g. spreadsheet or database).

Activity ideas

1. Year 1 children differentiate between objects used today (new) and objects used in the past (old). Using a content free package they categorise aircraft by dragging and dropping their images into the correct box.

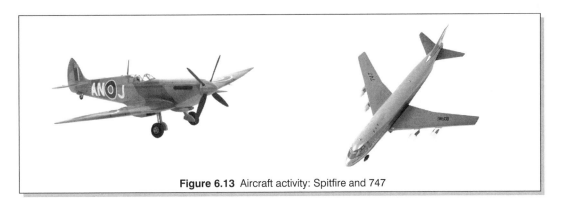

Figure 6.13 Aircraft activity: Spitfire and 747

2. Year 3 pupils research the Internet to find historic archives of their locality. Images and information are transferred onto an old map, printed out and placed on the classroom wall alongside the modern day map that they created in geography activity 1. Children compare the two and use a word processor to write about changes over time.

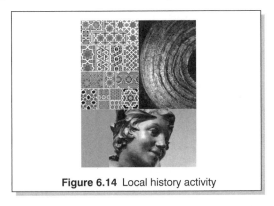

Figure 6.14 Local history activity

3. Year 5 pupils visit the local museum to investigate the influence of the Romans on their town. They capture images of artefacts and use an mp4 recorder to make verbal notes. They take the opportunity to interview the curator and record this too. Back at school the information collected is collated and added to the history section of the school website. Podcasts are created to provide supporting commentary.

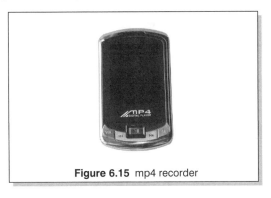

Figure 6.15 mp4 recorder

Music

In music, children use their own voices and musical instruments to make, change, order and combine sounds. They also explore how sounds may be used and the relationship between different sounds.

ICT can help pupils to: make and explore sounds; simulate the playing of musical instruments; compose musical scores; record for different purposes; structure music; and understand musical processes.

Resources

Useful resources for music include:

- tape-recorder with counter
- keyboard with a selection of voices
- focused activity software such as pitch and rhythm games
- simple pattern sequencing software
- digital effects units
- MIDI keyboard featuring a wide range of preset sounds
- software for recording and processing sound
- software for exploring style and structure.

Activity ideas

1. Year 5 pupils use the 2Simple's Music Toolkit to produce a simple radio jingle using two staves and two different musical instruments. The composition is developed over a period of six weeks using all the staves and different instruments. Pupils are then encouraged to develop and amend ideas and, at the end of each session, pupils evaluate each other's compositions.

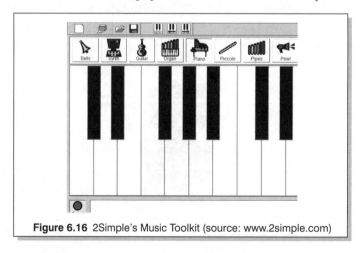

Figure 6.16 2Simple's Music Toolkit (source: www.2simple.com)

2. Year 1 children discuss features of sounds they might hear around the school (sounds such as the school bell, rain on a window, an aeroplane flying overhead etc. Features such as loud, quiet, long, short, high pitch, low pitch etc.). Then they locate the source of these sounds and record them using a tape recorder. The sounds are played back later and children have to identify each sound.

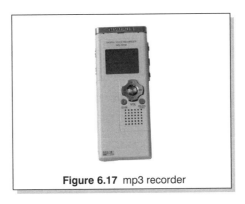

Figure 6.17 mp3 recorder

3. Having listened to several music samples, Year 4 pupils use simple drag and drop software to produce a structured music composition. A number of instruments are used and each is allocated its own track. The music is critically evaluated (against a set of criteria) and edited accordingly until the children are satisfied with it.

Physical education (PE)

The National Curriculum programme of study for physical education has four aspects:

1. acquiring and developing skills
2. selecting and applying skills, tactics and compositional ideas
3. evaluating and improving performance
4. knowledge and understanding of fitness and health.

Children will develop an understanding of why physical activity might be good for their general health and well-being. They will explore and perform movement with control, coordination, accuracy, consistency and fluency (from simple to complex) and they will evaluate their performance in order to improve the quality of their work.

Using ICT, pupils can use a sound system to provide the stimulus for their movement; digital photographs and videos of their gymnastics and dance sequences in order to bring about improvement; CD-ROMs and websites to compare their own movements to those of others (including gymnasts and dancers) and to increase their awareness of health issues; digital timers, heart rate monitors and mobile computers to monitor their performance; and software to record and analyse their progress and development.

Resources

Useful resources for physical education include:

- digital cameras with video and still facilities
- TV monitors, screens and interactive whiteboards
- sound systems with recording facilities
- laptops and palmtops
- digital timers, heart rate monitors and timing mats
- data-recording and analysis software such as spreadsheets
- CD-ROMs
- the Internet.

Activity ideas

1. In athletics, Year 4 children work on their running technique. The teacher introduces key principles and the children then explore the Internet for videos of athletes. They examine the athletes' running actions and attempt to emulate these on the playing field. Pupils take videos of themselves and use them to evaluate their own performance.

2. Year 1 children use images projected onto the wall (or onto an interactive whiteboard) to discuss the association between colours and moods and between the weather and our emotions. As part of a dance lesson they act out these emotions using a range of movements.

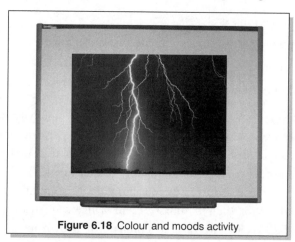

Figure 6.18 Colour and moods activity

3. Year 6 pupils design a 'beeping' stopwatch and a metronome using MS PowerPoint. They are projected onto the wall in the sports hall and can be used in a variety of races, games, gymnastics and dance activities.

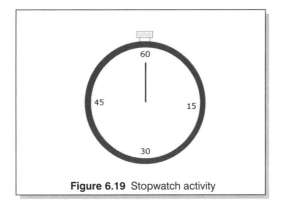

Figure 6.19 Stopwatch activity

 Activity

Link to the Primary ICT site and
1. read the pdf file 'Using Video Cameras in PE'
2. try out the PowerPoint Stopwatch.

Modern foreign languages (MFL)

Learning languages in primary school provides children with early access to foreign people and cultures. It may also improve performance in secondary school.

There's nothing new about teaching foreign languages in primary schools, however modern foreign languages is a contemporary addition to the National Curriculum at Key Stage 2. It is still to be fully embraced across all schools and yet the number of languages already taught by some is astounding. Alongside the familiar French, Spanish and German sit the likes of Japanese and Chinese.

As in English, MFL is organised under the language skills of speaking, listening, reading and writing. Children are taught to:

■ listen and respond to words and short sentences (with frequent repetition and visual or oral support as necessary);

■ speak slowly and with approximate pronunciation, using a narrow range of language that is related to topics of immediate personal interest;

■ read and write single sentences or very short extracts using a narrow range of language (with spelling and handwriting that can be understood by the teacher).

Research by Becta highlights a number of ways in which ICT might be used. Interactive whiteboards enable improved delivery and pacing, whole-class teaching, interaction and discussion. Digital resources from the Internet and CD-ROMs give access to a vast number of learning opportunities, allowing pupils to work at their own pace and replay audio/video repeatedly according to individual needs. International communication projects via video conferencing, email and discussion forums facilitate cultural awareness and impact positively on grammar, vocabulary and tenses. Multimedia presentation software enables a range of MFL skills to be practised. Digital video and audio recordings of students whilst speaking offers feedback on performance and the opportunity for critique and evaluation by teachers, peers and pupils themselves. Films in DVD format with subtitles and audio tracks in different languages are useful for language translation (Becta, 2008a).

Resources

Useful resources for modern foreign languages include:

- interactive whiteboards
- presentation software
- audio CDs
- CD-ROMs with phonetics and language activities (e.g. Fonetiks, Chatter Chatter, StarFrench, TextEase Language Packs, Talk Now! Italian, Sonica Spanish)
- web-based resources
- video conferencing, email, discussion boards and blogs.

Activity ideas

1. A Year 3 class use a web-based resource as part of their French lesson. The children watch the animated sequence which is projected onto an IWB. The sequence is repeated and the children repeat the phrases. The teacher supports the spoken word with speech bubbles created in the Smart Notepad. Later, children play individual parts and act out the sequence themselves.

Figure 6.20 French language software

2. Year 4 children take a PowerPoint talking story book of Goldilocks (which they previously created in English) and adapt it into a French language version (Boucle D'Or et les Trois Ours). As an extension, the class could be split into three groups with each group working on a different language (e.g. Spanish, French and German).

Figure 6.21 The three bears

3. A Year 5 teacher introduces German vocabulary and common phrases using the software title Chatter Chatter. Emphasis is placed on learning vocabulary in a fun and motivating way by listening to the spoken language on the two included CD-ROMs and practicing newly acquired words using some of the many games and focused lesson activities.

Religious education (RE)

For primary school children, Religious education is about knowledge of:

- religious and moral beliefs;
- religious teachings;
- religious practice and lifestyles;
- who we are;
- how we express ourselves;
- the difference between right and wrong.

They achieve this by exploring:

- religious stories;
- comparisons between religions;
- recognising religious symbols and words;
- their own experience and feelings;
- how they respond to the experiences and feelings of others.

Religious education can make use of a number of digital sources of information and activities on CD-ROM and on the Internet. They can also utilise a wide range of generic ICT resources for gathering, analysing and presenting data.

Resources

Useful resources for RE include:

- CD-ROMs such as: Kar2ouche Understanding Religion; BBC Faiths and Celebrations; Living Library; RM Colour Magic 3; World Religions; Christian Symbols; Ready Resources Religious Education [1 and 2]; and Year 1 [2/3/4/5/6] Religious Education

- websites including: Holy days and festivals; Religion online; Christianity [Hinduism, Judaism, Islam, Sikhism] for Children; and Teddy's day out.

Activity ideas

1. Year 2 children learn that religious organisations do work to protect our world. They use the Internet to access religious websites and explore threats to the environment and to the survival of people and animals in some parts of the world. Finally, they use MS Publisher to design a poster to draw attention to issues in the UK.

Figure 6.22 Pollution activity

2. Guided by a prepared activity sheet, Year 4 pupils use the CD-ROM Understanding Religion to develop an understanding of unfamiliar religions. In particular, they are required to identify a number of shared beliefs, values and practices within and between the religions.

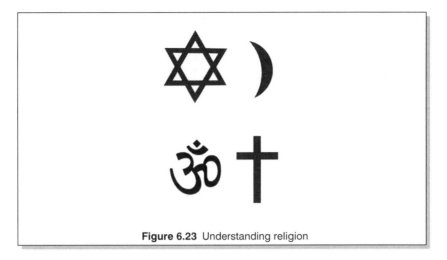

Figure 6.23 Understanding religion

3. Year 3 children carry out a school survey to ascertain individual's values and opinions on a number of moral issues. A simple spreadsheet is prepared and copied to personal digital assistants (PDAs). Pupils use the PDAs in the playground and dining hall, recording responses from children across school. The results are analysed and presented using a stacked bar chart.

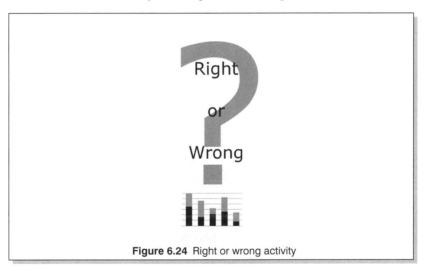

Figure 6.24 Right or wrong activity

Personal, social and health education (PSHE) and citizenship

Personal, social and health education (which now includes social and emotional aspects of learning) and citizenship are considered side by side. Although they are non-statutory elements of the curriculum, most schools teach them because they deal with important moral, social and cultural issues and help children to become healthy and safe, confident and active citizens, and to form good relationships and behave well.

Finding resources for these subjects can prove tricky. However, there are a number of appropriate CD-ROM/web-based offerings and Teachers TV provides some particularly useful coverage of a range of social and moral issues (such as how schools deal with bullying).

Resources

Useful resources for PHSE/citizenship include:

- CD-ROMs including: PSHE in the Playground; Kar2ouche PSHE [Bullying, Drug Awareness, Respecting Diversity, Relationships: School and the Wider World]; Growing & Developing; Keeping Healthy; Feelings & Worries; and You, your body and sex
- web-based materials such as: The Association for Teaching Citizenship; National Association for Pastoral Care in Education; Schoolzone; Grid Club; TeacherNet PSHE; World E-Citizens; Eco Schools; and It's Your Goal
- Teachers TV.

Activity ideas

1. Over a period of time, a primary school creates a collection of audio and video clips of children expressing their views on a wide range of moral and social issues. The clips form part of subsequent PSHE lessons and are used to stimulate discussion on a whole range of topics. Cameras are ideal in this respect for reflection and consolidation.

Figure 6.25 Camcorder activity

2. A Year 4 class use an interactive whiteboard to brainstorm ideas on reactive and preventive measures with regard to bullying. The file is saved and revisited from time to time so that children can review the topic.

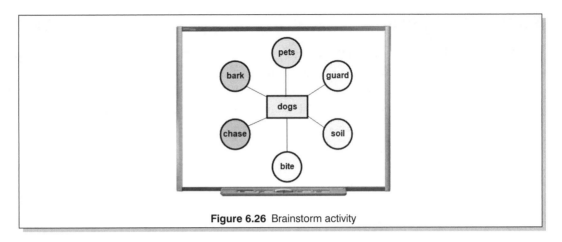

Figure 6.26 Brainstorm activity

3. Year 5 pupils use the Ace Monkey Drug Education Pack to explore the topic of drugs. They interview each other and record their responses to important questions using the podcasting package 'Podium'. The resulting mp3 files are shared on the school learning platform.

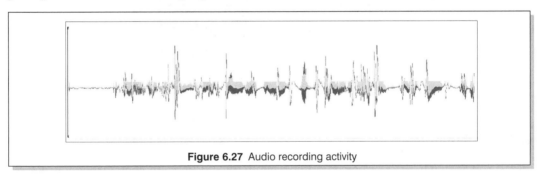

Figure 6.27 Audio recording activity

ICT

There are two aspects to ICT in schools:

1. ICT across the curriculum
2. ICT as a discrete subject.

The first has been covered in this chapter and the second was introduced in Chapter 3. The only remaining consideration is your own competence ('computer literacy') in using ICT in order that you can adequately support your own pupils. Computer literacy will not be covered here – if you need help in this area then there are several options available to you including:

■ e-learning courses which are made available on the Primary ICT website;

■ dedicated training courses such as Computer Literacy And Information Technology (CLAIT) and the European Computer Driving Licence (ECDL) which are offered by a number of providers;

■ other books which are dedicated to CLAIT and ECDL.

Subscription websites

Some schools invest in subscription websites either in addition to conventional software or as a complete solution in itself. There are a number of available sites that charge a small subscription per pupil per year. Some are devoted to specific topic areas whilst others cover the whole of the National Curriculum. Some are available online whereas others are downloaded to the school server and updated on a regular basis. Each has its own strengths and weaknesses. Perhaps the two most popular are Espresso and Education City. Other sites include At School, MyMaths and Spark Island.

Figure 6.28 Espresso (source: www.espresso.co.uk)

Resource guides

If you are the ICT Coordinator or you have an interest in technology then you may well know exactly what ICT resources the school holds, where to find them and how they can be used. However, this will not hold true for all staff, particularly new teachers or supply teachers.

It's a good idea therefore to produce ICT resource guides for each subject. These will list the resources you hold for the subject together with a brief overview/evaluation of each. Part of a resource guide for mathematics might look something like Figure 6.29.

List of resources

All the resources mentioned in this and other chapters are tabulated in Chapter 10. Many are common to all subjects whilst some are specialist (although the cross curricular approach to ICT does mean that many resources can be adapted to any topic).

ICT Resource Guide - Mathematics

 iBug Ladybird (Classroom 1)	The iBug Ladybird is an appealing remote control floor robot for KS1. It is very simple to use and extremely child friendly. It is ideal for teaching instructions, spatial awareness, angles, direction, estimation control and programming to primary school children. It can be adapted for use in English activities and other subjects too. *Requires two re-chargeable AA batteries*.
 Mathletics (web based) Source: www.3plearning.co.uk	Fun and motivating interactive software which covers all aspects of the Mathematics curriculum and improves speed and accuracy. It adapts to the ability of the child. Best introduced by teacher – children can then progress on their own (or with support from teacher or parents). Available via the school website 24 hours per day.
 123 CD (Computer Suite) Source: http://www.sherston.com	Software which effectively promotes children's learning of counting and early number, using a variety of activities to introduce, reinforce and consolidate these skills. Once explained, the program can be used by pupils without adult assistance. The program makes the world of numbers fun and the children enjoyed using it.

Figure 6.29 Resource guide

7

Models of e-learning

Introduction

Of the many definitions of e-learning, most refer to the delivery of learning online. For the purposes of this book however it is defined simply as 'technology-based learning' whether the method of presentation is in a face-to-face environment, at a distance, online or a blended approach.

There is no single 'best practice' when using ICT to enhance teaching and learning and, not surprisingly, a variety of 'models' have emerged. This chapter examines these models which may be used in isolation or in combination. They include:

- interactive whiteboards
- computer–mediated communication
- learning platforms
- video conferencing
- podcasting and vidcasting
- play-based learning
- computer games
- computer configurations
- mobile learning.

It must be stressed however that, whichever model is adopted, it is the learning which is important; the technology simply helps provide the means by which it is achieved. This is emphasised by Biggs (1999) who describes the task of good pedagogical design as one of ensuring that there are absolutely no inconsistencies between the curriculum we teach, the teaching methods we use, the learning environment we choose and the assessment procedures we adopt.

Interactive whiteboards (IWB)

Interactive whiteboards enable improved delivery and pacing, whole-class teaching, interaction and discussion, and relate to increased motivation for both teachers and pupils (Passey *et al.*, 2004).

Boys in particular, are captivated by the IWB. It is captures their interest, holds their attention and offers them a degree of control. (GTC 2006)

What is an interactive whiteboard?

An interactive whiteboard is a touch-sensitive screen that works in conjunction with a PC and a data projector.

This combination of technologies not only turns the IWB into a huge computer screen, it also provides a range of features which allow teachers and children to perform functions and carry out activities which would otherwise be impossible or inferior when reliant upon conventional whiteboards and computer displays alone. In the right hands, the IWB is a very valuable resource.

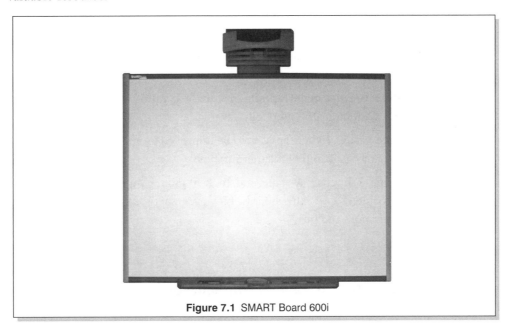

Figure 7.1 SMART Board 600i

History of the interactive whiteboard

The IWB has been around for many years (in one form or another) but only began to make a major impression in primary schools from the early part of the twenty-first century and particularly from 2003 when the Department for Children, Schools and Families (DCSF) Primary Schools Whiteboard Expansion project (PSWE) was launched. It provided substantial funding to 21 local authorities to support the acquisition and use of interactive whiteboards. The number of primary schools now using IWBs is over 95 per cent.

Becta's evaluation of the project (in 2007) reported the following key findings:

- The more experience the teacher has of using the interactive whiteboard, the greater the likelihood of positive attainment gains for pupils.

- In Key Stage 2 maths, average and high attaining boys and girls who had been taught extensively with the interactive whiteboard made the equivalent of an extra 2.5 to 5 months' progress over the course of two years. There was less effect on progress for boys and girls of low prior attainment.

- In Key Stage 2 science, all pupils except high attaining girls made greater progress with more exposure to the IWB, with low attaining boys making as much as 7.5 months' additional progress.

- In Key Stage 2 English, the presence of an interactive whiteboard does not appear to have a significant effect on attainment, though further investigation with larger data sets is required.

- In Key Stage 2 writing, boys with low prior attainment made 2.5 months of additional progress.

- At Key Stage 1, there are indications of attainment gains once teachers have embedded the use of the interactive whiteboard in their practice. In particular:

  - In Key Stage 1 maths, high attaining girls made gains of 4.75 months, enabling them to catch up with high attaining boys.

  - In Key Stage 1 science, there appears to be improved progress for girls of all attainment levels, and for average and high attaining boys.

  - In Key Stage 1 English, average and high attaining pupils benefit from increased exposure to interactive whiteboards. However, there is little effect on progress for low attaining boys and girls.

Becta (2008b)

What are the benefits of the interactive whiteboards?

Using your finger as a pointer, you can do anything that a mouse can do (including left and right click). You can also write on the board, on top of open applications and within applications which support writing. This makes IWBs ideal for whole-class teaching because everyone is able to see the large screen from their own seats.

IWBs have specific educational value and offer a whole variety of benefits (though some of these result solely from projection onto a large screen):

- They provide all the familiar features of a traditional blackboard or whiteboard without the mess, without the need to clean them and with an infinite amount of working space.

- Lessons can be enhanced by augmenting the teacher's personal presentation with a range of formatting and multimedia features.

- Anything on the screen can be saved or printed as required.

- Teachers and children can interact directly with the board creating lessons and activities that benefit from a graphical user interface including the movement of objects (drag and drop), input of text, navigation and hyperlinks.

- They allow learners to absorb information more easily.

- They promote better learner participation by freeing them from note taking.

- They allow learners to work collaboratively around a shared task/work area.

- When used for whole-class interactive testing of understanding, they can provide learner feedback rapidly.

- They link to other applications (e.g. MS PowerPoint), providing them with additional features.

- They are well supported by a huge assortment of interactive educational software packages (both free and commercial).

- They come with additional, advanced features, for example, you can record and playback a whole lesson.

- As with many other ICT resources they are extremely motivating both for teachers and pupils.

They do of course have their downside:

- Simply installing the technology doesn't guarantee its use. There needs to be a positive investment by staff in terms of training and practice.

- Some teachers can become prepossessed to the extent that:
  - ☐ They use the IWB at any available opportunity, whether it is appropriate to do so or not!
  - ☐ They 'hog' the board and don't provide sufficient opportunity for children to interact.

- Interactive whiteboards are more expensive than conventional whiteboards or projector/screen combinations.

- Their surface can become damaged, necessitating expensive replacement.

- Front projection boards can be obscured by the user.

- Inadvertent eye contact with the projector is potentially harmful. Children should be supervised at all times when a projector is being used.

- Fixed-height boards are often too high to reach the top or too low for their bottom to be readily visible.

It is also important to be aware of the health and safety implications of using IWBs and, in particular, the potential of eye injury caused by the intensity of the projector beam.

TeacherNet (2008)

Making good use of interactive whiteboards

To maximise the impact of IWBs, teachers should invest time and energy in training and practice. Before considering specific software resources, the inherent features of the IWB should be mastered.

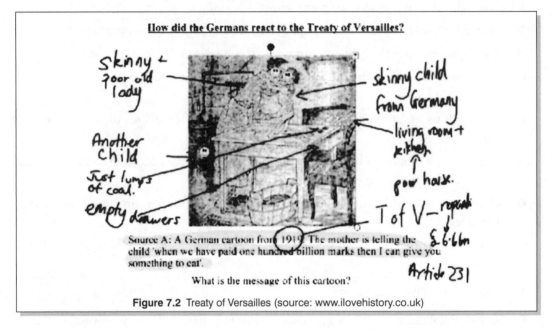

Figure 7.2 Treaty of Versailles (source: www.ilovehistory.co.uk)

Whatever you are projecting you can make annotations on top. Great for thought sharing, building up key points and highlighting text and images. The pens and highlighters have a wide range of colours and, of course, your notes can be saved, printed or wiped clean at a stroke. The 'floating tools' is a useful feature too.

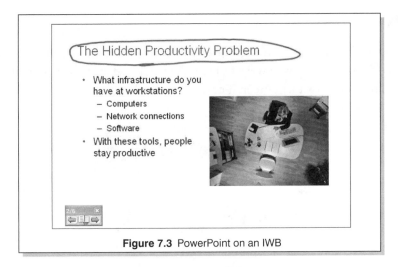

Figure 7.3 PowerPoint on an IWB

Make use of the features linked to MS PowerPoint. These include: a special toolbar with navigation and menu options, the option to advance (and rewind) the presentation with your finger (using single or double touch), pens or floating tools to make annotations (which may be permanently incorporated if desired), inserting notes and drawings on the fly and incorporating hyperlinks.

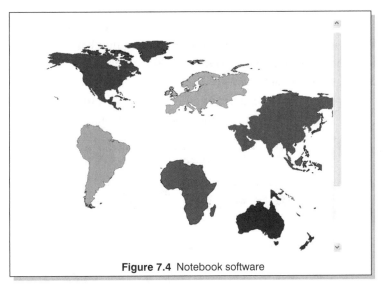

Figure 7.4 Notebook software

All boards come with useful software (e.g. Smart Notebook or ACTIVstudio). These are multi-page notebooks which include a variety of tools, such as drawing objects, photos, rulers, flipchart functions, protractors, playback features, diagrams, animations, backgrounds, text conversion, screen capture and more.

Activity ideas

1. Key Stage 1 children work in small groups on a number of interactive literacy activities provided free from the Crickweb website. Here they drag and drop the names of vegetables onto the picture. The name box turns green if correctly placed.

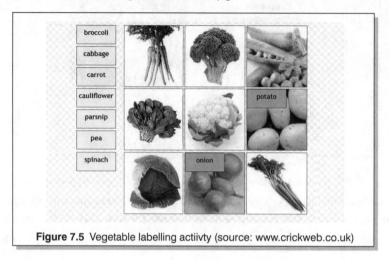

Figure 7.5 Vegetable labelling actiivty (source: www.crickweb.co.uk)

2. A Year 1 teacher designs her own simple maths activity using the Smart Notebook. Children count green and red apples (whilst dragging and dropping them from baskets into the answer box). The children are invited to write the corresponding numbers below each group of apples. More able children do the same with words to form a number sentence.

The words and numbers are then grouped and dragged onto a separate slide so that the exercise can be repeated over and over for all number bonds to 10. Other than the apples, all objects are fixed to the screen to prevent them being accidentally moved.

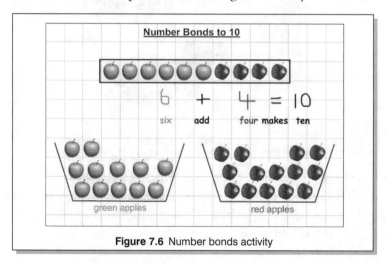

Figure 7.6 Number bonds activity

3. Using one of Smart Notebook's handwriting backgrounds, a KS1 group practice their writing skills (given pictures and typed words as clues). Their writing is then converted automatically into typed text in order to provide confirmation that they are achieving their goal.

Figure 7.7 Handwriting background

4. A Year 6 teacher uses several features of the IWB to demonstrate forces and movement. Using a content free software package she imports a number of useful images and builds up a word bank. With these objects, and some built in drawing tools, she builds up key points as the demo progresses. Using hyperlinks to pre-selected science websites, children are invited to carry out further reading and research and to confirm the knowledge and understanding they have acquired.

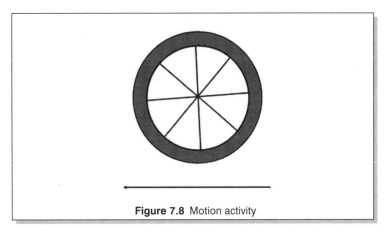

Figure 7.8 Motion activity

5. Year 5 children participate in a mind-mapping activity on the effects of smoking. They use MS Word to organise their ideas and input them using a radio-linked remote keyboard. Their hand

writing is then converted to text, formatted, colour coded and printed as an aide-memoire for a subsequent off screen activity.

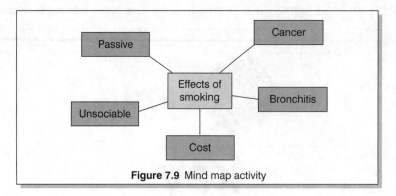

Figure 7.9 Mind map activity

6. A primary school uses Whiteboard Wizard's Time Teller, one of many commercial packages designed specifically around the national numeracy strategy. It is used in whole-class teaching for time-telling on analogue and digital clock faces. Tasks are made incrementally more difficult to suit ability and progress through years 1 to 6.

Figure 7.10 Analogue to digital time telling activity

7. A Reception/Year 1 teacher uses TextEase to set up a lesson on small numbers and number order using money as the theme. The available clipart provides the drag and drop money images and the features of grouping and rotating are used to help establish the principles involved.

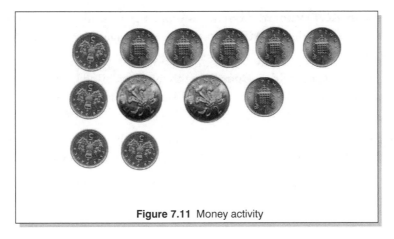

Figure 7.11 Money activity

8. A Year 5 teacher uses the IWB to make annotations on top of a spreadsheet in order to help explain the use of tables, formatting and simple formulas. When used with the whole class (or to overcome problems for small groups) this saves the time which would otherwise have been expended dealing one-to-one with each pupil in turn.

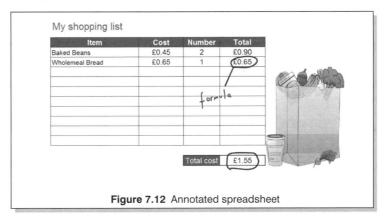

Figure 7.12 Annotated spreadsheet

Types of interactive whiteboards

There are several types of IWB to choose from (albeit you may well be tied into the brand offered by your local authority). Options include front projection, rear projection, interactive displays, boards incorporating projectors and adjustable height boards (very useful when you need to position the board close to the floor for young children at circle time). The main brands are:

- **Smartboard** from www.smarttech.com: probably the most popular. It comes with the Smart Notebook and a wide array of other associated software and hardware resources are available too.

- **Promethean ACTIVboard** from www.prometheanworld.com: it comes with a good range of resources including ACTIVstudio for Key Stages 3–4 or ACTIVprimary for Key Stages 1–2.

- **Hitachi board (Cambridge Board)** from www.hitachi-education.com: claims to be the best value and best quality whiteboard available for education today. It utilises Starboard software.

- **RM Classboard from** www.rm.com: comes with Easiteach Studio software it offers a powerful teaching software product for both primary and secondary schools.

- **Clasus** from www.adaptedlearning.com: with A-migo software specifically developed for training and education.

Interactive whiteboard resources

There are many IWB resources to be found on the Internet. A number of extremely good tutorials can be found on Promethean's Activprimary2 at (http://movies.atomiclearning.com/uk/activprimary_2_pc) and on the Smart Notebook (http://smarttech.com/trainingcenter/tutorials.asp). Other materials are listed in Appendix 2.

Mobile learning

Introduction

Mobile learning (m-learning) refers to the use of mobile and handheld devices in teaching and learning. These include mobile telephones, personal digital assistants (PDAs), laptops/notebooks, net books and tablet PCs.

Education now benefits and, to some extent, relies on ICT and the Internet. As a result, technologies have become more portable, cheaper and user friendly. Mobility offers opportunities for widening participation in learning. Many devices now offer similar functionality to a PC itself and can provide access from remote locations or from within the classroom.

In January 2007 the government announced 'The Home Access Taskforce', whose remit is to advise on ways in which children can use technology to access learning whilst away from school. The extent to which this is possible for primary school children is debatable however, since 51 per cent of all 10 year olds own their own phone or other mobile device (Bhat, 2006) then mobile learning is certainly a possibility.

Some of the benefits are (QIA 2008):

- Learners can interact with each other and with the practitioner instead of hiding behind large monitors.

- It's much easier to accommodate several mobile devices in a classroom than several desktop computers.

- PDAs or tablets holding notes and e-books are lighter and less bulky than bags full of files, paper and textbooks, or even laptops.

- Handwriting with the stylus pen is more intuitive than using keyboard and mouse.

- It's possible to share assignments and work collaboratively; learners and practitioners can e-mail, cut, copy and paste text, pass the device around a group, or 'beam' the work to each other using the infrared function of a PDA (or a wireless connection such as Bluetooth).

- Mobile devices can be used anywhere, anytime, including at home, on the train or bus, in hospital etc.

- These devices can engage young people who may have lost interest in education.

- The size, shape, weight and portability of mobile devices make them particularly effective for users with disabilities.

- This technology may contribute to combating the digital divide, because it is generally cheaper than desktop computers.

There are of course a number of potential disadvantages:

- Small screens limit the amount and type of information that can be displayed.

- Small buttons can be difficult for people with little manual dexterity to manipulate.

- Some devices have limited storage capacities.

- Batteries have to be charged regularly, and data can be lost if this is not done correctly.

- Bandwidth may degrade with a larger number of users when using wireless networks.

- The stylus pens are often narrow and small, and require accurate use to work correctly.

- Attachable keyboards for PDAs are available, but these are also quite small, and options for switch or mouse access are limited.

- Some devices have restricted functionality in the operating system and in the applications too.

- It's a fast-moving market, especially for mobile phones, so devices can become out of date very quickly.

Mobile phones

> There are one and a half billion cell phones in operation around the world, and a large percentage of them are in the hands of students. Yet these phones are barred in most classrooms because they interrupt lessons and can enable cheating.
>
> Prensky (2005)

Mobile phones are more than communications devices, they are mini computers which, for most pupils are indispensable and always turned on. So why not make use of their redeeming features, treat them as powerful learning devices and use the opportunity to everyone's educational advantage? Even with the existence of a digital divide, most pupils have already bought their own phone.

Pupils will undoubtedly welcome using their phones, just as they have done with other technology. However, making effective use of mobile phones in learning will require considerable rethinking by teachers.

Opportunities for learning with phones will depend upon their included features. Most phones have text input and voice recording facilities and the latest (including the iPhone and Blackberry) provide a whole lot more.

Activity ideas with mobile phones

1. Year 5 and 6 children took mobile phones on a field trip to the Black Country Museum. The features of the phone were used to capture images and short video and to store textual descriptions of some of the museums artefacts. Back at the school, all the information was uploaded to PCs and used to compile a web page which served as a portfolio of work to share with all the children and their parents.

The trip was all the more interesting and motivating. The quality of the images was surprisingly high and it served to demonstrate how such small mobile devices can be used without the need for larger laptops or notebooks.

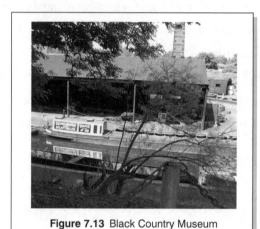

Figure 7.13 Black Country Museum
(source www.bclm.co.uk)

2. A school in Australia, looking for ways to connect with their disengaged pupils, decided to employ mobile phones in literacy. The pupils, who found writing difficult, were invited to use their phones to develop their writing and reading skills: capturing images, writing about them, and emailing the work to friends, families and teachers. The school's principal said he had been overwhelmed by the pupils' enthusiasm and resulting progress.

Figure 7.14 Mobile literacy

Personal digital assistants (PDAs)

A PDA is a handheld/palmtop computer with a touch-sensitive screen and a writing stylus. It will have a Windows Mobile operating system and Windows Mobile Office tools such as Pocket Word, Pocket Excel, Pocket Outlook, MSN Messenger, Windows Media Player, Pocket Microsoft Reader, Pocket Internet Explorer and Voice Recorder. It has wireless networking capability and can therefore connect to the school network and to the Internet. It is also capable of 'beaming' data from the PDA to the network or from PDA to PDA using its built-in infra red system and/or Bluetooth. The latest versions also act as a mobile phone and camera.

PDAs are useful for viewing and editing Word, Excel (and other documents), making handwritten notes and recording and playing audio and video files. The PDA can be synchronised with a PC to allow files to be transferred in both directions – quite a step up from a mobile phone!

Many PDAs have a range of available peripherals including the option to plug in a miniature keyboard and mouse.

Some local authorities are aiming to give every learner in their region access to a handheld computer.

Activity ideas with PDAs
1. KS2 children use the handwriting recognition facility of a PDA to develop their literacy. They use the stylus to form letters and words on the touch sensitive screen. The software then translates the words into typed text.

2. A Year 3 teacher has found that some pupils prefer reading from handheld devices rather than from books (particularly boys). He splits the class into groups and encourages them each to write a part of a story using the PDA. They 'beam' their work to each other and then piece the individual parts together to form a complete story. He has also created a number of pre-written stories which he beams to the class. The pupils then read the stories and discuss aspects by using the built-in email feature.

Figure 7.15 Personal digital assistant

3. Staff in a primary school are issued with PDAs for administrative purposes. Amongst other things they coordinate their diaries and tasks using the handheld device (which is frequently synchronised with their office PCs). The head teacher is able allocate tasks to staff and to access their diaries remotely.

Tablet PCs

A tablet PC is a slate-shaped mobile computer, equipped with touchscreen technology which allows the user to operate the computer with a stylus or digital pen. Some are 'hybrids' and also include a keyboard (which can be hidden beneath the screen as required).

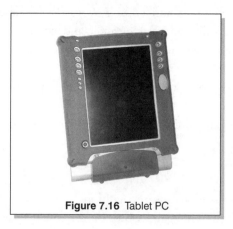

Figure 7.16 Tablet PC

The benefits of tablet PCs include:

- compactness when space is an issue;
- portability between classes;
- robustness;
- motivation;
- useful for note-taking;

- successful with reluctant writers;
- good for handwriting practice.

Some tablets can be housed in a docking station which provides floppy disc, CD drive and additional ports.

As with other laptops and notebooks, tablets can be stored and charged using a charging trolley.

Tablet PCs offer the same features as a PC or laptop but they take up less space and are less imposing. Therefore they can be easily used in class alongside other 'non-ICT' activities. This helps to embed ICT across the curriculum (in contrast to computer suites which encourage discrete and separate ICT).

In its early days the tablet showed great promise and Microsoft's Bill Gates predicted that, because it is a PC that is virtually without limits, it would become the most popular form of PC on the market within five years (Gates, 2002). However, the tablet has not really taken off in a significant way since then. The main reason appears to be the somewhat prohibitive cost, particularly for the swing-screen versions with a keyboard attached. Some would say that the tablet PC is now 'dead' but perhaps it is simply 'dormant' and awaiting reintroduction when 'the price is right'.

Netbooks

Mobile computing is a compromise between the usability and features offered by the larger devices such as laptops and the convenience and portability of the smaller devices such as PDAs. If there is to be a solution which meets somewhere in the middle then it is surely the netbook. Some retailers have already stopped selling PDAs in favour of netbooks.

Netbooks are quickly capturing the interest of many teachers as an affordable way to achieve their desired pupil-to-computer ratio (half the price of an average laptop).

They are smaller and more portable than laptops – the screen size ranges from 7 inches to 10 inches and they tend to use low power processors in order to maximize battery life. They are chiefly intended for browsing the web, light computer work and cloud computing[1].

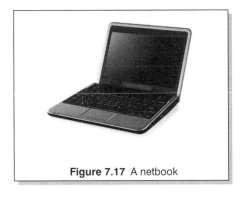

Figure 7.17 A netbook

---

1 The concept of cloud computing is that vast computing resources will reside on the Internet or other central location rather than in your own computer and network servers.

The netbook realises its full potential for mobility when equipped with mobile broadband which is either built in or achieved using a plug-in USB 'dongle'. The netbook then becomes a 'webbook' which provides Internet connectivity from anywhere that is covered by the mobile network provider.

An alternative to the netbook might be an ultra-mobile PC (UMPC) which is of slightly smaller size and with a keyboard which slides away under the screen. However, UMPCs are currently prohibitively expensive for most of the potential customers.

Play Station Portable (PSP)

Not long ago, gaming consoles like the Sony PSP would not have merited a place in a book such as this. At most they might have been offered space in a section relating to the educational value of games. However, the PSP has recently taken to the stage as an educational tool in its own right and is referred to, by some, as a 'mobile learning platform'.

 Activity

Link to the Sony site at: http://uk.playstation.com/education and watch the PSP video. It relates the experiences of several practitioners who have trialled PSPs in an educational context. How do you rate the PSP as an educational tool?
Perhaps the video says it all: unique; high quality; robust; portable; connects children directly with technology they use every day; accepts teacher-devised learning content using open standard technology; a great visual stimulus; interconnects with other devices such as the IWB; parental involvement; children value them; audio and video recording capability further empowers children as learners; facilitates self- and peer-assessment; features video conferencing; lessons can be downloaded automatically at specified times using RSS feeds.

The deployment of PSPs in schools may be recent but, already there are many reports on the positive impact they make on teaching, learning, personal development and well-being. As with any technological enhancement to a school's provision, its success will be enhanced through well planned and judicious use.

The PSP is of course not the only device on the market. However, according to Boxer (2008) it is becoming the games platform of choice in British schools.

Case study: A window to the world

Longwill School for the Deaf use PSPs for visual impact.

Technology has the power to enhance learning – but for deaf children it can be transformational. This has certainly been true in Longwill School for the Deaf in Birmingham where learning to read is particularly hard; not only is English the children's second language, but they are unable to work out the words on the page from the sound they make.

'Because the children are deaf, we think about how we can really exploit that visual strand', says Alison Carter, Longwill's deputy head. 'Every classroom has an interactive whiteboard, and we have visualisers; a lot of the teaching is through that visual channel, because it gives them a window to the world. I think children, specifically deaf children, need to be able to learn experientially; it's no good talking about a fire station to a deaf child – you need to take them there.'

The PSP project began in Sept 2007 working closely with Birmingham East CLC and ConnectED – a close and valuable partnership. From then on Alison's ideas kept on developing, and she realised the potential is as wide as your imagination can take it. Since then the school has found all sorts of uses for the PSP. For example: teaching spelling to the older children by filming BSL signs that can be displayed next to the written word; and creating 'dialogue journals' between teachers and individual children on the child's PSP.

Figure 7.18 Sony PSP

The PSPs are also being used effectively for home-school links, allowing children to take their experiences home to the parents and to bring work done at home back to school. Older children can film activities at home, and show them on the interactive whiteboard back at school. For younger children 'we film the nature centre trip using the PSPs and that goes home with the children that night, so the child and the parents can share that visit, talk it through and have a shared understanding of what's going on'.

Not only have the children been enthusiastic about the PSPs, but the parents have too. One parent told Alison that it had brought home and school life together, enabling her to share her child's experiences in school in a completely new way.

Figure 7.19 Deaf children using the Sony PSP

Longwill has a Monday morning session where Foundation Stage children talk about what they did at the weekend. Small children can find this hard because their signing skills are still emerging – but now the children can visualise their exploits by getting their parents to film them using the PSPs. 'The parents are filming them going out to the park. A lot of parents filmed Christmas morning, opening presents. Another mum came home with a new baby, and that came into school. Now the news session is enhanced – they sit in front of the interactive whiteboard and look at what their friends are doing.'

Despite early concerns, children have taken great care of their PSPs and not one has yet been lost or damaged. Giving responsibility to children in this way has been one of the biggest benefits: 'We want them to be independent learners. We don't want children who are spoon-fed; we want them to be thinking and creative. For any school that has that sort of aim for their children, PSPs can play an enormous role.' She is now hoping to acquire PSPs for all the children, and certainly isn't stuck for ideas about how to use them.

The children are proud of their achievements too. Mustafaa Basharat (Y6 child) said. 'I really like the PSPs because I can take photos and videos of my family and my home and show them to my friends. My mum looks at the videos and learns signs from them with me'.

Zeeshan Khan (Y6) is equally enthusiastic and says, 'I use the PSP to help me with my English, maths and spellings. I take the PSP home and I use it there to video friends and family. I sign my video diary into the PSP every night. My brother watches with me and he learns BSL [British Sign Language]'.

Alison believes that other schools can learn from Longwill's experience. 'Good practice in special education is good practice everywhere', she argues. Her dream is that 'a PSP becomes an entitlement for every Deaf child at Longwill. … We look upon the PSPs as a twenty-first century learning tool which can really enhance home school links and engage pupils in their learning. They are an effective, inspirational bit of mainstream technology, which is highly motivating and which enables deaf sign bilingual to access the curriculum in their first language.'

For more detail about this exciting project visit the Primary ICT website and read the documents 'Action for Inclusion' and 'Top tips for lessons using PSPs with Deaf Sign Bilingual pupils'.

With kind permission of futurelab.org.uk and Longwill School for the Deaf

For further insight into mobile learning visit:

- the Mobile Learning Network (MoLeNET) at www.molenet.org.uk; and

- Wolverhampton's award-winning Learning2Go initiative at www.learning2go.org.

Learning platforms

The evolution of online learning

Online learning is not a new phenomenon. It dates back to the advent of the Internet in the early to mid 1990s and before that on network-based learning environments and CD-ROMs. However, the notion of online education in schools is more recent and is now becoming formalised as part of the government's e-strategy.

The majority of schools have networked resources and broadband connectivity to the Internet. Not only can pupils and teachers access learning and share information and resources within the school, the possibility exists to do this from outside the school too – via a learning platform.

The school learning platform initiative

The government initiative expects that:

1. As from spring 2008 every pupil should have access to a personalised online learning space with the potential to support an e-portfolio (provided by their local authority) and that the space should:

    ☐ be Internet-based; secure, anytime, anywhere;

    ☐ be able to upload/download files;

    ☐ provide each pupil with an individual online working space;

    ☐ have basic communication tools and discussion boards;

    ☐ enable both peer-to-peer and peer-to-mentor dialogue;

    ☐ have the potential to support an e-portfolio.

2. By 2010 every school should have integrated learning and management systems (a comprehensive suite of learning platform technologies) including:

- learner support;

- learner tools;

- publishing tools;

- VLE (virtual learning environment);

- digital curriculum management;

- management and tracking of learner activity;

- assessment.

There are real benefits to be gained with such an initiative and as the South West Grid for Learning (2008) stress, 'The development of a learning platform appropriate for your school, may be one of the most important strategic planning decisions that can be made.'

This is perhaps a tall order for many schools whose development with regard to ICT is still relatively primitive and for which a longer timescale would be more feasible. That said, some schools have been using learning platforms for several years to good effect and, as learning platforms become more commonplace for everyone, they will fade into the background and become the norm.

There is also an issue with the 'digital divide' – those pupils who do not have access to a computer or the Internet from home. This is however being addressed with the 2009 launch of the government's Home Access Programme which aims to provide practical and financial support for low-income families to get online, and training for teachers and parents on how to help school-aged children access the Internet from home.

What is a learning platform?

A learning platform isn't necessarily a single entity. The term describes a broad range of ICT systems used to deliver and support learning (DfES, 2005). It might involve the school website and/or intranet, shared folders, collaboration tools and conferencing systems, virtual learning environments (VLEs) and portals (though strictly speaking a portal will be a means of bringing together resources from a number of disparate sources).

The heart of the learning platform is most often a VLE, which, when linked to the school's management information system, becomes a managed learning environment (MLE).

There are many learning platforms on the market. As part of their Learning Platform Services Framework, Becta provides a list of authorised providers that have shown themselves to be capable of supplying quality learning platform services to education. These include:

- Core Projects and Technologies Ltd - (TALMOS Learning Platform)

- Etech Group – (Studywiz)

- Fronter – (talk2learn)

- Netmedia Education – (Primary and Secondary Learning Platforms)

- Pearson Education Ltd – (Pearson Learning Platform)

- Ramesys – (Assimilate)

- RM Education plc – (Kaleidos)

- Serco Learning Solutions – (Skillspace)

- UniServity – (UniServity Learning Platform)

- Viglen Ltd – (Viglen Learning Platform)

Becta (2007c)

This list is far from exhaustive and other platforms currently in use in UK primary schools include:

- Kowari

- Frog Teacher

- Knowledge box

- Digital Brain

- MOODLE

- Learnwise

- DB Primary.

MOODLE has particular significance because it is not only a powerful learning environment but it is Open Source software and is essentially free.

Most schools have been able to either buy a learning platform of their choice or to opt in to a platform made available at local authority (LA) or regional broadband consortium (RBC) level. The options at LA level vary from region to region. For example, the South West Grid for Learning have employed their own system known as Merlin whereas the Cumbria & Lancashire Education Online (CLEO) RBC has employed MOODLE as the platform for all schools across Cumbria and Lancashire

 Activity

Link to the Primary ICT site, and watch the Learning Platforms Video (courtesy of Teachers TV). This may help to generate some ideas with regard to the choices of platform available and the uses that they can be put to.

Benefits of a learning platform

A learning platform not only promotes learning but serves a number of other purposes too. It helps promote extended learning and, in doing so, connects with parents and the outside community. Within the school it provides a range of features which are helpful to administration and management. The main benefits are summarised in Table 7.1

Table 7.1 Benefits of a learning platform (derived from the South West Grid for Learning, source www.swgfl.org.uk)

Teachers will:	Learners will:
Deliver on-line tutorials, access email and hold on-line discussions with learners and colleagues. Participate in a collaborative approach to the development of lesson plans, schemes of work and learning plans. Access learning resources and content designed to support learners in groups or individually.	Access learning materials and tutor support before, during or after school. Study from home or other locations. Submit homework and assessment activities in electronic format. Work in a secure and safe virtual environment. Take part in discussions with other children (perhaps live!).
Management/administration will:	**Parents will:**
Have on-line access to up-to-date learner data, thus improving efficiency and effectiveness. Communicate quickly and effectively with parents via email, electronic bulletins and discussion groups. Deliver personalised learning plans and materials. Contribute to the adaptation and development of web-based and electronic learning resources.	Access on-line portfolios and information. Support children accessing on-line resources and homework. Access school bulletins on-line and join discussion groups. Feed back information to school and contribute to the school community. Play a greater role in supporting their children's learning.

The evidence is clear, when parents engage with their children's education, achievement levels rise. The issue goes well beyond technology, but technology can have a vital role in energising the dialogue between schools, parents and their children. We know that when parents have timely and accessible information about their children at school it has a significant effect in stimulating this engagement. Real time reporting means parents have secure, online access to information about their child's learning, available to them wherever and whenever they want it.

Next Generation Learning (2009)

Ideas for using a learning platform

Learning platforms are extremely versatile and can be used for any number of learning activities from bitesize chunks (e.g. homework exercises and revision) to full-blown learning units (e.g. a history project or a self-paced module on PSHE). Here are a few ideas:

Staff Room
Staff share ideas and resources using an area of the learning platform which they have named the 'Staff Room'. The Staff Room has several functions: it acts as a repository (for lesson plans, presentations, videos etc.), as a discussion area; and as a collaborative space which can be used for team working (e.g. joint contributions to a policy document).

The Tudors

A KS2 teacher sets up a learning space as part of a history project. The space is available to pupils, teachers and parents so that children can carry out some of the work from home and parents can take an active interest in what their children are doing.

The space contains guidance on how to go about the project, choices of tasks they might perform, links to resources (both on the school server and on the Internet), and how they will be assessed (in this case they are to compile a short presentation).

Noticeboard

Children from Year 1 to Year 6, by way of an exercise in social interaction, are given ownership of an area of their learning platform. Each week the children contribute useful information to their electronic 'noticeboard' including reviews of books they have read, films they have seen, recipes for healthy eating, etc. They are responsible for deciding the content and for updating it on a periodic basis. The area also contains a safe chat room which allows them to discuss issues they have raised.

My Parents

A primary school identifies their learning platform as an ideal way to communicate with parents. The announcements page of the 'My Parents' area provides parents with their first point of contact and acts as an up to the moment message system. Discussion forums allow parents to have their say on a variety of issues. Their comments are constructive and they feel involved in the development of the school and can truly influence proceedings.

Case study: How to unleash your student's inner Tolkien

Shaldon Primary School use the Netmedia Learning Platform to have a positive impact on pupils' writing.

How to engage pupils in writing

Shaldon Primary School, an Outstanding OFSTED school in Devon, is one of the first schools in this area to implement a Learning Platform. Although the school had excellent SATs results in the summer of 2006, the school found that Year 6 pupils were not engaged with their writing and these results were much lower (77% level 4 compared with 93% for reading). As a result, the school identified Y6 literacy as a priority for the academic year 2006-7. The curriculum approach in Y6 was theme based and creative with literacy being taught through cross-curricular links. However, the teachers involved felt it was not as exciting as it could be. A Learning Platform was seen to be the way to re-engage pupils with writing and after some research the school identified Netmedia as the most appropriate solution. In September, three staff members had two days of training: the head teacher (who also teaches Y6 literacy alongside the teacher), the ICT Coordinator and the teaching assistant (who is in the IT suite full time).

Introducing the Learning Platform to pupils, staff and parents

The first stage in this process was the practical issue of introducing the Learning Platform to Y6. Initially each year group agreed to donate one of their slots in the ICT suite to provide additional access. This extra time enabled Y6 to focus on using the Learning Platform and their literacy work in these sessions.

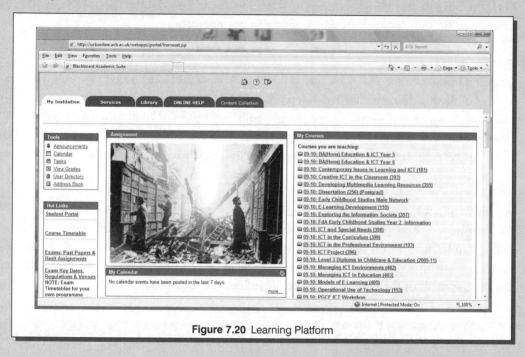

Figure 7.20 Learning Platform

This demonstrated there was a need to purchase additional laptops for the school if the Learning Platform was to be used effectively throughout the school. The school also conducted a survey amongst Y5 and Y6 pupils to find out their ICT usage. A few children did not have access to a computer at home, so they created the opportunity to use school computers during lunchtime and in an after school club each week. At the beginning of the term parents were also invited into school to understand how and what their children could do at home and the arrangements made for children to engage in their learning outside class.

Supporting learning objectives with MyClasses

The key element of the Learning Platform used to support this project was MyClasses, which provides teachers with a flexible set of tools to enhance the planning and delivery of lessons. As the autumn term theme for Y6 was World War 2, a 'Class' page was created to support the children undertaking a unit of work learning about an evacuee's life. On the page, various 'Properties' were created to help them try and understand what it might have felt like to be an evacuee in WW2 including:

- Text and Image Property – used questions and photographs to stimulate discussion and help children look for evidence to support their views.

- Discussion Forum – allowed the children to ask an evacuee who lived in Portsmouth about her personal experiences.

- Noticeboard Property – set up as a glossary to which pupils added any words or phrases linked to the war as they came across them.

- eLearning Folio – created a page with prompts for children's writing and links to appropriate resources. This was followed in the second half of the term with a 'WW2 Poetry Class', with the objective for pupils to write their own war poems.

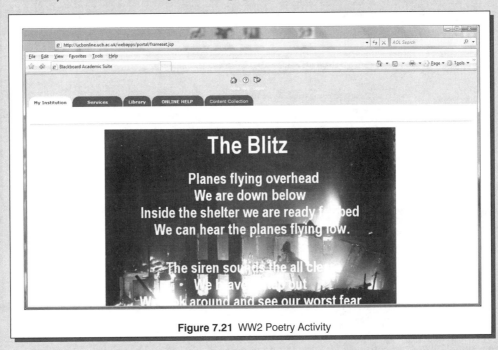

Figure 7.21 WW2 Poetry Activity

Adding depth to pupils' understanding

The school found that pupils responded well to using the Learning Platform as a primary learning resource and tool. They enjoyed it so much that they were even logging on to the Learning Platform in the evening and during the weekend to add to the pages. It was also found that pupils generally stayed on task when using the Learning Platform, unusual during Internet work. The children responded to the interactive nature of the Platform and were asking further questions when posting answers on to discussion forums. By the end of the topic, pupils were backing up their thoughts with evidence they had learnt which demonstrated higher level thinking skills. A vote conducted via the Learning Platform by the teachers at the end of the topic showed that 59% of the pupils thought that 'war was worthwhile because countries must fight for their freedoms', a very surprising result that showed pupils used critical judgment in drawing their conclusions.

Enjoyment, engagement and attainment

The quality of poems produced showed pupils had learned and understood what it would have been like to live during WW2. Furthermore, feedback from pupils included comments such as 'It was fun to communicate with others, sharing pinions and ideas' and 'I liked being able to log- on at home and find out more' showing a level of engagement beyond initial expectations. At the end of the year the school achieved 100% Level 4 in their English SATs, but more significantly this was 100% for both reading and writing – a clear indicator of the project's impact on attainment.

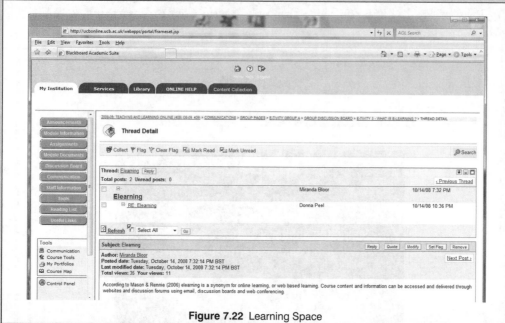

Figure 7.22 Learning Space

Extending use of the Learning Platform: Pupil Voice

The school want to extend usage of the Learning Platform beyond just using MyClasses for literacy. Pupils at the school are encouraged to talk about and reflect on their learning to help them see the development of their work and to help with goal-setting. One objective will be to implement online journals and a portfolio for pupils to use. An advantage of this feature is the ability to transfer the student work when they move school, providing an ongoing record of achievement. The Learning Platform has already had a positive impact on teaching and learning within Shaldon Primary School. As confidence amongst staff and excitement among pupils grows, the Learning Platform will become an even more important teaching tool across the whole school.

With kind permission of netmediaeducation.com and Shaldon Primary School

Activity

You will find more case studies on the Primary ICT site. Perhaps these will give you further ideas for using your learning platform.

Content creation

Increasingly, learning platform providers are offering their own content packages (either pre-loaded or as add-ons). Many teachers will however create their own content in familiar formats such as MS Word documents, PDFs, PowerPoint presentations, images, audio and video (including podcasts and vidcasts), and so on.

To help create units of learning and assessment there are a number of available content creation tools (some free, some at a cost).

You will find an extensive list of authoring tools at the Centre for Learning and Performance Technologies (www.c4lpt.co.uk/Directory/Tools/authoring.html).

 Activity

Link to the Primary ICT site and look at the simple Course Genie learning unit.
Lesson creation is simple with packages like this. Type the content and assessment into MS Word and Course Genie will do the rest. The word document is instantly converted into a series of linked web pages together with a SCORM-compliant zipped version which can be uploaded into many learning platforms.

Computer-mediated communication (CMC)

Computer-mediated communication, mainly in the form of discussion forums, has become an integral part of many e-learning courses. It is seen as an effective means of providing students and teachers with a means for discussion (often the only means) and, more appropriately, a way to collaborate in order to construct and confirm learning. Communication is mainly asynchronous with students and teachers posting messages (threads) to online forums. The discussion can be between teacher and students (one-to-many), between students themselves (many-to-many) and between the teacher and a single student (one-to-one). Messages posted are visible to the entire group and can be searched, sorted and archived (Garrison and Anderson, 2003).

What started out in further and higher education has now begun to spread into primary schools. After all, children make much use of social interaction and are equally able to construct learning. Since most all learning platforms incorporate discussion boards then the opportunity exists to employ CMC as one means of promoting learning.

A CMC activity for Year 1

Kowari is a learning platform designed specifically for very young children and can be used by those who are not able to read yet because everything is linked to pictures as well as words. Using the integrated chat feature, children share their ideas and thoughts about characters from traditional stories. They can continue the chat from home because the platform and its features are accessible remotely – they are however secure and the children are therefore protected.

Podcasting and vidcasting

In Chapter 4, podcasting was hailed as a candidate ICT resource in support of literacy. In truth, podcasting, and indeed vidcasting, lend themselves well across the curriculum. Podcasts can be used independently as part of the mobile learning revolution or incorporated into the school learning platform. The use of RSS feeds (really simple syndication or rich site summary) further extends their capability allowing automatic downloading of 'episodes' of learning as and when they become available (or at a pre-determined time). For example, a pupil with a PDA or PSP which incorporates an RSS reader could automatically receive 'chunks' of learning which are periodically downloaded from their school learning platform or website.

There are many potential benefits both for teachers and for pupils (Podium, 2008).
For teachers:

- a new and dynamic element to teaching and learning;

- convenience of listening anywhere, anytime;

- teacher absence – when away at a conference etc., a podcast could replace a conventional lesson;

- economic on resources – most resources are freely available;

- may suit particular learning styles – most children are 'plugged in' to mp3/mp4 players everywhere they go;

- supports or extends the work of any pupil with special needs – useful for those with a reading difficulty or for English as a second or third language;

- useful for children who miss lessons (e.g. disengaged or ill);

- great community/school link potential and an effective way to communicate with parents (e.g. regular broadcasts instead of/as well as newsletters);

- new approach to homework (e.g. audio notes to reinforce learning);

- enables schools to celebrate their school's achievement and events.

For pupils:

- The benefits of podcasting extend much further than simply listening to educationally charged content. The process of creating podcasts themselves gives children a whole new outlook and opportunity to exploit their creative talents, share what schools are doing with other schools as well as the wider community, and showcase their work with a potential audience of thousands.

- Pupils concentrate on their speaking and listening skills which will have consequential effects on their writing skills (writing scripts, setting up interviews etc.).

- Publishing their own podcast is hugely motivating for pupils and also gives them a sense of ownership.

- In learning how to create a podcast, pupils are extending their ICT skills and capabilities to embrace new technologies.

- Podcasting can be tailored to a number of curriculum areas and is also great for developing teamwork skills.

 Activity

There are two podcasts on the Primary ICT site which are part of a literacy activity. If you have not already listened to these you may like to do so now. These may give you some ideas for the next activity in this chapter.

Creating a podcast

Creating podcasts is quite simple. You can use your mobile phone or mp3 recorder to make a recording and then upload it to your PC as an .mp3 or a .wav file. These are convenient, ready-made solutions for recording when out in the field, however, for better quality recording, and editing capability, you will need podcasting software and a good quality microphone. There are lots of free software packages (e.g. Audacity) and commercial packages (e.g. Podium). A podcast usually comprises one or more mp3 files, each file representing an 'episode' of the podcast.

For the following activity you will need Podium software installed on your PC. If you don't own it you can download a 30-day evaluation copy from www.podiumpodcasting.com/trial/index.html or you can perform a similar activity using the free Audacity from http://audacity.sourceforge.net.

Finally, if you want to go a step further then you could produce the video version of the podcast – the vidcast (or vodcast). The principles are much the same but the video will be captured using a camcorder, webcam, mobile phone etc. and the format will likely be .mp4, .avi. or .wmv.

Playing podcasts and vidcasts will rely on you having an appropriate player installed on your PC. The most common are Windows Media Player, QuickTime (by Apple) and Flash (by Adobe). If you don't already have these they are free to download from the Internet.

Activity

Link to the Primary ICT site and carry out the Podcasting Activity. You will also find a collection of other useful podcasting files. Do you think you might use podcasting in your teaching and learning?

There are plenty of plus points with podcasting but there are some disadvantages too:

- as with all ICT activities, their creation is time consuming and schools may need to invest in training for their staff;
- without reasonable resources quality may be jeopardised;
- broadcasts are one-way only – there is no immediate opportunity for interaction;
- file size can be large and downloading consumes bandwidth.

In addition, some staff are not comfortable recording their own voices and there may be issues around intellectual property rights.

If you are beginning to feel that this discipline is the preserve of the real enthusiast then do keep in mind the many benefits that are to be had and, all said and done, it won't harm to have a go.

Even if you don't create your own learning podcasts, you should strongly consider allowing children to develop them as a class or school project.

As listeners to popular radio stations will already know, podcasts can also be made available as RSS feeds (really simple syndication) from a website. Doing this from your school website will allow pupils, and others, to subscribe to your podcasts by linking their RSS reader (e.g. iTunes) to your website. Many school websites already provide RSS feeds.

Video conferencing

Benefits of video conferencing

Video conferencing has become quite commonplace in many primary schools and enriches learning by (Northwood, 2008):

- giving children easier access to distant people and places;
- elimination of travel costs and subsequent time saving;
- allowing several schools to share the same teacher;
- developing speaking and listening skills;
- developing questioning skills;
- encouraging collaboration between schools (both locally and worldwide);
- bringing expertise into the classroom;
- and, of course, it's fun!

Setting up a video conferencing system

You may decide to set up your own conferencing system independently but, before embarking on such a project, you should check with your Local Education Authority to find out what expertise they have to offer and whether they have a regional conferencing service available to you.

Equipment needed

There are a several options from cheap 'low end' systems to expensive 'high end' systems (Table 7.2).

Table 7.2 Comparison of video conferencing systems

Type	Equipment	Comments
Basic	Flash Meeting software and a webcam	Cheap, cheerful and reliable – a good place to start. A good quality webcam can be purchased from £50 upwards.
Intermediate	Polycom PVX software and webcam	Runs on fast PCs. Picture quality depends on webcam. Software and camera bundles cost around £200 upwards.
Higher	Video Phone	Like a telephone with a built in screen. Allows you to call other video phones or other intermediate and higher systems, but is only really suitable for one-to-one conferences. Cost around £500.
	All-in-one camera and monitor	A flat-panel monitor with a built in camera at the top that works independently of a PC. Better for one-to-one or small group. From around £1700.
Top	Desk Top Video Conferencing Unit (DVC) e.g. Polycom or Aethra	Top of the range all in one solutions with frills such as ability to zoom and pan camera from remote end. Cost from around £2000 upwards. Now available with High Definition video (HD) – at a higher price!

Source: Hertfordshire Grid for Learning, derived from: www.thegrid.org.uk/learning/ict/technologies/
videoconferencing

To some extent, quality depends on price. However, many schools, having invested in an expensive system, have found that it doesn't get the level of use that its cost would justify. As a start up you may find an intermediate system to be perfectly adequate.

Intermediate solutions such as Polycom PVX run from a PC or laptop computer with a broadband connection. DVC solutions do not require a PC or laptop, they connect directly to a TV or data projector and have a network point to access the school's broadband.

Connectivity

Video conferencing was originally conducted over leased telephone lines and, whilst this is still an option (known as ISDN video conferencing), it is relatively expensive. You are most likely to use your broadband connection and conference across the Internet (known as IP video conferencing).

Conferencing sessions can be set up between any two parties that have video conferencing systems. You will most likely participate with other schools and video content providers such as the many museums and galleries that offer videoconference programmes to schools.

It is possible to connect directly to another party but this will often give you problems resulting in picture and sound break up. You are better advised to make use of the National Education Network (NEN) which has been set up to connect schools in England and Wales. The NEN uses the JANET network (or superJANET) to allow video conferences to take place between sites around the world. (JANET – Joint Academic Network – is a private British government-funded computer network dedicated to education and research.)

Video conferencing connectivity is managed by the JANET Video Conferencing Service (JVCS) which is based in Edinburgh. You first need to register with them (at www.ja.net/services/video/jvcs) and then you may book a connection in advance of each of your intended conferencing sessions. JVCS provide support during the school day. There is no charge for this service.

Activity ideas

1. As part of its MFL programme, a local authority employs a language specialist to teach French to several primary schools from a small conferencing room in a central location. The class teachers observe the lessons with a view to taking on the role themselves the following year. Classes are often delivered to individual schools but occasionally, more than one school joins in the same lesson. Equipment can be expensive though simple systems such as webcams and Skype/MSN Messaging can be effective too.

Figure 7.23 Webcam activity

2. Year 5 and 6 pupils learn about the solar system and space travel via a pre-booked video conferencing session with the National Maritime Museum. They also take the opportunity to question an expert from the Royal Observatory with astronomy-related questions (which they have prepared in advance).

Computer games

A limited amount of research has been carried out on the use of computer games in education and, whilst it has provided much food for thought, the results are not yet conclusive.

Computer games are accessible in a number of forms including: CD-ROM based games (which are played on a computer); television-based consoles such as the Sony PlayStation® and Microsoft's Xbox®; handheld devices such as the Nintendo DS™ series; Sony PSP; PDAs; mobile phones; and online games via the Internet or other network.

There is much concern that computer games are bad for children. They expend an inordinate amount of time; they can become addictive; many include unnecessary violence; they can be sexist and promote stereotypical views; they can have physically harmful side effects; and they can deny children the benefits of a fully active lifestyle. But are there any advantages?

Most games are produced for entertainment but some aspects of these are inherently educational: responding to challenge; achieving goals; applying logic; reasoning, problem solving; and, in some cases, literacy skills. Above all they are extremely motivating. Whilst it may be possible to adapt some of these 'off the shelf' products to the classroom, it can be difficult to measure successful achievement of desired learning outcomes.

If however the favourable aspects were to be incorporated into the design of bespoke educational games, they would better match the requirements of the curriculum whilst still having a degree of commercial appeal.

Becta rightly advise us that educational software should be based on accepted educational philosophy and valid educational objectives. They suggest that:

- Teachers should be involved in the design and evaluation process.

- Software should be inclusive of a wide range of aptitudes and abilities.

- Support and guidance should be provided for learners and teachers.

- Learners should be provided with opportunities for reflection and evaluation.

- There should be access to feedback on performance.

- The route through the software should be clear.

- Interactivity should be purposeful.

- There should be the chance to correct and to learn from errors in order to improve performance and achieve goals.

Becta (2007d)

Success stories

1. As part of an experiment on 600 pupils in 32 Scottish schools, test groups of pupils used the commercially available 'Nintendo's Brain Training' for 20 minutes every day over nine weeks. A control group continued their lessons as normal.

Testing, before and after the experiment, revealed that all groups had improved their scores but those using the game had improved by a further 50 per cent and had taken less time to complete tests. Teachers also intimated that a combination of good teaching and the impact of the computer games had brought about marked improvements in behaviour, class morale, time-keeping and even handwriting.

Critics might argue that a maths game, whether done on a computer or done by paper and pencil, is going to improve pupil capabilities. However, the success of the trial is attributed to a number of factors: children responded to the targets set and the desire to improve with each successive attempt; the games were simple to use; and the children were motivated to play (Cairns, 2008).

2. The fantasy puzzle game 'Myst III Exile' was introduced to a primary school class who used it as part of structured lessons for over a year. It has helped to improve their literacy, particularly boys who are reluctant writers.

Teachers have described it as 'Motivational and inspirational … Pupils are so engaged with the game that they were writing without any pressure'.

The game, which was also used for music, art, science and problem-solving, has had a number of benefits including: promoting collaborative working; inspiring creativity through drawing, writing and discussion; encouraging children's art; promoting prolonged writing; improvement of vocabulary; and the acquisition of better speaking and listening skills (McLeish, 2008).

For additional ideas on gaming, try the Marc Prensky website at www.marcprensky.com.

Play-based learning

When playing, children experiment with new ideas, develop their physical abilities and practice social and language skills. They use their imagination and learn to think and express themselves creatively, enhancing their self-confidence and increasing their sense of self and identity. There is much written about what children may learn through play (Vygotsky, 1978; Clements and Fiorentino, 2004; Montessori, 2007) and there are those who adopt the Reggio Emilia approach, a philosophy where children delight in taking responsibility for their own learning (Brunton and Thornton, 2005).

However, few would argue against the premise that play-based activity is an important way to promote active learning – where children use their brains in lots of ways. Play is the means by which young children make sense of their world. In this respect, children may be self-directed (unstructured play) or may follow pre-determined rules (structured play). There are sound reasons for doing both, just as there are for playing on their own, alongside others in independent parallel play or with other children in cooperative play.

The government believes that play has a key role in learning for younger children and, in December 2008, launched their new 'Fair Play' strategy. It recognises children's right to play and sets out fully funded plans to improve and develop interesting and free play facilities in every residential community throughout the country (DCSF, 2008b).

Even so, critics have expressed concern that children are denied imaginative play because of the demands of the curriculum. They believe it to be too strict a learning regime whose outcomes are evidenced only by the completion of a learning profile comprising 117 tick-boxes per child (Eason, 2006).

Teachers can facilitate play by programming opportunities into the curriculum and by allowing it to develop and flow naturally during more formalised activities. The teacher's role will be one of supporting children's development, observing their actions and responding where necessary. They should raise children's awareness of technology in the world around them and create safe settings which model a range of real world scenarios and include a choice of appropriate resources such as safe household items and materials.

> There are many suitable ICT resources that lend themselves well to role play situations and, with adult support, children can:
>
> * develop an interest in ICT equipment and apparatus;
>
> * identify and explore everyday uses of information technology in a meaningful context;
>
> * talk about uses for ICT in their own lives and represent experiences through role-play;
>
> * understand how to operate simple equipment and perform simple functions independently;
>
> * turn to appropriate equipment in their play in order to communicate information;
>
> * be aware of the dangers associated with some equipment, such as electrical switches, and of the need to work within simple safety guidelines;
>
> * use correct technical vocabulary.
>
> (Drake, 2002)

Resources

Possible resources, from a cast of hundreds, include:

* Battery operated toys
* Food mixer/blender
* Electronic till
* Telephone/mobile phone
* Washing machine
* Walkie-talkies
* Computer/keyboard
* Drill/screwdriver
* Heart monitor
* Tape recorder/headphones
* X-ray light box
* Clock radio
* Television/remote control
* Patient buzzer
* Microwave
* Telephone/answer phone
* Digital microscope
* Calculator
* Digital weighing scales
* On/off controls
* Digital camera
* Video/DVD player
* Scanning equipment
* Buzzers/lights

- Credit card/ticket machine
- Franking machine
- Radio
- Metal detector

- Cash dispenser
- Light toys
- Traffic lights
- Sensory devices

Activity ideas

These activities are aimed primarily at the Foundation Stage/Reception Classes.

1. Children set up a role play shop by assembling a selection of readily available items (for purchase) and a model electronic till with electronic keypad and display, swipe card facility and toy money. The items are labelled with price tags which have been prepared in a previous lesson using the simple software toolkit – Tizzy's First Tools.

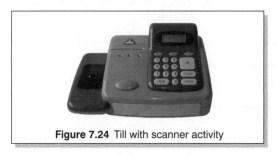

Figure 7.24 Till with scanner activity

2. A set of model traffic lights (fully working) are set up in the safety of the school playground and used to help children conduct a role play activity on traffic awareness and how to cross the road safely. A prior walk around the local area has already raised the children's awareness of traffic lights and pelican crossings and they are familiar with their sequence of operation.

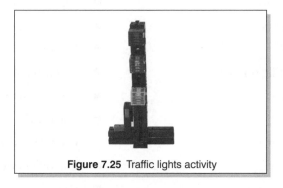

Figure 7.25 Traffic lights activity

3. Airport security is maintained when children adopt a range of roles and utilise familiar equipment such as walkie-talkies, metal detectors, light systems scanners, security systems, mobile phones, TV monitors, and buzzers.

Other role play situations include: 'the bank', 'the office', 'the supermarket', 'the café', 'the music studio', 'the hospital', 'the post office', 'the travel agent', 'outer space', 'the police station' and so on …

The World Wide Web

The Internet

The Internet has become an increasingly important feature of the learning environment for pupils and teachers. Despite concerns over e-safety (see Chapter 9), it is now an essential and often vital study aid both inside and outside the classroom, an important means of communication and a way to access and share resources.

Most schools have fast Internet access via services provided by their regional broadband consortium (RBC) and many pupils now use the Internet as their primary source of information. Some of the many uses are shown in the Table 7.3.

The Internet is most frequently used as a tool for 'searching and learning' and, whilst children are particularly adept, there are some useful rules to be followed if searches are to be effective. Google and other search engines provide basic and advanced tips.

The World Wide Web Consortium (W3C) are developing an extension to the web known as the 'semantic' web where intelligent agents will help to sort search information and present it in a useful format.

Web 2.0

The term Web 2.0 describes a number of developments on the World Wide Web that mark a shift in the way it is used. Most notably it signifies a move from accessing static content (information) to dynamic, interactive participation by way of communicating, collaborating and sharing. Examples of services include: social networking sites, weblogs (blogs), wikis, social bookmarking and media sharing sites.

Whilst accessing these services is predominantly a leisure pursuit, many teachers have identified benefits for young learners including: enabling access anytime and anywhere, encouraging participation and online collaboration, extending children's use of media, providing opportunities for assessment and extending learning beyond the school. The ensuing 'sense of ownership' promotes increased attention to detail and an improvement in the quality of work.

It is true to say however that most teachers have yet to use Web 2.0 services in their teaching and learning because they are not yet familiar with the technology and they have concerns about using the Internet in class.

Social networking

Social networking sites provide new and varied ways to communicate via the Internet and mobile phone. Users can easily create their own online page and personal profile which they

Table 7.3 Uses of the Internet

School related use of the Internet
(Pupils and teachers)

General research by searching ('Googling').

Information for a school project.

Accessing museums and art galleries.

Downloading a study aid, image, sound or video.

Creating a web page for a school or pupil.

Pupils / parents emailing teachers.

External access to school learning platform.

Electronic submission of work.

Email project with other schools.

Collaborating in group work.

Social networking (blogs, profiles, discussions etc.).

Accessing teacher resources (e.g. schemes of work from QCA).

Downloading shared activities (e.g. from TRE).

Linking to web-based activities (e.g. Cbeebies).

Sharing school resources with others (e.g. Coxhoe Primary).

Keeping abreast of policy and practice.

Linking the school MIS to the local authority.

Using LEA portals and Grids for Learning.

Instant messaging – pupil to teacher (e.g. Skype and MSN).

Video conferencing.

News and current events.

display to a network of contacts ('friends'). Users of these sites can communicate with friends and others and share resources. Communication may be one-to-one (like email) or one-to-many (postings, comments etc. that everyone can see). In truth, networking could be kept within the confines of the school network/learning platform for extra safety.

Social networking services (SNS) have been around for over a decade. They began with services that allowed users to build personal profiles (for a variety of reasons) and have now grown to include media sharing. The term networking relates to contact with people who share similar interests and pursuits and not to making deliberate contact with strangers. Some of the more popular examples are:

- Facebook and MySpace – the two leaders in social networking websites that provide users with personal profiles, a network of friends, blogs, photos, music and videos.

- YouTube and TrueTube – video sharing websites where users can upload, view and share video clips.

- Bebo – a popular social networking website.

- Twitter – a social networking and micro-blogging service using mobile phones to send text-based posts of up to 140 characters in length.

- Flickr – a photo and video hosting and sharing website.

- LastFM – an Internet radio and music community which shares listening habits.

Most schools block access to these sites although the 2008 research report by Childnet suggests that there is good reason to explore their potential.

 Activity

Childnet's mission is to help make the Internet a great and safe place for children. If you'd like to look at the Childnet report in more detail, then visit their website (www.childnet-int.org). You can also find a copy on the Primary ICT website (www. primaryict.org.uk/roict.htm).
The report looks at how social networking services can support learning in schools and colleges. The report also includes an evaluation tool, produced in conjunction with major service providers, designed to walk teachers through key features of sites that they are considering for use in support of their teaching and learning practice.

The Childnet report finds that young people are well acquainted with social networking services and regard them as just another part of their social and school-related activities. Approximately 50 per cent of children from 8 years up are believed to have a profile on a social networking site (Nightingale, 2008) and there is an indication that education-related topics are the most commonly discussed. However, teachers are often wary about social networking because of the negative press. They may not recognise the educational potential of social networking and are more likely to need support than their pupils.

What are the risks?
The two most obvious risks are making friends with strangers who turn out to be predators and the opportunity for cyber-bullying (not to mention the downside of increased time spent online and over exposure to advertising). This presents teachers (and parents) with a dilemma; banning social networking completely may appear to be the only safe option but it also denies any opportunity to exploit possible educational potential (more on risks in Chapter 9).

What are the benefits?

Despite the concerns, children are really enthusiastic about social networking and independent research shows that it has significant benefits and helps raise standards.

Communicating via personal profiles, emails and blogs builds friendships around the world and, in doing so, promotes reading and writing skills and allows children to present information in a variety of formats.

Forums get pupils involved in discussing ideas on a variety of topics of personal and educational interest. They can collaborate on projects, building and confirming knowledge. They can form partnerships and buddying schemes with other schools in the UK and abroad, broadening their understanding of local, national and global issues. Children can also join (or set up) shared interest groups.

Social networking helps to encourage creativity and develops authoring and publishing skills through the creation of personal websites on hobbies, personal interests and school work.

Doing all this improves children's knowledge and skills in ICT – and there is often support for teachers too!

 Activity

You may wish to read a report conducted by the School of Psychology, University of Hertfordshire in October 2006. It assesses the educational and social benefits to children when participating in an online social networking community (copy available from the Primary ICT website).
Whilst the report examines a specific system (SuperClubsPLUS), its findings are extremely positive and may well be generalised to other systems too.

Safe social networking

It may be that your school will err on the safe side and stay clear of general social networking services. A good compromise, which has been adopted by many, is to use a system which is designed specifically for schools. This will help to overcome most of the problems.

The main advantages are that only the school itself can register users and every user can be monitored. Good systems will incorporate both automatic and manual monitoring in order to identify inappropriate material and possible instances of bullying. The best systems will also provide real time intervention and someone to contact.

However, the very features which make such systems attractive to teachers (e.g. control) often make them less attractive to children because they will not be the systems of choice (like Facebook and Bebo).

There are several systems available, some are web based and others are run from the school server. Examples include:

LEARNING LANDSCAPE FOR SCHOOLS (LL4SCHOOLS)

Learning Landscape for Schools is a safe social network designed for schools using the award-winning Elgg open source platform. It is not a replacement for a VLE/MLE but is complementary to it. It includes: a range of Web 2.0 tools (blogs, forums, wikis, file storage, podcasting, social bookmarks, etc.), the ability to create communities of users (locally and globally) and, of course, a way to make 'friends'. All accounts are created at the request of subscriber schools so there is complete traceability which allows staff to have confidence that it is a safe environment in which to explore the educational potential of social networking. Users can also create communities of common interest: they can create a community and ask other LL4S members to join and they can request to join communities created by other members. Teachers, and others involved in Education, can now freely try out the facilities available in LL4Schools by signing up to LL4Education: www.ll4education.co.uk (LL4S, 2009).

SUPERCLUBS PLUS

SuperClubs Plus is a safe social learning network where 6–12 year olds can meet friends across the UK and around the world, be creative, have fun and learn ICT, literacy and global citizenship together. All members are validated through their own schools. Professional mediators monitor all communication and content and constantly watch out for your children and keep them safe. The communities are available from breakfast to bedtime – on school and home computers and mobile devices, so it's non-stop learning for children at school and at home. Children from different backgrounds and cultures keep in touch with friends, share interests and help each other. The home-school projects help parents get involved with their children's school work. The communities are ideal for elective home education (Intuitive media, 2009).

Computer configurations

In an ideal school, the preferred teaching approach of staff would dictate the deployment of their ICT resources. However, in some cases it is the other way around! Typical organisational models include:

- *Computer suites*: large numbers of computers assembled in one dedicated teaching space.
- *Computer clusters*: small groups (clusters) of computers in areas close to the classroom or teaching space.
- *Classroom computers*: a small number of computers within the classroom itself.
- *Mobile computing*: sets of notebook or laptop computers which can be moved from classroom to classroom as required.

Activity

Given the choice, which model of computer configuration would you prefer?
It is certainly a matter of preference but hopefully you would base your decision on some sound fundamental criteria including: the learning experiences you want for your pupils; their preferred learning styles; the range of teaching methods you wish to employ; the balance between individual, paired, small groups and whole-class teaching; the balance between discrete ICT subject teaching and the use of ICT to support learning across the curriculum; and health and safety issues. All these should be reflected in the school's ICT policy and its vision for the future (Becta, 2008c).

You will of course be faced with practical constraints which will ultimately dictate the outcome. The availability of appropriate accommodation, cost of building or refurbishment, cost of ICT resources (capital and maintenance) and availability of technical support will all play a part. Your main aim however should be that there is appropriate and equitable access to ICT resources. This is not necessarily about the quantity of resources but more importantly it is about their organisation (Pelgrum, 2001).

Computer suites

If you want to allow large groups or whole classes to work simultaneously in ICT 'lessons' then computer suites offer a solution. They are self-contained environments which, together with a data projector and interactive whiteboard, lend themselves nicely to the teaching of ICT as a discrete subject and the acquisition of important basic skills. Some however would argue that if these skills are to be taught in isolation then this is best done within the context of chosen curriculum areas. The question which then arises is 'who is best placed to teach it?'. This will be explored in more detail in Chapter 10.

Computer suites offer significant organisational advantages. They can be timetabled to allow whole classes to have access to a PC at the same time (whether or not all pupils are working on the same project). In a networked computer suite, software is available which lets the teacher take control of all the screens in the room. This allows them to monitor pupil performance and to view each individual's work (and even help them remotely if desired). The contents of any screen can be switched to the IWB allowing individuals or groups to showcase their own work.

However, suites do not offer the best pedagogical model because pupils are removed from their customary working environment and they may perceive computer work as something separate and out of the ordinary.

The reverse is of course true for classroom computers and clusters which better facilitate the embedding of ICT into the curriculum but restrict ICT activities to fewer pupils at any given time.

A good compromise is a portable trolley full of laptop computers. There are several types on the market and various sizes. They provide secure and rechargeable stowage for up to 20 laptops and can easily be wheeled from one classroom to another. They connect to the school's existing network via a wireless access point and, overall, provide a significant saving over a cable network solution.

Figure 7.26 Laptruk computer trolley

They allow existing classrooms to be turned into temporary computer suites with minimal disruption and are much less obtrusive than desktop PCs. It makes it easier to integrate ICT into the curriculum, easy to expand the system (additional PCs and trolleys can be added as required) and there are no obtrusive cables. In addition, the laptops can be used in other locations. For example, pupils and teachers could take them home.

There are of course some disadvantages too. Laptops can be less robust, they can be slower in operation due to the bandwidth limitations of their wireless connection and they need to be recharged on a regular basis. They too need to be booked in advance if they are to be fairly distributed.

Overall, the advantages generally outweigh the disadvantages and issues such as bandwidth are improving steadily as technology continues to develop.

Another option is to incorporate a space-saving cluster(s) such as the Hexacom system from OFM. The desk can be used as an IT work station and also as a paper-based work station. The desk folds down to a convenient size and can be stowed away conveniently in a corner and is also transportable between rooms. The six screens are all connected to a single server.

Whatever your choice, research shows that ICT resources have maximum impact when organised around whole-class or small group work which allows for differentiated learning (Becta, 2004). In addition, 'staff are more likely to use ICT as part of their teaching when they have access to both ICT suites and clusters of computers in their classrooms' (Ofsted, 2004).

ICT infrastructure

Having covered various models of e-learning, and the deployment of assets, this chapter would not be complete without at least a mention of the infrastructure that supports it. That is to say, a computer network and other associated equipment, applications, services and data.

Most schools will already have a network in place but those still considering the purchase, upgrade or expansion of ICT infrastructure are recommended to do so through their local authority. LEAs, together with regional broadband consortiums (RBCs), may have a collective policy for networking and broadband connectivity. If your local authority doesn't purchase equipment on behalf of all schools then you can seek advice from Becta who provide guidance on the types of service available – 'managed' or 'individual' (Becta, 2008d).

Before completely relinquishing control to others it would serve you well to compile your own 'outline specification' for the school's infrastructure based upon your organisational and pedagogical needs. This will avoid having to accept something you don't actually want or need. The specification will include the types of resource, their deployment and your preference for cabled networking, wireless or a hybrid (and perhaps in the future a cloud). The most important point here is that the resulting change should bring about significant improvement to teaching and learning and afford everyone reasonable access to, and sharing of, resources.

It should also, enhance communication and improve connectivity with the outside world. This is not simply about linking to the Internet, it is also about accessing the school learning platform and thus increasing the possibilities for extended learning. In addition, if you have access to the National Education Network (NEN), you will benefit both from the widening access it provides and the high bandwidth dedicated connections provided by the SuperJANET backbone.

Health and safety

ICT resources pose specific health and safety issues. These issues are outlined in Chapter 8 and you may also seek advice from more appropriate sources such as the Health and Safety Executive (HSE) and the Schools Building and Design Unit (SBDU). Becta also offer some useful guidance relating specifically to the safe installation and use of ICT equipment (you will find links in Appendix 2).

Visualisers and document cameras

The visualiser is a major item of ICT equipment and, whilst it is not a new technology, it has become popular in some schools in recent years. It's more of a teaching aid than a learning resource and it's not exactly a 'model' of e-learning. However, it is very much a favourite with a number of teachers and is used on such a frequent basis that it is perhaps deserving of a place in this chapter.

What is a visualiser?

If you haven't come across one before, a visualiser is essentially a movable digital colour camera mounted above a display platform. It is similar in appearance to an overhead projector but it is a much more powerful device in terms of its technical and pedagogical capabilities. Solid objects on the platform can be displayed on a computer and/or projected onto an IWB or large screen. The resulting images have superior clarity. The camera can zoom in to magnify the object and display it in microscopic proportion.

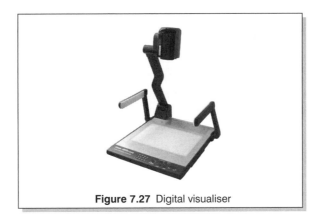

Figure 7.27 Digital visualiser

Visualisers come with a whole range of additional features such as: the ability to freeze a screen shot whilst still displaying the object, allowing the object to be moved and captured in a sequence of different positions; splitting the screen into two or more areas thus allowing the user to display a complete object whilst simultaneously viewing a portion of it in fine detail; capturing still and moving images; and displaying 'negatives' of an object.

How can a visualiser be used?

Some examples of use include (HGfL, 2008):

- Numeracy: place coins under the visualiser to practise counting money; easily add and remove coins to change the amount.
- Literacy: display the page of a book and zoom in on particular paragraphs or words.
- Science: use the zoom to display an insect in great detail to observe its features.
- History: display artefacts to the class quickly and easily.
- Geography: display maps, zoom in on particular features and symbols.
- Music: display sheet music and zoom in on features such as clef, key signature, rests etc.
- Art: use the visualiser to highlight different brush stroke techniques in great detail.
- Assembly: if you have a projector in your assembly hall you can use a visualiser to present certificates, good work etc. to the whole school.

Visualisers have not attracted widespread use. As with the tablet PC, this is probably attributed to their cost which, for many schools will be prohibitive. A reasonable visualiser will cost in the region of £500 upwards. There are cheaper versions known as document cameras but, as the name suggests, these are lacking in features by comparison.

8

ICT and special educational needs

Introduction

One in every five children is considered to have special educational needs (SEN) because they either have greater difficulty in learning than the majority of children of the same age or they have a disability which prevents or hinders them from making use of educational facilities (DfES, 2001).

Within the last few years, moves have been made to include all SEN children, other than those with severe problems, into mainstream schools. This has placed additional demands on teachers and teaching assistants who are now responsible for pupils with a diverse range of personal needs. Staff need access to a greater range of tools, and the use of ICT in advancing and enabling access to learning is therefore pivotal in meeting the needs of these learners (at all educational levels).

This chapter will briefly outline each of the recognised areas of SEN and introduce a number of ICT resources which can be used to support each of them. The main areas of SEN covered are: communication and interaction; cognition and learning; behavioural, emotional and social; sensory, physical or medical; English as an additional language (EAL); and children identified as gifted and talented (G&T).

It should be recognised that children with SEN rarely fit into one specific category. Similarly, many ICT resources can be used for a multitude of needs – and for all children who just require that bit of additional support!

Communication and interaction

Children with communication and interaction problems may have difficulty understanding others and/or making others understand them. Problems include delayed speech or language development, inability to articulate or to form certain speech sounds, speech impediments (such as stammer) and those who do not speak at all.

There are also those with language difficulties who cannot understand words or cannot use them in the right context. They will generally have limited vocabulary or find it hard to recall words and express ideas.

Technology can aid these children in order that they can participate in lessons and gain access to the same curriculum as their peers.

For some learners with speech and language difficulties, ICT is a lifeline, enabling them to communicate with the world around them. For others, it can support their classroom work and therapy.

Becta (2007e)

Augmentative and alternative communication (AAC).

Those with speech problems may benefit from AAC resources. These range from high-tech voice output communication aids (VOCAs) and software equivalents, to simple paper-based symbols which illustrate words or phrases.

Symbols

There are a number of sets of symbols; The most common are the Widgit Literacy Symbols (previously know as Rebus) and the Pictorial Communication System (PCS). Others include Makaton, PECS and Bliss. Teachers can of course make their own symbol set if so desired.

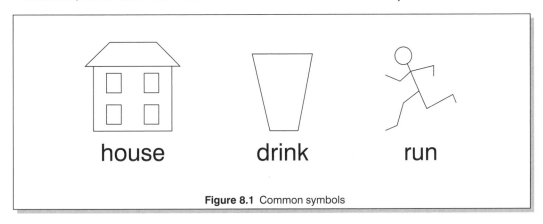

Figure 8.1 Common symbols

There are also graphic symbol systems associated with specific high-tech communication aids, for example, Minsymbols (multi-meaning icons) and Dynasyms.

Practitioners and pupils will need ready access to printed symbols. There are several publications available to purchase though many teaching assistants create their own books, wall posters, laminated flash cards and streamers (which they hang from their belts).

Children can make use of software programs such as Widgit's Writing with Symbols 2000, SymWriter and Communicate in Print 2. These symbol-based word processor programs not only associate words with a choice of symbols, they also include speech, writing grids, word banks and scanning capability.

If you don't own a copy of SymWriter you can download a 21-day evaluation copy from the Widgit website at www.widgit.com/support/symwriter/download.

Activity

Visit the Widgit website at www.widgit.com and browse the resources. You can try some out for free (look under Teaching and Learning). You might also look at the Online Resources which provide links to websites that use symbols or provide free resources.

Voice output communication aids (VOCAs)

These hardware devices come in a number of formats displaying up to 128 symbols at a time. Symbols are provided on sets of overlays (with some devices, additional overlays can be self-designed using specific software).

Teachers can record words and messages which are replayed whenever a symbol is touched (either with the finger or using external switches). These devices are designed to be durable but come at a hefty cost.

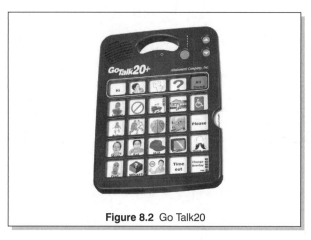
Figure 8.2 Go Talk20

Software communication aids

Software versions of communications devices can be created easily and cheaply using familiar applications such as MS PowerPoint.

Children with communication problems often suffer from other learning difficulties or physical disabilities. The type of communication solution selected will therefore depend on their ability to interact with devices and their understanding of the spoken word.

Activity

Visit the Primary ICT website and try out the PowerPoint communication device. What are the advantages and disadvantages of developing simple resources of this type?
The PowerPoint communicator emulates the expensive high-tech devices. It is simple to make, scalable and low cost. Resources of this type lack mobility although they could be loaded onto notebook computers (which are much cheaper than VOCAs and have the added versatility to host other software solutions too). They won't be suited to all children because they are not robust, keyboard keys are small and they lack switch access. In addition, software equivalents may need their own set of symbols if copyright is an issue.

Language difficulties

Children who have difficulty in formulating language will benefit from the visual stimulus that can be provided by software. Care must be taken when selecting software because it is not always suitable.

> Many content rich software programs for young children are rich in visual stimuli and offer too many distractions to make them suitable for children with SEN … [however], using well designed software can have huge benefits.
>
> (Sparrowhawk and Heald, 2007: 21)

Applications such as concept mapping can help them to plan and organise their ideas before moving on to communicate them vocally and in writing.

Up-to-date packages like Rationale include tools to guide, develop and enhance thinking, questioning and reasoning skills. These help pupils to build projects using visual objects which can eventually be converted to textual (essay) format.

Children with writing problems will benefit from word banks, talking word processors, talking books, overlay keyboards, predictive words and spelling and grammar checkers.

Word processors with banks of words and phrases together with story grids can be used to support structured language activities. A popular title in this respect is Clicker 5, a switch compliant writing-support tool for every subject area (including EAL). It builds sentences (by selecting words, phrases and pictures) and speaks them back using a selection of voices.

Most word processors include predictive text and spelling/grammar checkers. These can be extremely helpful for children with speech and language difficulties though practitioners should be cautious not to overuse them. Examples include Co:Writer, Penfriend and WordAid.

Another extremely versatile and well respected package to help pupils with reading and writing is textHelp Read & Write Gold. It works alongside mainstream Windows applications and offers a wide range of features including text-to-speech, word prediction, phonetic spell checker and a speaking dictionary.

The Visual Learning For Life website offers a subscription database of over 1000 downloadable worksheets which cover ten visual perception areas, each with three levels of difficulty. They are designed to strengthen weak areas of visual perception and sharpen mental skills.

Autistic spectrum disorders

Autistic spectrum disorder (ASD) is a lifelong condition that affects how a person communicates with, and relates to, other people. It also affects how they make sense of the world around them.

ASD is the term that is used to describe a group of disorders, including autism and Asperger's syndrome. The word 'spectrum' is used because the characteristics of the condition vary from one person to another. Those with autism may also have a learning disability. Those who have Asperger's syndrome tend to have average, or above average, intelligence, but still have difficulty making sense of the world (NHS, 2007).

Autistic children are often unable or unwilling to engage in activities which rely on social or verbal interaction. The computer will therefore offer an attractive alternative. However, whilst ICT can offer a range of useful tools, the National Autistic Society (2006) stress that ICT does not by itself provide a magic solution for people with autism; it must be embedded in a wider care and/or educational system to be effective.

Software

There isn't a great deal of software for people with autism aside from a small number of titles which focus on specific aspects of the condition. For this reason, the computer should be used purely as an occasional support tool and not allowed to become a dominant part of learning activities. Care should also be taken not to overuse the computer as a means of curbing bad behaviour as this may ultimately appear to condone it!

The main advantages of computers are that:

- they don't require interaction with other people;
- they offer autonomy and a 'safe' environment;
- they are non-judgemental;
- they provide a focal point to hold concentration;
- they are consistent and predictable;
- they enable errors to be easily corrected;
- they can provide instant feedback;
- interacting with a computer can create an awareness of self;
- simple games promote communication with others.

Here are some ideas:

The company 'Raising Horizons' has researched and produced training materials specifically to help people with ASD. Your School Day is aimed at children aged 5–12 years and, with teacher assistance, takes them through the school day – ranging from getting ready for school, recognising 'danger zones' when travelling to school, recognising faces and working with others.

Figure 8.3 Your School Day (source: www.raisinghorizons.com)

Social and life skills training software for younger children includes software packages like Smart Alex which can be used to learn how to recognise facial expressions and emotions from an animated character. At a higher level, keyboard users can hold a simple conversation with Alex and talk about their likes and dislikes. Try also Streetwise.

Figure 8.4 Smart Alex (source: www.inclusive.co.uk)

Researched by professionals, Gaining Face helps people with Asperger's syndrome, high-functioning autism and similar issues to learn to recognise facial expressions and associated moods and emotions. A free demonstration can be downloaded from www.ccoder.com/GainingFace.

Figure 8.5 Gaining Face
(source: www.ccoder.com/GainingFace)

Other titles include Mouse Trial, Mind Reading, Being Me, Connections, ISPEEK at home, ISPEEK at school, Blooming Kids (series), Story Builder, Just Like (series) and Out and About.

Video conferencing

Pupils who experience difficulty interacting with others have been shown to respond much better when communicating using indirect methods such as video conferencing. They seem to feel less intimidated and are able to open up more freely. As a result, they can work together on projects and build up strong relationships with pupils in other schools.

Figure 8.6 Webcam

Computer-mediated communication

Computer-mediated communication (CMC) was covered in Chapter 7. Children on the autistic spectrum should excel using CMC because they can work in an environment which does not require face to face interaction and is therefore more comfortable for them. In addition, some of the weaknesses of CMC are implicitly turned to advantage. For example, children with autism rarely have the ability to read body language and are therefore not penalised by its absence.

Video cameras

A KS1 child with Asperger's syndrome is given a simple video camera as a tool for self-expression. She is asked to explore the classroom and talk about the things she likes and dislikes about school. The activity motivates her and the outcome is astonishing. The audio is very clear and she expresses herself in a way that she would never do when talking to the teacher or to other children.

Figure 8.7 Flip video camera (source: www.flip-video-cameras.co.uk)

Cognition and learning

Children requiring help in this category come under the general headings of specific learning difficulty (SpLD), moderate learning difficulty (MLD), severe learning difficulty (SLD) and profound and multiple learning difficulty (PMLD).

> SpLD pupils may have a particular difficulty in one learning area (e.g. reading or writing) but not in others. They may also suffer from short-term memory loss and with coordination. Pupils with SpLD cover the whole ability range and the severity of their impairment varies widely. Specific learning difficulties include dyslexia, dyscalculia and dyspraxia.
>
> MLD pupils will have difficulties with most or all areas of the curriculum and with basic literacy and numeracy skills. They may also have associated speech and language delay, low self-esteem, low levels of concentration and under-developed social skills. Their needs cannot be met by normal differentiation.
>
> SLD pupils will have significant intellectual or cognitive impairments which have a major effect on their ability to participate in school without support. They will need support in all areas of the curriculum and they may also require teaching of self-help, independence and social skills. Some pupils may use signs and symbols but most will be able to hold simple conversations and gain some literacy skills. Their attainments may be within the upper P scale range (P4–P8) for much of their school careers (that is below level 1 of the National Curriculum).
>
> PMLD pupils have severe and complex learning needs. In addition they have other significant difficulties, such as physical disabilities or a sensory impairment. They require a high level of adult support, both for their learning needs and also for personal care. They are likely to need sensory stimulation and a curriculum broken down into very small steps. Some pupils communicate by gesture, eye pointing or symbols, others by very simple language. Their attainments are likely to remain in the early P scale range (P1–P4) throughout their school careers.
>
> (DCSF, 2008c)

This section will address the needs of SpLD/MLD children. The more specialist needs of SLD/PMLD children are not addressed specifically in this book except where they overlap with other needs such as sensory, physical and medical requirements.

Dyslexia

Dyslexia is a term to describe a learning difficulty associated with words (reading, writing and spelling). It affects some 4 per cent of the population severely and a further 6 per cent have mild to moderate difficulties across the whole ability range. Symptoms are wide ranging and children with dyslexia may have poor reading comprehension, handwriting, spelling, punctuation and pronunciation. They may also reverse or jumble letters and sounds in words and mistake similarly shaped words. As a result, their work may be untidy and full of errors and crossing out and they may become reluctant writers. They can suffer from memory loss, have difficulty organizing thoughts and manage time poorly.

ICT can help with these issues and can also be directed toward the strengths of dyslexics which include innovation, lateral thinking and creativity.

Memory loss

One very simple idea is to provide an area on the computer to store ideas, notes and reminders to help with memory loss. Windows Vista includes 'Sticky Notes' and there are several, similar free packages for download from the Internet. Try sticky-notes.net or the interactive screen saver mycorkboard.com.

Figure 8.8 Sticky Notes

Organising

Mind mapping helps children to organise, plan and present ideas in pictorial form using words which they find are familiar. This provides a structure for writing. Some software titles provide tools to transform mind maps into sequential text which helps begin the writing process. Titles include Inspiration, IdeasMap, Kidspiration, Visual Mind and 2Connect.

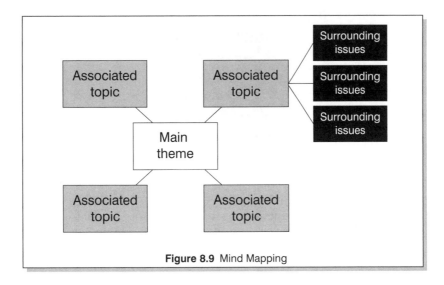

Figure 8.9 Mind Mapping

Writing

Touch typing and keyboard skills are invaluable for dyslexic children. They reduce the need for handwriting (which is commonly a disliked or a challenging area for many) and help children to learn spelling, word recognition, comprehension and vocabulary. Effective products include 2Type, Englishtype Junior, First Keys to Literacy, Speedy Keys and Nessy Keys.

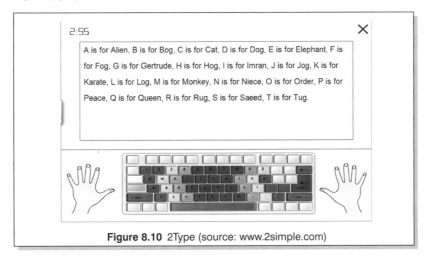

Figure 8.10 2Type (source: www.2simple.com)

Dyslexic children who struggle to scribble down notes will benefit from electronic note-taking devices. There are plenty to choose from. Sound recording can be done using dictaphones, mobile phones, mp3 recorders and most handheld devices. Notebooks and Alphasmarts with spellcheckers and other useful features can be used to type notes directly.

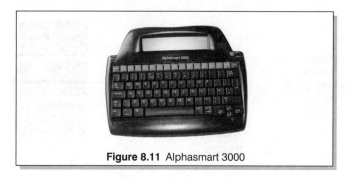

Figure 8.11 Alphasmart 3000

Pupils with dyslexia are often frustrated because they know what they want to write but they have great difficulty in committing it to paper. Word processors and 'add-ons' provide a range o f features to alleviate the problem. Programs such as Co:Writer SOLO add word prediction, word banks, a dictionary and other tools to any word processor or email program.

For severe dyslexia, voice recognition may provide a much needed alternative input (these are covered fully in the section 'Sensory, physical and medical' below). However, these should not be used frequently for mild dyslexics or it my impede development.

Reading

Reading can be improved in a number of ways. When presenting written material, try to keep to continuous and consistent lines of text. Avoid centre and right justification, try to reduce unnecessary clutter on the screen and don't wrap text around images. Block capitals and underlining are often tricky for children with dyslexia too.

Reading rulers will help to focus readers on specific lines of text either as paper versions or free screen utility programs such as VU-Bar 4.0 or Virtual Reading Ruler.

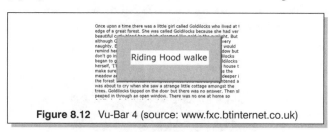

Figure 8.12 Vu-Bar 4 (source: www.fxc.btinternet.co.uk)

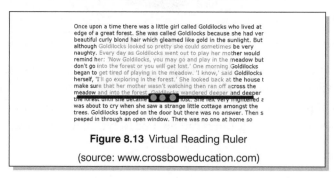

Figure 8.13 Virtual Reading Ruler

(source: www.crossboweducation.com)

Changing background colours and fonts can be beneficial and each individual will have their own preference. Computer operating systems will have limited features. For example, one of the Windows Control Panel accessibility options is 'high contrast' which offers a range of colours and fonts for easy reading. However, it is cumbersome to change settings and limited in operation. Individual software applications may have reading options as do some websites. There are also a number of software programs which provide more efficient solutions.

Screen Tinter Lite, one of a number of useful products by Thomson Software Solutions, is a free download which allows for easy adjustment of the colour properties of a Windows display. It helps with reading difficulties and reduces glare from the screen. Changing a screen's colour scheme can also motivate learners with cognitive difficulties.

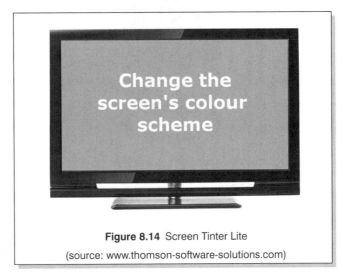

Figure 8.14 Screen Tinter Lite
(source: www.thomson-software-solutions.com)

A large and ever-increasing number of e-books are available to download from digital bookstores such as ebooks.com and there is also a large collection of free out-of-copyright e-books available at Project Gutenberg.

Pronunciation

Reading pens (scanning pens) help children to read words that they can't spell, pronounce or comprehend. The pen is scanned across printed text and the word is displayed on an LCD screen and spoken (or spelled out) using clear English voices. Oxford Dictionary pens can recognise up to 240,000 definitions from the Oxford Concise Dictionary.

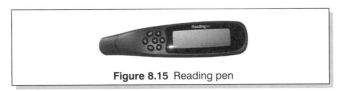

Figure 8.15 Reading pen

Screen readers and text-to-speech converters can perform the same function with on-screen text. Text can also be scanned in from printed documents if required (these are covered fully in the section 'Sensory, physical and medical' below).

Another way to help with pronunciation and spelling is to provide materials such as podcasts together with accompanying printed copy and a reading ruler. Children play the files using an mp3(4) player, iPod or mobile phone. They can work at their own pace, in their own time and repeat the process as many times as they require.

Figure 8.16 mp4 recorder

Other software and teaching programs

A number of computer teaching programs have been designed to provide multi-sensory support. Examples include:

- The Nessy Learning Programme: a complete teaching scheme including worksheets, puzzles and activities for developing reading and spelling skills.

- AcceleRead AcceleWrite: a complete programme using speech output to develop reading.

- Spinout Stories: talking stories to get poor readers reading the same information as their peers.

- Eye Track: visual discrimination, pattern recognition, memory and spatial relationships.

- Phoneme Track: relates sounds to letter combinations and phonemes.

- Wordshark: reinforces spelling rules through fun games.

- Starspell: look-cover-write-check approach to spelling (words are spoken).

- Oxford Reading Tree Talking Stories: reading scheme for infants.

- Lexion: helps children to unravel the reading and spelling process.

- Learning Access Suite: a complete learning suite for reading, writing and accessibility.

Dyscalculia

Dyscalculia is a condition that affects the ability to acquire mathematical skills. It is not as widely understood as dyslexia, perhaps because there is less shame attached to being poor at sums than there is to not being able to read.

Dyscalculic learners may have trouble learning and recalling number facts, counting up or down, relating multiples of ten, dealing with money, rote learning the times tables, telling the time and understanding direction. There is no direct link between dyscalculia and dyslexia though some dyslexic children have difficulty with maths because of the language surrounding it.

In terms of ICT resources you might begin by listing the general ways in which teachers can help dyscalculic learners. For example, you could provide fact sheets, encourage children to set out work neatly, offer pictorial representations of numbers and provide physical (or virtual) objects which can be manipulated. With these in mind, consider whether ICT can be used to create these types of resource. It may be that you simply use basic office packages to produce printed materials or perhaps you can be more ambitious.

Fact sheets

It is helpful to provide basic fact sheets (number grids, times tables, formula lists) to help children to visualise number pattern and position. ICT is useful here because fact sheets created using word processors and spreadsheets can be stored and printed out easily and will not be lost as frequently. There are also many websites that provide free sheets together with other useful resources. Try the BBC Skillswise site for fact sheets, work sheets, quizzes and games.

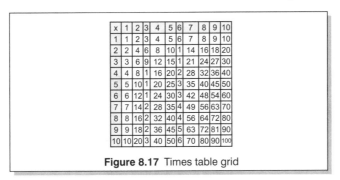

Figure 8.17 Times table grid

Number lines

Number lines can be created in a variety of formats to help with number position and counting up and down. Sets of numbers and mathematical symbols are available commercially though you can improvise and create your own printed and laminated versions (children could make them as part of a structured activity). The use of ICT here is highly appropriate because you are in a position to create individual solutions which fit the personal requirements of children with particular needs. If you are ambitious and creative then you might also consider designing simple on-screen versions using software which allows drag and drop. The Smart Notebook and TextEase are two contenders.

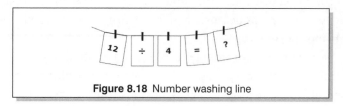

Figure 8.18 Number washing line

Websites

If experimenting isn't your style or you simply don't have the time on your hands then search the Internet or visit some of the sites listed in Appendix 2. English and maths resources are abundant and many of them, whilst not necessarily designed with SEN in mind, are quite suitable for dyslexic and dyscalculic children. Two good examples from the popular Primary Resources website are Number Line and Number Order. Both have a range of activities which are both effective and very motivating.

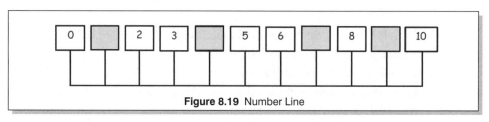

Figure 8.19 Number Line

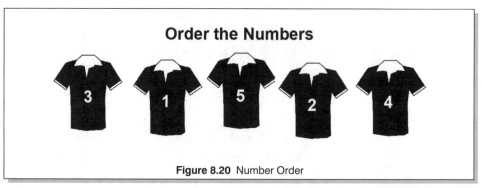

Figure 8.20 Number Order

 Activity

Link to the Primary ICT site and try out the Numbers to 10 activity. This is an example of a game you can create yourself using TextEase. You can also use the Number Bonds Spreadsheet. If you don't own a copy of TextEase you can download a trial version from www.textease.com.

Such games are simple to design and easy to adapt. Once you have created one game or activity you quickly realise that the possibilities are endless.

Calculators

Using a calculator can be very helpful. The keys provide a guide to number order and it can be easier to perform simple calculations than using pencil and paper. However, there are more issues than solutions with calculators. Whilst most people can estimate what to expect for an answer, dyscalculic learners cannot. One remedy is to perform the calculation more than once and see whether the answer comes out the same each time. Computer keypads are laid out as the inverse of calculator keypads (7,8,9 at the top rather than 1,2,3). This leads to confusion as do the numerous superfluous keys. Talking calculators are available but these are extremely expensive.

Commercial software

There are many maths software titles which are suitable for dyscalculic learners. There are also programs for identifying children who might have dyscalculic tendencies. One example is Dyscalculia Screener, designed by Professor Brian Butterworth, a leading UK authority on dyscalculia.

Some software applications rely on reading skills and will therefore require teacher support. Others, like Numbershark 4, include audio instructions. Popular titles include The Number Race, Bubble Reef, Knowlsey Woods, Star Fractions, Time and Money and Dynamo Maths. Try also some of the school websites such as Priory Woods (www.priorywoods.middlesbrough.sch.uk).

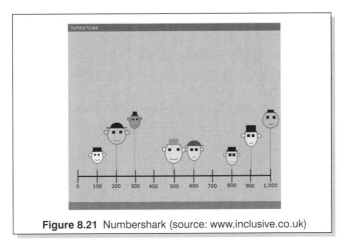

Figure 8.21 Numbershark (source: www.inclusive.co.uk)

Dyspraxia

The term dyspraxia is used to describe impairment or immaturity in the organisation of movement. Children with dyspraxia have difficulty developing fine motor skills and often appear clumsy. As a result, they may have problems with handwriting, drawing and articulation. This will often lead to a lack of confidence and poor social skills.

With some dyspraxic children there is a definite overlap with dyslexia and dyscalculia and the ICT solutions that can be applied to these will often help dyspraxic children too. In addition, ICT can help with:

- fine motor skills: mouse, keyboard and graphic tablet activities;

- presentation: word processors, DTP applications, presentation software, etc.;

- privacy: computers allow for self-paced work without fear of embarrassment or intimidation;

- social interaction: the motivational impact of ICT draws children naturally into group participation.

As a result there may also be an accompanying increase in motivation and self-esteem.

Behavioural, emotional and social difficulties

The SEN Code of Practice describes children with behavioural, emotional and social difficulties (BESD) as children who demonstrate behaviour such as: being withdrawn or isolated, disruptive and disturbing, being hyperactive and lacking concentration, having immature social skills or presenting challenging behaviour arising from other complex special needs.

BESD includes children with emotional disorders and hyperkinetic disorders including attention deficit disorder or attention deficit hyperactivity disorder (ADD/ADHD). It also includes children with anxiety, school phobia, depression and those who self-harm.

Pupils with BESD cover the full range of ability and a continuum of severity. They are considered to have SEN if their behaviour presents a barrier to learning and persists despite the implementation of an effective school behaviour policy and personal/social curriculum. They may be withdrawn or isolated, disruptive and disturbing, hyperactive and lack concentration, have immature social skills or present challenging behaviour.

With this category of pupil, ICT in general can have a positive impact on motivation, self-esteem and achievement, just as it can with any pupil. The level of impact will depend upon the capability of teachers in making effective use of ICT to provide exciting lessons and to offer opportunities for autonomous learning. As a result, pupils become more engaged in their work, their standards rise, they become motivated to continue learning in their own time, and behaviour improves.

Interactive whiteboards

When considering how to use ICT to help BESD pupils a good starting point is the interactive whiteboard. Teachers indicate that the IWB is especially motivating for pupils who respond badly, or choose not to take part in, whole class activities. The success of the IWB is in part due to its striking visual impact and also to its numerous interactive features. BESD pupils, particularly visual or kinesthetic learners, relish the opportunity to carry out exercises involving writing and moving objects on the board. This in itself improves concentration and participation and the incentive to take part has a tendency to improve behaviour. For very bad behaviour it can act as both carrot and stick!

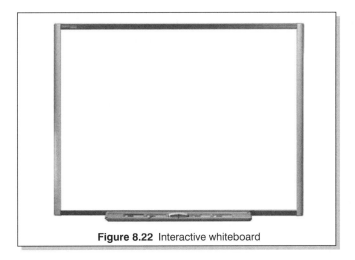

Figure 8.22 Interactive whiteboard

Several teachers report spectacular initial results with children with attention deficit disorder and those on the autistic spectrum; the highly visual nature of the tasks [on the Interactive Whiteboard] seems to attract their attention and keeps them attentive in ways that tasks presented at a desk cannot.

(Sparrowhawk and Heald, 2007)

Software

Garagouni-Areou and Solomonidou (2004) carried out a controlled study which involved primary school pupils with and without ADHD. Both groups worked on computers on a series of specially designed software activities. The results indicated that the software's specific features stimulated the ADHD students' attention far more than it did the other group. Such software will have sound, graphics and animations that hold a pupil's attention in a way that the teacher cannot. In addition, computers allow greater independence, privacy and are non-judgemental – 'the computer doesn't shout at me!'.

Several suitable software titles have already been mentioned in this chapter. Here are just a few more:

- Talking Animated Alphabet: presents letters of the alphabet, with graphics and sound feedback, to help children learn letter sounds and shapes.

- Tizzy's Toybox / Tizzy's First Tools: stimulating and enchanting resources that introduce early learners to essential basic literacy and numeracy skills.

- Wellington Square: talking books including supporting activities.

- Clockwise 2: practice telling and perceiving time.

- Making sense with number: provides practice in early number work.

- Maths Circus Act: practice and enhance a wide range of maths and problem solving skills.

- Think About: helps develop literal, inferential and evaluative comprehension and aids concentration and memory skills.

- Letter Olympics: cover recognition, discrimination and differentiation of lower case letters b and d, with auditory and visual instructions emphasising accurate sound production of the b and d phonemes.

- Penfriend: helps children with words they can't read or spell.

- SUMone: eight activities to practise basic number skills.

- NumberTrain: over 20 carefully structured practical and mental maths activities.

You might of course consider designing activities yourself.

 Activity

Link to the Primary ICT site and try out the Emotions game. It was created by a PGCE student and has yet to be finished. You might like to do this yourself.

The activity was designed using MS PowerPoint to augment a social use of language programme (SULP). If you evaluate it you will find plenty to criticise. For example, you may feel that there is far too much distraction and that the synthetic voice could be improved. There are plenty good points too. Evaluation of software and hardware will be covered fully in Chapter 10.

Interactive voting systems

Interactive voting systems are an ideal way to motivate pupils with learning difficulties and engage them in lessons. They are suitable for a range of activities including quizzes, multiple choice mental arithmetic (or spelling), surveys on their own preferences for music and discussions stimulated by posing a question and then voting on the possible answers. Since responses during most activities are quite simple (Yes/No; A, B or C; etc.), the majority of pupils will not have difficulty in operating the hand held devices. Pupils who normally lack confidence and are reluctant to respond in conventional lessons are able to provide anonymous answers.

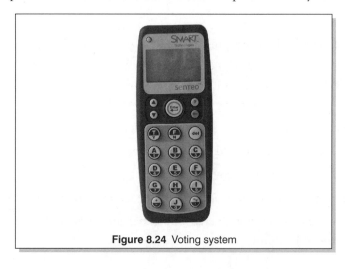

Figure 8.24 Voting system

Case study : Using Audacity and Movie Maker to support a Y4 child with MLD and ADHD in language development

A practice developed in Tameside Authority, which have developed and are cataloguing a wide range of effective uses of ICT to support inclusion.

Pupil description
Child A is a boy aged 9. Child B is a boy aged 9.

Learning objective
Strand 9 – Summarise and shape material and ideas from different sources to create convincing and informative non-narrative texts.

Show imagination through language used to create emphasis, humour, atmosphere or suspense.

Strand 11 – Clarify meaning and point of view by varied sentence structure using phrases, clauses and adverbials.

Additional/special need
Child A is at school action plus for moderate learning difficulties (MLD). He is below the national average for his age group in reading, writing, spelling, and speaking and listening. Child A has previously received speech and language therapy from the CLASS team and has made good progress over the current year at school. He has a short attention span and finds writing for the time periods expected in his year group difficult and frustrating. Child A is often supported in class during Literacy. He has some interesting ideas and can express them coherently to the teacher.

Child B is also at school action plus for moderate learning difficulties and attention deficit hyperactivity disorder (ADHD). He is below the national average for his age group in reading, writing, spelling, and speaking and listening. Child B finds concentrating during a 30-minute lesson difficult. He has previously received support from the BESD team and has taken medication for his ADHD which has been withdrawn recently. His short attention span results in him being distracted and distracting others which consequently has a knock on effect on his learning and attainment.

The role of ICT in addressing the learning objectives
Both children are fully engaged during ICT lessons and by the use of ICT during lessons. Consequently to support them in moving their learning forward ICT was used to motivate, excite and inspire them thus raising their self-esteem and confidence during the literacy lesson. Throughout the year both pupils have used Audacity on a regular basis developing their competence and gaining confidence in both their ability and use of Audacity. During this three-week unit the teacher has provided extra support and guidance for the two pupils on using Windows Movie Maker.

The topic was persuasion and involved using persuasive language and key features of persuasion. The ICT outcomes were taken from the renewed literacy framework. The medium through which the children were using their knowledge was by writing their own voice-over for a pre-selected film trailer. They also had to add sound effects and music appropriate to the film clip. This was then put together on Windows Movie Maker to create a final film trailer. Children worked mainly in mixed ability pairs, however the children with MLD worked with TA or teacher and their outcomes were solely based in ICT, rather than written, to break down many of the barriers these children face when asked to do a written piece.

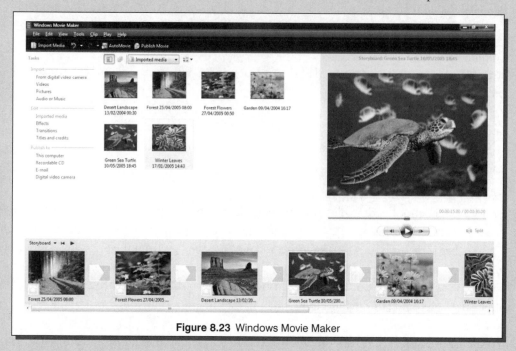

Figure 8.23 Windows Movie Maker

Outcomes

This unit of multimedia work was extremely successful and promoted excellence and enjoyment for all members of the class. It certainly exemplifies how media other than pencil and paper can be adopted to include children who have additional needs. It gave rise to a better use of language and expression. Also the use of Audacity allowed them to effectively and quickly edit and re-edit their work. The two pupils are now capable of using Audacity with Windows Movie Maker to create a sound multimedia presentation with minimal support. For these two pupils to show their class a super piece of work that they have produced by themselves was a real achievement and boost to their self-esteem.

What next/follow up?

Both children will continue to use Audacity and Windows Movie Maker in class to encourage and motivate them during literacy lessns and give them a sense of independence and achievement. The class teachers aim to employ the use of multimedia where possible into their planning and share their ideas with other staff members.

With kind permission of Tameside Authority: www.teachingandlearningtameside.net/ict

This allows teachers to facilitate learning and assess outcomes in a way that they would otherwise find tricky. In order that this approach remains effective over time it should not be overused and should be one element of a blended system which incorporates a range of ICT and non-ICT activities.

Mobile devices

Mobile phones and other handheld devices provide opportunities for autonomous learning. They can also motivate and include pupils who fail to attend.

> Learners nowadays are mobile, and with good pedagogy and good support, handheld devices can help them fulfil their full potential.
>
> (Education Business, 2008: 63)

Examples of mobile activities include:

- A mobile phone activity: pupils are sent instructions for a literacy activity using SMS (text messaging). The activity requires them to read a passage of text and summarise its meaning. Each summary is returned, via a specified mobile number, to a website which collates and presents the results. These are used to stimulate a subsequent group discussion once the pupils return to school.

- Nintendo DS: together with its associated packages, Brain Training and Big Brain Academy, this handheld game console helps to improve numeracy skills.

- Weather Willy: pupils with learning difficulties use this simple wireless device to help in choosing what clothing to wear prior to setting out on a nature trail. Some children use a map and compass to navigate and others make use of a personal digital assistant (PDA) with a built-in global positioning system (GPS).

For further ideas, visit the Mobile Learning Network (MoLeNET) site at www.molenet.org.uk.

The choice of teaching method, whether it be whole group (using the IWB, video conferencing and interactive voting systems) or individual (using PCs and mobile devices) will depend on each child's preferred learning style. This is something which needs to be established at the outset. In some cases, the degree of privacy required by a child might warrant the use of screening around the computer (this could be achieved by setting up your suite as a number of carousels).

Sensory, physical and medical

Visual impairment

Visual impairment includes a range of difficulties from partial sight through to blindness. For educational purposes, a pupil is considered to be visually impaired if they require adaptations to their environment or specific differentiation of learning materials in order to access the curriculum.

As with other special needs, the first step should be to establish the exact nature of the impairment and the problems faced by each individual pupil. Some pupils are registered as blind whilst others will have partial sight which manifests itself in a number of ways including: poor central vision; poor peripheral vision; blurred vision; a mixture of blank areas and defined areas; and colour blindness. It may therefore be necessary to obtain medical advice from health professionals and qualified teachers for the visually impaired before exploring possible solutions.

This section presents a number of resources which may prove useful in enhancing the learning of children with visual impairment. The best place to start would be the computer display settings. However, since this applies to all users, it has been incorporated into the final section of this chapter 'Environmental health and safety'.

Windows accessibility options

Windows operating systems incorporate a number of accessibility options. It would be prudent to explore these first since they are available free of charge. The options have grown with the release of each new version of Windows. This section includes the options available in Windows XP and Windows Vista. You will find them via the Start button → Control Panel or Start button → Programs→ Accessories.

XP includes an Accessibility Wizard, but in Vista this has been replaced by the Ease of Access Center.

MAGNIFIER

Magnifier (XP and Vista) enlarges selected text and other on-screen items for easier viewing. When launched, the enlarged view appears in a designated pane which has magnification up to x16. The magnified portion can also invert colours (i.e. black on white becomes white on black)

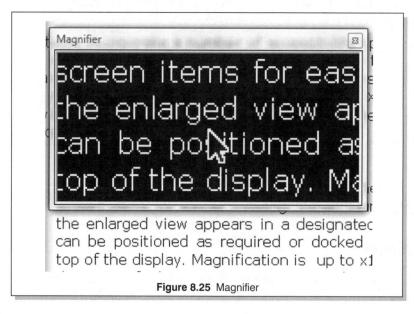

Figure 8.25 Magnifier

NARRATOR

Narrator (XP and Vista) reads on-screen text, dialogue boxes, menus and buttons. It will also read text as it is typed. A choice of synthetic voices are available and, whilst they might seem unrealistic at first, frequent users will quickly get used to them.

SPEECH RECOGNITION

Speech Recognition (XP and Vista) allows the user to dictate text and control the computer using voice. The user can train his/her voice and, the more training carried out, the more accurate the conversion process. The same feature is available in Word 2003 and 2007.

DISPLAY OPTIONS

Display options which can be modified: font style, colour, and size of items on the desktop; icon size; screen resolution; high-contrast schemes (for colour combinations that are easier to see); cursor width and blink rate (to make the cursor easier to locate); plus other personalised settings.

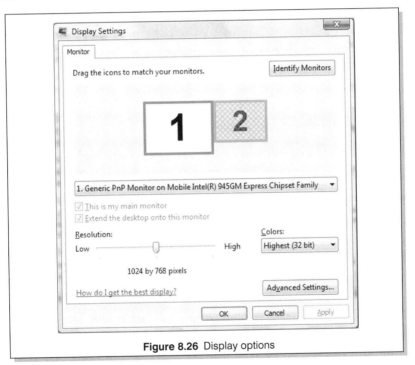

Figure 8.26 Display options

INTERNET EXPLORER

Internet Explorer includes a number of useful features: zoom – to magnify text, images, and controls; change colours of text, background, links and hover; change text size from small to medium to large; and Internet options to change font and accessibility settings.

SOUND SCHEMES AND THEMES

Sound schemes/themes (XP and Vista) can be assigned to many program events. Every sound scheme consists of a set of events and sounds associated with them. These will benefit pupils who rely on sounds to get information from their computers including those who are blind or have other vision impairments.

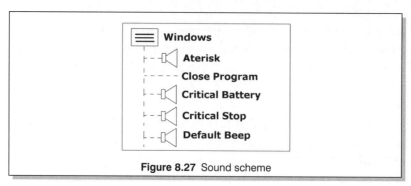

Figure 8.27 Sound scheme

Pupils who have difficulty with printed materials can obtain the documentation for many Microsoft products in more accessible formats at www.microsoft.com/enable/products/docs/default.aspx.

Educational materials

When presenting materials for your pupils you can:

■ provide access to existing electronic materials (e.g. websites and e-books);

■ create your own electronic texts (e.g. word processed, PDF and html);

■ convert existing printed materials into electronic format (by scanning with optical character recognition);

■ produce printed materials which are more accessible than the norm;

■ produce audio materials (and/or allow pupils to record lessons and dictate their own notes);

■ produce Braille books.

Electronic materials are a good option because they are readily accessible using good screen reading software. The Windows Narrator will suffice for some pupils but those who are heavily dependent on such software will benefit from a better offering. There are several on the market including, Lookout, Window-Eyes, ProTalk 32, JAWS, Wordread and SuperNova; but perhaps the best is HAL.

If you create your own texts and web pages then you should incorporate alternative text in order that your chosen screen reader can decipher images too (all good authoring packages, including MS Word will provide this feature).

Converting printed materials to electronic format is quite simple and requires a flatbed scanner and optical character recognition (OCR) software. Most scanners will include OCR software but it may not entirely meet your needs. If you are to avoid tedious editing, a quality package will be needed; titles include OmniPage 16, FineReader and IRIS. For 99+ per cent accuracy choose Kurzweil 1000.

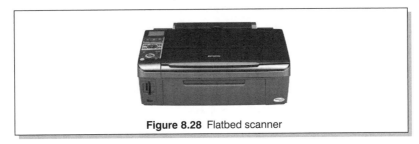

Figure 8.28 Flatbed scanner

Blind children may rely heavily on quality OCR software which will allow them to scan books (and other documents) and have them read back directly using a screen reader (or a standalone reading machine which integrates a scanner, OCR software and speech software).

Partially sighted pupils will still need access to printed materials. It's all too easy to administer standard materials which have been prepared for other children in the class. However, it is very important for the partially sighted to receive materials in clear print. Each individual's needs will differ but, in general, print should be of adequate size (12–14 point), contrasting with the background colour (e.g. black on green), simple typeface (e.g. Arial), and consistent word and line spacing. The Royal National Institute of Blind People (www.rnib.org.uk) offer more detailed advice on the topic.

You should also be conscious of any colour deficiency (colour blindness); red and green are the most common colours affected. Blue on yellow and white on black are best for significant features.

Braille

Developments in ICT have led to the emergence of many useful resources for the visually impaired; these have augmented, though not entirely replaced Braille. However, for many people, Braille is their natural way of working and it is an essential medium for the deaf-blind (RNIB, 2008).

Braille note takers assist the blind in several aspects of their work including note taking, sending emails; and acting as personal organisers they come in a variety of forms. The essential features are a refreshable Braille display and a Braille keyboard with voice output. Some have a computer style keyboard. Using screen reading software the BrailleNote can also be used as a Braille terminal.

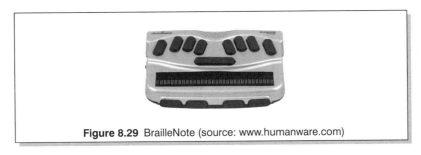

Figure 8.29 BrailleNote (source: www.humanware.com)

Braille translation software (such as the Duxbury Braille Translator) will convert text from any type of document into Braille. Reading the converted Braille will require either an electronic Braille display or a Braille printer (embosser).

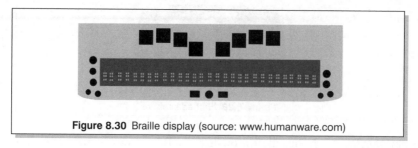

Figure 8.30 Braille display (source: www.humanware.com)

For more information on electronic Braille readers, Braille note takers, Braille embossers and Braille conversion software you should look at the RNIB fact sheets at www.rnib.org.uk/xpedio/groups/public/documents/PublicWebsite/public_withoutvisinfosheet.hcsp.

Voice recognition

Voice recognition is useful for pupils with physical access difficulties, reading, writing or spelling difficulties and for those with visual impairment. There are two types of recognition system – discrete and continuous.

Discrete systems require words to be spoken one at a time with a distinct pause in between. These are useful for pupils with speech impairments that are due to other problems such as cerebral palsy or dysarthria. The most widely known system is DragonDictate.

Continuous systems are now the most widely used because they allow pupils to speak in a more natural way. The most popular continuous speech systems are Dragon NaturallySpeaking and IBM ViaVoice. Microsoft has incorporated speech recognition into Windows XP and Windows Vista although it is not as accurate as the dedicated products.

Whichever system is used it must be trained by each individual user. This usually takes a small number of 10–15 minute sessions – the more training carried out, the more accurate the system becomes.

Hand-held computers

Hand-held computers are also available for blind people. They come with an integrated tactile keyboard, audio recording, voice playback, wifi, infrared, Bluetooth and Internet access. In theory they are comparable to a standard PDA. Some will have built in GPS too, which can afford users increased independence.

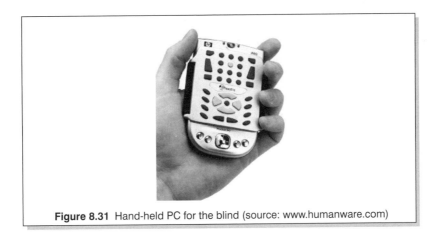

Figure 8.31 Hand-held PC for the blind (source: www.humanware.com)

Global positioning systems (GPS)

A GPS has many applications and can be invaluable to a blind or partially sighted person who may find it difficult to read signs and maps. Users can tell exactly where they are at the touch of a button, navigate their way around with precision and follow familiar, pre-stored routes. Directions are given using voice announcements and these devices offer a much valued degree of independence, freedom and dignity which may otherwise be denied.

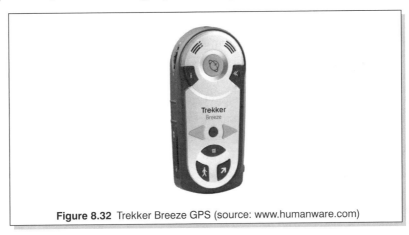

Figure 8.32 Trekker Breeze GPS (source: www.humanware.com)

Hearing impairment

Pupils with a hearing impairment range from those with a mild hearing loss to those who are profoundly deaf. They may have a complex range of needs and those with significant impairment will receive support from a specialist teacher of the deaf. Some children will rely on lip reading, some will use hearing aids and some will have British Sign Language (BSL) as their primary means of communication.

There are also emerging derivatives of sign language which are used in conjunction with lip reading and known as 'Visual Phonics'.

In education, children are regarded as having a hearing impairment if they need communication aids or alternative approaches to teaching in order to access the curriculum. Most will require help with communication and associated language and literacy support.

Windows accessibility options

Recent versions of Windows operating systems include a number of accessibility options that are suitable for those with hearing impairment. They are available via the Control Panel.

SHOWSOUNDS

ShowSounds is an accessibility feature which instructs programs that usually convey information only by sound to also provide all information visually, such as by displaying text captions or informative icons.

SOUNDSENTRY

SoundSentry is an accessibility feature designed for people who have difficulty hearing system sounds generated by the computer. SoundSentry allows them to change the settings to generate visual warnings, such as a blinking title bar or a screen flash, whenever the computer they are using generates a sound. They will be able to choose visual warnings (for example, a flashing border) for sounds made by windowed programs and for sounds made by full-screen text programs.

Software

Since hearing impairment results in communication difficulties, much of the software already covered for reading, writing and language difficulties is useful here too. Content free packages, especially word processors, allow text, images (and clipart), animations and symbols to convey information. This mixture of media gives additional meaning and visual clues to written material.

Hearing impaired children may not be able to work at the same pace as other pupils because they may require more time to assimilate information. Electronic delivery of information allows pupils to work at their own pace and to revisit parts of lessons they do not fully comprehend.

Good examples of content free packages are Writing with Symbols 2000, Symwriter, Communicate in Print, Clicker, Co:Writer and TextEase. Content rich packages include Wordshark, Fun with Texts and THRASS.

Sign language

Images or video clips of signing (BSL or letter signing) can be added to software activities, multimedia presentations, TV programmes and other media which incorporate sound as a means of conveying information.

Deaf books are a good example. There are lots available to purchase from commercial vendors and plenty of free offerings too if you care to search the Internet. Most will have been created on CD-ROM or using simple multimedia packages such as PowerPoint. Examples include: Let's Sign (series), Centre Stage and Level 2 BSL Stories. Some software activities have built in signing. A good example is To Market, To Market.

Activity

Link to the Primary ICT site and look at the Five Little Ducks. It is one example of a multimedia deaf book produced using MS PowerPoint and incorporating BSL images (sign boxes).

This is yet another instance of a type of resource that you can easily develop yourself and tailor to the exact needs of your own hearing impaired learners. You can add sign boxes to your printed materials too in order to aid the learning of sign language.

There are also multimedia dictionaries, software and online courses for learning sign language. These include *The Standard Dictionary of The British Sign Language* (multimedia dictionary), Sign to Me (software) and Introducing British Sign Language (online course by www.british-sign.co.uk).

Text and video communication
Email, discussion forums and SMS (text messaging) facilitate easy text communication using computers and mobile phones. Video conferencing and video capable hand-held devices allow children to communicate using sign language. Learning platforms and associated systems can ensure that children receive all information, even if they miss out on other visual clues.

Interactive whiteboards
Once again, this versatile device can prove extremely useful. It facilitates clear presentation of information and, by its very nature, it allows teachers to face the class while delivering a lesson and this will help lip-readers.

Hearing aids
The term hearing aid now applies to conventional hearing aids and also to technologies such as loop systems and sound field systems which can greatly improve the range and quality of sound received by pupils in the classroom. With induction loop systems the teacher will communicate with hearing impaired pupils using the amplified signal from a radio microphone to connect with pupils' hearing aids via a pre-installed loop (wire installed around the classroom being served). An alternative is an infrared induction hearing system.

With the sound field system, the teacher communicates using a microphone which links, using Bluetooth, to a number of pre-positioned loudspeakers around the classroom. The idea is that all children will receive the same volume of sound regardless of their position.

For small numbers of hearing impaired children the teacher can use a radio microphone to transmit to individual receivers which hang around pupils necks.

Not only do these systems provide sound amplification, they also remove the need to continually lip read and, if teachers occasionally turn their backs on the class, pupils can still hear what they have to say.

Physical disabilities

The traditional mouse and keyboard provides suitable access to a computer for most pupils but not for those with physical disabilities or impaired fine or gross motor skills. ICT can however provide these children with assistive technology which can enhance their learning.

Windows accessibility options
Windows provides a number of accessibility options which may be suitable for some pupils with physical disabilities.

Children with motor impairments including Motor Neurone Disease (MND) and cerebral palsy may need help with devices such as the mouse and keyboard which require motor control. Mouse options include:

- *Double-click speed* allows control over the speed of a mouse click. It may be beneficial to slow the process down (particularly when it comes to double-clicking).

- *ClickLock* allows users to highlight and drag objects without having to continually hold down the mouse button.

- *Pointer schemes* alter size and colour of the pointer for better visibility.

- *Pointer speed* controls the speed of the mouse pointer as it moves across the screen. Slowing it down allows for easier location of objects.

- *Pointer trails* gives better visibility when set to 'long'.

- *SnapTo* helps users to locate buttons by forcing the pointer to move to the default button in a dialog box.

- *Button reversal* allows the functions of the right and left mouse buttons to be reversed if users are more competent with their left hand.

Keyboard options include:

- *Character repeat rate* sets how quickly a character repeats when a key is struck.

- *StickyKeys* removes character repeat and allows one key to be pressed at a time.

- *Dvorak keyboard layout* offers alternative keyboard layouts for people who type with one hand or finger.

- *FilterKeys* ignores brief or repeated keystrokes and slows down the repeat rate.

- *MouseKeys* allows the mouse pointer to be moved using the four arrows on the keyboard.

- *On-Screen keyboard* displays a virtual keyboard on the computer screen. It has scanning capability which allows users to type data by using switches or a pointing device.

Keyboard access
Poor motor skills may result in pressing the wrong key or fingers slipping from one key to another. A standard keyboard fitted with a key guard can help prevent unintended key presses and can provide support for the hands between key presses.

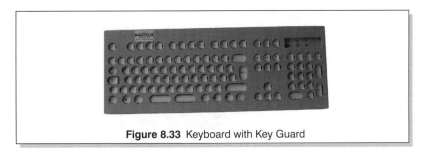

Figure 8.33 Keyboard with Key Guard

Another way to cater for unsteady hands is to choose a keyboard with bigger keys – this model has 1-inch square keys with striking lettering and helpful colour coding. It has a simple ABC layout (though some would argue that children should use QWERTY layouts to avoid confusion). The best judge is you.

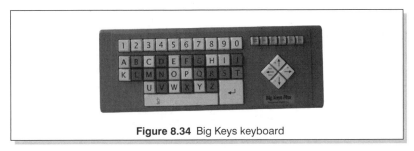

Figure 8.34 Big Keys keyboard

Keyboard gloves are an inexpensive way to turn an existing keyboard into a more accessible option. Gloves will normally come in sets with picture symbols and colour coding. Additional blank gloves and stickers allow you to add colour coding, convert a standard keyboard to lower case or to 'ABC'. They also offer protection to the keyboard from spills and drips.

Figure 8.35 Keyboard glove

If your children are learning lower case letters and words then you can also obtain lower case keyboards. Again, colour coding and other options are available.

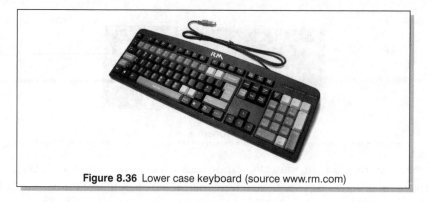

Figure 8.36 Lower case keyboard (source www.rm.com)

A standard keyboard can be converted to lower case by using a keyboard glove.

Ergonomic keyboards compel users to continually adjust their hand and arm position. They were originally designed to prevent repetitive strain injury (RSI) but were subsequently found to be helpful to SEN children with limited hand control or who suffer pain when typing.

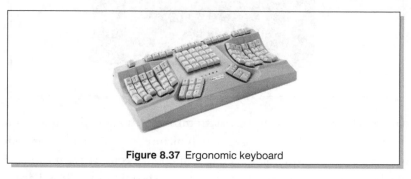

Figure 8.37 Ergonomic keyboard

Pointing devices

A conventional mouse is often difficult for children to use because of their small hands. A number of alternatives exist including rollerballs (including those with a large ball such as Big Trak) and joysticks. There are also mice for very small hands and ergonomic mice too.

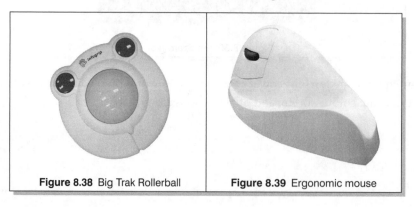

Figure 8.38 Big Trak Rollerball   **Figure 8.39** Ergonomic mouse

Special software exists to make clicking a mouse easier (e.g. one click to select and move without having to hold the button down and then a second click to release; or make a single click equivalent to a double click).

Switch access

Pupils with severe disabilities may not be able to use a keyboard or mouse at all. They can however interact with a computer via a combination of one or more switches. Switches are provided in a number of different forms suitable for all parts of the body. They can be mounted on furniture or on a wheelchair (with adaptations if required). Switches are normally connected via a USB switch interface which allows for connection of multiple switches (up to 6).

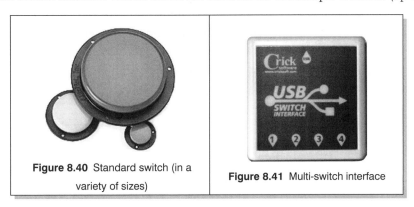

Figure 8.40 Standard switch (in a variety of sizes)

Figure 8.41 Multi-switch interface

Switches may also prove useful for children with learning difficulties because they simplify the menu selection process.

Existing buttons such as the spacebar and mouse buttons can also be used as switches.

Scanning access

Switches interact with any software that has 'scanning' access. Scanning refers to the process of highlighting consecutive menu options or items on the screen (not to be confused with scanning of documents).

When the desired item is highlighted, the switch is pressed in order to select it. The principle extends to the selection of letters, words, punctuation and images such that pupils are able to carry out word processing and other activities. One of the best examples of SEN software with scanning capability is Clicker 5.

Most scanning software applications provide a number of scanning options. Autoscan puts the computer in control and automatically cycles through items on the screen (with an adjustable pause between items). Some children become anxious when using this method and better alternatives might be Userscan and Stepscan which put the user in control, allowing them to start, stop and pause the process.

Scanning can be 'simple scan' where individual items are highlighted in succession or 'group scanning' where complete rows or columns are highlighted followed by individual items within the row or column once it has been selected. Group scanning speeds up the selection process.

A pupil's ability to successfully operate one or more switches will depend upon the degree of their disability, the speed and method of the scanning process and the pupil's positioning with respect to the switch and the screen (seating, comfort, switch mounting etc.). Children's capability should always be assessed prior to engaging in scanning activities in order to make them as effective as possible and to avoid frustration.

All scanning software is capable of accepting single switch access. Some however will permit two or more. If a child is capable of using two or more switches then this can speed up the scanning process.

Software with scanning access

Wide provision has been made with regard to scanning software and, as with other applications, it comes in both content rich and content free forms (including online offerings).

Much of the commercial software (e.g. Clicker 5 and Communicate in Print) and some of the Windows accessibility options (e.g. the onscreen keyboard) already mentioned in this chapter incorporate scanning. For more comprehensive listings, visit the SEN suppliers listed in Appendix 3.

There are plenty of free resources too. For example, you might try the SEN Teacher website at www.senteacher.org.

 Activity

Link to the NGfL Cymru site at www.ngfl-cymru.org.uk/vtc-home/vtc-als-home/ vtc-als-switch_users and try out some of the colouring activities (you can use the spacebar as a switch).

These are not the easiest activities for children yet they do show that scanning activities reach beyond literacy activities and provide opportunities for creativity too.

If you would like to get stuck in then you can create scanning activities yourself using packages such as SwitchIt! Maker 2 which includes sample pictures, videos, music and Picture Communication Symbols.

Overlay keyboards

Overlay keyboards such as the Concept and Intellikeys can provide for easier access because not only can the 'keys' be made much larger, the overlays can be whole words, pictures and symbols. Concept also allows teachers to design their own overlays to suit the particular needs of their children.

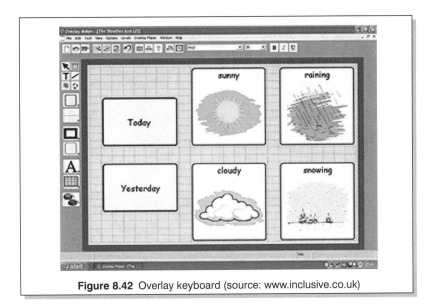

Figure 8.42 Overlay keyboard (source: www.inclusive.co.uk)

Touch screens

A touch screen allows data to be input by touching it with a finger or stylus. Touch screens can also provide SEN pupils with easier access than keyboard or mouse though they tend to be quite expensive. You can purchase a touch screen monitor or convert an existing monitor by hooking on an attachment.

Multi-sensory rooms

Multi-sensory rooms offer a safe, relaxing and fascinating environment which potentially stimulates children to explore, develop awareness and learn. They can also reduce behavioural difficulty, stimulate conversation and act as a reward.

The concept of sensory rooms is accepted by practitioners as an effective therapy for special needs children if they are designed well and used correctly because learners are affected by their environment.

Having spent a limited amount of time in a sensory room, the effects can carry over into other learning spaces and other activities.

Correct supervision is essential and staff should always be adequately trained to ensure that they are conversant with technical, pedagogical and health and safety issues.

Figure 8.43 Multi-sensory room (source: www.experia-innovations.co.uk)

Sensory rooms have been used for people with learning difficulties, physical disabilities, autism, ADHD and other problems. The potential benefits include: developing a sense of cause and effect; controlling events; improving hand/eye coordination; developing language; promoting communication and sharing; encouraging human touch; reactivating hearing, sight, smell, touch and taste; and relaxation.

Sensory rooms may be designed to cater for a range of needs or for one specific need. They may take the form of light rooms, dark rooms or soft play areas and general multi-sensory rooms. In some schools the sensory environment takes up only part of a room or other designated area and, for those with restricted facilities or funding, a sensory 'trolley' or 'tub' may be the preferred option.

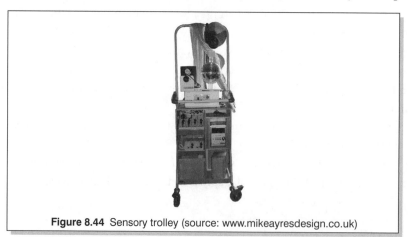

Figure 8.44 Sensory trolley (source: www.mikeayresdesign.co.uk)

The focus in sensory sessions may be on calming, relaxing and generally having fun or it may be to achieve a number of specified objectives. Equipment will include:

- Lighting effects such as projectors, spotlights, UV lights, bubble lamps, mirror balls, fibre optics, glow lines, glow sticks, torches and visual software. They are often used in conjunction with wheels and other devices which disburse light patterns throughout the room.

- Sound effects such as music, nature sounds, animal sounds and soothing rhythmic music.

- Cause and effect equipment such as switches and sensors (including remote controlled).

- Sensory surfaces which comprise interactive floor and wall projection systems.

Sensory equipment can be expensive though you can start quite cheaply with some soft lighting, simple torches, switches and your own existing sound system.

English as an additional language (EAL)

There are many children in mainstream schools for whom English is an additional language. They may already speak a native tongue or they may be learning their native language and English together. It is challenging for teachers to accommodate these children because no two children will be at the same stage of language development and, as they are developing a mastery of a second language, they may fall behind in terms of progressing through the curriculum. In addition, teachers are expected to plan their lessons so that all children can take part. This may mean that some children will need to use their first language at times.

ICT can help with EAL learners because it not only offers a range of useful resources, it also offers a common medium through which learning can be effected. Children who are struggling to learn another language may not struggle with the basic computing skills required to give them access to language tools.

Here are some of the ways in which ICT might enhance the provision for EAL pupils.

Word processors

Word processors provide a number of support features which are advantageous to EAL pupils. Spelling and grammar checking highlights mistakes in a non-threatening way and this reduces anxiety and encourages experimentation. Dictionaries and thesauruses aid and extend the learning of vocabulary. Text manipulation tools such as cut, copy and paste allow writing to be redrafted without the need to rewrite lengthy passages. Some word processors, including MS Word, offer this support in a range of languages and can perform limited language translation too.

Alternatively, specialist individual language software can be used (usually to augment MS Office) which may provide better script quality and additional support.

If you need to type in a foreign language then a special keyboard may be required though you can buy keyboard gloves for English keyboards and a number of virtual keyboards are available too.

Overlay keyboards

An overlay keyboard may be used in place of or alongside a standard keyboard. The preferred option would be a keyboard that allows teachers to design their own overlays (e.g. the Concept keyboard). The keyboard can then be divided into areas in order to create any number of 'buttons' (from 1 to 255). Words, sentences, pictures and sounds can be assigned to each button. Words can be associated with pictures, English and first language can be used side by side and words can be spoken as they are typed.

Cross-curricular software

First, it should be noted that one of the main advantages of ICT is that it typically combines textual, audio and visual representations in learning materials. This lends itself well to a range of learning styles (including those of EAL pupils) and therefore the general incorporation of ICT resources across the curriculum will have benefits for language learning too. Multimedia authoring software is particularly effective because it enables text, images, animation, video and sound to be combined and this is useful for teachers when creating learning materials and for pupils when completing activities and projects. Simple packages include MS PowerPoint, HyperStudio, Mediator, Opus Pro, Story Maker and Kids Animation Maker. The more ambitious author might try Adobe Authorware.

Visual aids

Visual aids play an essential role and ICT can be used to generate a wide range of materials including: signs, drawings, diagrams, charts, tables, flash cards, posters, labels, picture dictionaries, matching games and worksheets. Competence in one or two basic multimedia authoring or DTP packages will go a long way here. MS Word, MS PowerPoint and MS Publisher may be all a teacher needs in this respect. As ever, the interactive whiteboard excels here (see the Becta ICT Test Bed Evaluation of EAL at www.evaluation.icttestbed.org.uk/learning/research/ primary/ interest/eal for research on the IWB).

Pictorial and audio software

ICT is particularly effective in providing pictorial support. Many software packages include pictorial support for learning basic vocabulary such as food, clothing, travel, the body, colours, home, family, pets, numbers, shapes, time, weather, animals and familiar places. Examples include: Picture This, Junior World of Words, Games Box, Windows Box, Play & Learn, Living Books, Oxford Literacy Web – Sound Stories, Wordshark, Lexia, Smart Talk, Flash!Pro 2, MatchWord, Colour Magic, My World, Listen & Learn English, Talk Now, World Talk and Rosetta Stone.

Any software with visual and audio representations, signs, symbols, word banks, grids and speech will be beneficial. Talking word processors like TextEase, Clicker, Writing with Symbols 2000, Communicate in Print and Talking First Word are obvious choices.

Audio recordings made with simple recording software can provide useful revision aids which speak native words and their English equivalents. Windows Sound Recorder, Audacity and Podium are good creation tools. Children will need audio players (e.g. Windows Media Player, Real Player and Quicktime) or a mobile mp3 player to play them back.

Mind mapping

Graphic organizers, mind mapping and concept maps are powerful tools which help children to organise, plan and present ideas in pictorial form and they help children to understand and remember. They are particularly useful for pupils with EAL. Examples include Inspiration, IdeasMap, Kidspiration, Visual Mind and 2Connect.

Reading schemes on CD-ROM

Reading schemes on CD-ROM provide practice at learning to read, listening and pronunciation in a second language. Animations, sound cues and other interactive features enhance the process. Examples include: Oxford Reading Tree, Wellington Square, Rainbow Stories, Listen and Learn English and Planet Wobble.

Digital story telling

Following traditional story telling, children can capture the main points in a story board (perhaps using simple multimedia authoring software) or using simple Duplo models. They can then record or animate their stories using video cameras, visualisers or other devices which can capture still or moving pictures. Their own versions of the stories can then be replayed and narrated. Group interaction such as this immerses the EAL learner in the English language, language structure and vocabulary in an informal way (Niace, 2006).

Email and chat rooms

A school's learning platform will provide controlled email and chat room features which provide great opportunities for learners to communicate with first language speakers.

Web-based resources

There's plenty of stuff on the web that's worth considering too (some free). See Appendix 3 for details.

What else can you do?

Given the resources and a little creativity there are many things that you could create for EAL pupils. The DCSF advise on what to do with new arrivals. For example, a buddy system, introductory booklets, a dictionary, bilingual school word lists, phrase books and other support materials. How much of this could you develop using ICT. Would it be possible to design a pack of resources which are published to CD-ROM or the school learning platform (and shared across other schools perhaps?).

Gifted and talented (G&T) children

Gifted and talented (G&T) refers to pupils that demonstrate, or have the potential to demonstrate, an outstanding level of ability in one or more fields of activity and whose needs may not be served by the normal curriculum (e.g. Key Stage 3 pupils who are comfortable meeting the demands of the Key Stage 4 curriculum). It is important to remember that they may not be gifted in all subjects or in all aspects of any one subject.

A review of literature conducted by Roehampton University in 2008 concluded that:

> there does not appear to be any evidence to support a claim that any single strategy is more effective for this heterogeneous group of pupils. The diversity means that personalised, differentiated provision is needed. What works for gifted and talented pupils in the classroom depends on the student, the teacher, the curriculum and the classroom context.
>
> (DCSF, 2008d: 1)

Pupils may benefit from the use of ICT to support their learning (including integrated learning systems) and may also be able to use more advanced features and techniques of ICT itself. They will also benefit from a wider degree of freedom and flexibility in order to enhance their own learning and meet their own individual needs.

There are some specific ICT resources for G&T though it is more about the way in which pupils are encouraged, how their learning is facilitated and how the uses of resources (ICT and other) are extended to provide challenging enrichment activities. Schools might audit their existing ICT provision (in all subjects) in order to ensure that they do have resources which are capable of extending G&T pupils.

In terms of ICT as a subject, pupils who are gifted in ICT are likely to:

- *Demonstrate ICT capability significantly above that expected for their age.* For example, Key Stage 2 pupils may be comfortable meeting the demands of the Key Stage 3 curriculum.

- *Learn and apply new ICT techniques quickly.* For example, pupils use shortcut keys for routine tasks effectively and appropriately; they quickly apply techniques for integrating applications such as mail merge and databases.

- *Use initiative to exploit the potential of more advanced features of ICT tools.* For example, pupils investigate the HTML source code of a website and apply features such as counters or frames to their own web designs.

- *Transfer and apply ICT skills and techniques confidently in new contexts.* For example, having learned about spreadsheet modelling in a mathematical context, they recognise the potential of applying a similar model in a science investigation.

- *Explore independently beyond the given breadth of an ICT topic.* For example, they decide independently to validate information they have found from a website; having learned control procedures for a simple traffic light model, they extend their procedure to include control of a pedestrian crossing.

- *Initiate ideas and solve problems, use ICT effectively and creatively and develop systems that meet personal needs and interests.* For example, they create an interactive fan club website that sends out a monthly newsletter to electronic subscribers (either working on their own, or collaboratively with peers).

(QCA, 2008d)

When using ICT in other subjects, teachers should:

- have high expectations of pupils and make this known;

- encourage pupils to make more use of packages, exploring and utilising advanced features;

- introduce pupils to a wider range of resources and technologies;

- encourage pupils to be critical about, and to explain and justify, their approach to tasks, and to evaluate the resources and methods used;

- extend tasks in order that pupils attain a deeper understanding;

- expect pupils to transfer skills to differing contexts;

- provide pupils with tasks that involve the higher order skills of analysis, synthesis and evaluation;

- expect pupils to use a wider range of source materials;

- encourage pupils to build knowledge and skills through collaboration with others;

- Promote a greater degree of independent working whilst affording opportunities for formative appraisal;

- provide increased access to ICT (timetable constraints permitting);

- provide opportunities for extended learning including homework and out-of-hours use of school resources (including ICT) by way of breakfast clubs, lunchtime clubs and after school sessions;

- consider facilitating some of the learning alongside older pupils;

- challenge underachievement (not all G&T pupils are eager to enhance their education).

 Activity

If you want more guidance on teaching G&T pupils using ICT, link to the Primary ICT Website and read the document 'gifted.pdf'.

Enrichment activities

You will find a number of useful websites which offer free enrichment activities and ideas in Appendix 2. Here are just a few possibilities.

■ Simon Tatham's Portable Puzzle Collection comprises 27 different abstract puzzles. Neat re-packaging of some well-known (and some not so well-known) puzzles in a portable format (executable files). They are challenging and an ideal extension for the gifted and talented. Find it at www.chiark.greenend.org.uk/~sgtatham/puzzles.

■ An intriguing online resource, Escher Web Sketch, allows pupils to experiment with symmetry by drawing repeating patterns. This is just one of a number of cross-curricular resources available from the Brightonline website: www.brightonline.org.uk.

■ The Young, Gifted and Talented website (http://ygt.dcsf.gov.uk) provides a range of resources for every subject in the primary curriculum. The school history section is an incredibly popular site with many history teachers. The content on this can be used by learners and teachers as a means of enhancing and enriching the study of history.

Commercial software

From the limited offerings from commercial retailers you might try the following:

■ From r-e-m: Activities for Able Mathematicians, Brain Academy (series), Maths Challenges for Able Pupils, MissionMaker, Power Maths and PredICTion.

■ From the Chalkface Project: Extension Activities for More Able Students, Thinking Skills for G&T students, and more.

And finally, you might like to take a look at some of the videos provided by Teachers TV.

 Activity

Visit the Primary ICT website and view the Teachers TV video about SEN resources (SEN_Resources.wmv).
There are other videos about SEN and ICT on the Teachers TV website at www.teachers.tv and search for 'SEN'.

Environmental health and safety

ICT health and safety is extremely important for children with SEN and this should perhaps be your first consideration. Prior to deciding on access methods and appropriate resources it is important to remember good basic practice when working with children in the ICT room. Just a few points:

- Is the room tidy? Adequate space, free from clutter, no trailing cables, no dangerous objects, adequate well-labelled storage for computer equipment, books, software etc.?

- Is the seating appropriate and comfortable? Legs, back and arms should all be at right angles with feet flat on the floor, chairs should be adjustable.

- Is the screen positioned correctly and at the right height for the child? Top of the monitor should be level with the eyes, monitors should tilt and swivel.

- Is the screen clean and free from glare? Back to the window, use non-reflective screens, use window blinds if necessary.

- Is the ambient lighting correct to provide good contrast? Adjust lighting, turn the brightness of the screen as low as possible and the contrast as high as possible.

- Can the child comfortably reach the access device? No sharp edges on the computer table, use keyboard and mouse rests.

- Is there adequate space at the computer? Space for reading/writing materials, space for more than one child in order to facilitate pair work.

- Would the child benefit from working in a quieter area?

- Can all children see a demonstration clearly? Room layout should provide adequate view of teacher/IWB.

- Are children supervised when using the IWB? Keep back to the projector beam, never stare at the projector.

- Is the room at the correct working temperature? $18-24^0$C, well ventilated, low humidity.

The SENCO

Responsibility

The SENCO will have responsibility for advising on special needs provision across the school (though responsibility for SEN pupils within each class lies with the class teacher who should liaise closely with the SENCO and ICT coordinator).

The DfES, SEN Code of Practice, 2001 provides a framework within which the SENCO can operate and the framework includes the use of ICT as a tool for the following:

- assessing pupils' abilities;

- assisting in the administration of the SEN Code;

- providing direct support for pupils with special educational needs;

- accessing information, advice and support.

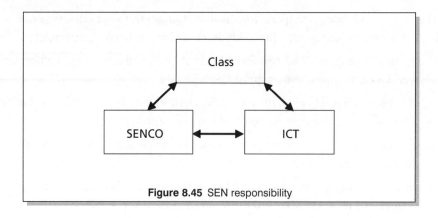

Figure 8.45 SEN responsibility

Assessing pupils' abilities

Periodic assessment of pupils provides up-to-date information to measure progress and inform the teaching and learning process.

Assessment software is available to help assess and analyse pupils in basic skills (literacy and numeracy and short-term memory) and learning styles. There are several recognised tests covering a range of needs. Some can be taken online or they can be administered in school using CD-ROMs. Examples include: Lucid Baseline Assessment; Lucid KS1 CoPS; Junior LASS; LASS; and Instines IDEAS.

Pupils who are not making satisfactory progress may require Individual Education Plans (IEPs). This currently includes those pupils at 'School Action', 'School Action Plus' and those with statements. IEPs document targets, level of support, parental input and evidence of achievement between reviews.

There are a number of IEP software packages available including IEP Writer, IEP Manager, IEP Developer, IEP Pro and B Squared which are used by thousands of schools.

It must be stressed that, whilst some pupils will have IEPs, *all* pupils will have their own individual needs.

Assisting in the administration of the SEN Code

The majority of management information systems (MIS) used in schools facilitate the collection and sharing of information on special educational needs. This can be a real time saver for SENCOs and it also means that all staff can be actively involved so they feel ownership. Some include special features to help schools meet the requirement of the SEN Code of Practice. MIS software includes SIMS, CMIS, Integris G2 and Hebron Engage. When choosing a package it should be understood that there is no 'one size fits all' and the system must fit the school's own requirements. Some of the features to be considered are:

- Can the system be customised to suit the school's needs?
- Can the system bring together assessment, IEPs and monitoring?

- Is it easy to produce data and tables for reports?

- Can you compare data easily?

- Can information be presented in different forms for letters to parents and so on?

- Is data transferable from existing school management systems?

- Can graphs and data analysis be produced?

Becta (2003)

Providing direct support for pupils with SEN

Having established the individual needs of all pupils, the SENCO will need to work in conjunction with the ICT coordinator and other key staff in order to identify and make appropriate provision of ICT resources. Previous sections have outlined resources which can be used for a wide range of special needs. In addition, the Northern Grid for Learning has produced a matching of ICT competences to P scales for pupils with severe learning difficulties (www.northerngrid.org).

Accessing information, advice and support

There are many websites which offer useful information and guidance on the entire spectrum of SEN. These are listed in Appendix 2. There are also online courses covering various aspects of SEN. For example, the Institute of Child Education and Psychology: www.icepe.eu/dyslexia.html.

9

ICT management and leadership

Introduction

This book has presented a range of ideas for using ICT resources in primary schools. However, it is only when such resources are used within a sound strategic framework that schools will achieve and sustain maximum benefit in terms of enhancing learning and teaching, and supporting management and administration.

This chapter examines the requirements for successfully managing ICT processes and links closely with the Becta Self-Review Framework. Each primary school will differ in its current practice, provision and level of ICT experience. The guidance offered here should therefore be treated as general rather than specific (though examples of best practice will be offered throughout).

The approach taken will be simplistic and 'top-down' – first identifying the basic components and then gradually breaking them down into more detail. It will work on the principle of bridging the gap between 'where you are now' and 'where you would like to be in the future'.

The Becta Self-Review Framework

The Becta Self-Review Framework (SEF) was launched in 2006 to help schools to employ strategies to bring about the most effective use of ICT resources.

The framework is broken down into eight elements:

1. Leadership and Management

2. Curriculum

3. Learning and Teaching

4. Assessment

5. Professional Development

6. Extending Opportunities for Learning

7. Resources

8. Impact on Pupil Outcomes.

Each element has a number of detailed strands.

Becta offer the 'ICT Mark' award to schools that are assessed as successfully attaining level 2 in each of the elements where:

Level 1 = Nothing in place
Level 2 = Made a start
Level 3 = Strategy in place
Level 4 = Coherence
Level 5 = Aspirational

To date (2009), over 1000 schools have already achieved the ICT Mark and many more are working towards it.

Schools can also sign up to the 'Next Generation Learning Charter', a commitment to the strategic and effective use of technology across the school.

 Activity

Visit the Primary ICT site and skim through the Becta SEF guides (there is a guide for each of the eight elements). Get a flavour for what you are required to do to achieve the Becta ICT Mark.

Each strand of an element is split into five levels. The levels provide a brief outline of what the school will have in place when they are assessed as being at that level. To be awarded the ICT Mark a school would need to aspire to level 2 throughout. Even if you are not applying for the award, the self review framework is a useful guide to help you improve your school's position. You will note from the level descriptors that, whilst employing good ICT resources has merit, focussing on resources alone will not raise you to level 2.

Each of the eight elements will now be examined in turn (though it must be stressed that all the elements dovetail together and cannot be treated in complete isolation).

Leadership and management

There is no specific order in which to tackle each of the eight elements. However, since the development of ICT will follow a pre-determined strategic plan, then leadership and management must be the first port of call.

ICT Team

With the exception of very small schools, managing ICT is too big a prospect for just one person. Most schools will appoint an ICT leader (e-learning manager) to lead a small team.

Activity

Who do you think should be in your school ICT Team and who would lead it?
Your team needs to include those people who are able to effect the necessary changes which you will ultimately agree to implement. A member of the headship, the ICT coordinator and subject representatives are likely candidates.

In many schools, the deputy head leads the team – in others, it is recognised that, whilst the head and/or deputy should be a member, he/she is already extremely busy and responsibility for leading the team is better invested in the ICT coordinator.

The composition of the team can vary enormously but should adhere to sound management principles. If the team is too small you will deny yourself vital expertise but if the team is too large it will prove difficult to manage. A compromise is to form a core team and an 'extended' team.

For example, the core team might comprise:

- ICT leader (deputy head)
- ICT coordinator
- Subject leaders
- SENCO
- Technical representative
- Teacher representative
- Teaching assistant representative
- Pupil representative

An extended team might include one or more of:

- Teachers
- Teaching assistants
- Pupils
- Parents
- Governors
- LEA
- Commercial partners

It is important that you include all key stakeholders in one way or another and that, in order to obtain maximum 'buy in' to your polices, you consult with members and make them feel included. This is absolutely essential for teachers, particularly those who are not ICT 'enthusiasts' and those who are technophobes.

It will be helpful to the team if:

- its task is clearly defined;
- the roles and responsibilities of the individual members are agreed;
- it is clear who the team will report to and what will happen to its recommendations.

Choice of the ICT coordinator

The traditional role of the ICT coordinator in primary schools has changed enormously over the last two to three years because of the widening impact of ICT on the whole school and beyond (Wright, 2007). The choice of ICT coordinator used to be quite straightforward – choose someone with good ICT skills. However, the role is now becoming increasingly complex and it may require someone with a goodly amount of teaching experience and good people skills.

Team roles and responsibilities

When deciding on team responsibilities it may be a good idea to carry out the exercise of listing (brainstorming) all the things that the school will be required to do. These will range from the simple to the complex. Here are some examples (the list is far from exhaustive):

- Writing policies and procedures
- Audits
- Planning
- Purchasing hardware
- Purchasing ICT consumables
- Repair and maintenance of hardware
- Evaluating software
- Purchasing software (and licensing)
- Using ICT for administration and management
- Network issues
- Sourcing of funding
- Using ICT in each subject area
- Using ICT for assessment
- Replacing printer cartridges
- Managing information
- Staff training
- Review and evaluation
- Health and safety
- Data protection
- Extended learning

This exercise can be carried out over a period of time and you would be wise to consult school-wide as a first step toward involving everyone. Indeed, now may be a good time to benchmark yourself against other schools, particularly one or two that have already achieved the ICT Mark.

Once you've decided who should do what, duties can be further delegated. For example, it may be a good idea to involve the pupils – they could replace printer cartridges and keep the paper topped up. Sharing responsibility in this way also reduces the dependency and the burden on the ICT coordinator.

Roles, responsibilities, duties and so on should eventually be documented in an ICT handbook.

The vision

The starting point for a school is to express its vision for ICT, not in terms of assets or resources, but in terms of measurable benefits. Such a vision might be summarised in a 'vision statement' which is written in quite general terms, owned by all key personnel and shared with all stakeholders. An effective vision should support and enhance the school's aims in terms of learning, teaching, management and administration (i.e. all aspects of the school). It would need to be periodically updated as part of the normal management cycle.

In this respect an ICT vision is no different from an organisation's vision.

 Activity

Do you know the ICT vision for your school?
Hopefully the answer is yes. Ideally it will be properly communicated and prominently displayed in easily accessible places. At the very least, you should be aware that there is a vision and know where to find it.

If you are starting from scratch then it would be wise to keep your vision simple and achievable. Some of the issues that might be included are: pupil entitlement, the value of ICT as a teaching and learning tool, cross-curriculum use, improving attainment, promoting learning styles and extended learning. Here is one example.

> ICT will be used effectively to raise awareness of the benefits and uses of technology, to enhance learning and teaching in all subjects, to improve school management and administration processes, to promote home-school links and, overall, to improve the attainment of all pupils.

ICT audits

Once you know where you want to be (the vision), you need to know where you are now. This may seem obvious but you should do it systematically in order that you don't miss something important. To establish your current position you should carry out an audit. The audit is effectively a quantitative and qualitative analysis of all aspects of ICT.

Activity

How would you carry out an ICT audit in your school – what aspects would you need to consider?
Essentially you will need to find out what resources you have, where they are, how they fit together, how they are being used, who is using them and how often. You will need to break each of these down into as much detail as you think you will need.

You may need to break your audit into several chunks. Some will require physical inspection in order to draw up inventories and others will take the form of interviews, observations, discussions, document inspection etc.

The questions you need to ask, and the evidence you will expect to find, will become evident as you proceed though the subsequent sections of this chapter. However, sources of evidence will include:

- schemes of work (all subjects);
- individual lesson plans;
- classroom observations;
- teaching and learning policy;
- INSET and staff development planning;
- discussions with pupils, teachers and support staff;
- IEPs and other learning programmes for pupils with special needs;
- documents relating to individual self-evaluations;
- personal development plans/action logs/learning logs/pupil diaries;
- cross-curricular ICT planning, including minutes of meetings;
- student peer review and evaluation documentation;
- inventories of ICT resources.

These are certainly the sources of evidence which will be examined by a Becta assessor who is awarding the ICT Mark!

Development plan

Having collated the information collected you can compare what you have in place now with your vision for the future (if you haven't yet done so then you need to break the vision down into more detailed elements).

This difference is the 'strategic gap' and, to bridge it, you need to compile a development plan. The plan will set targets in terms of: *what* needs to be done; *how* it will be achieved; *who* will be responsible for it (and who will provide support); and the timescale for completion (*when*). You might also include possible indicators which you can use to monitor progress.

A few words of caution. DON'T be too ambitious with your plan – it could easily take on unmanageable proportions and become ineffective. Prioritise what needs to be done and do it in phases. You can further modify it as part of a continuous cycle of improvement. DON'T give everything to the ICT coordinator; involve other staff too – it helps to include people. DON'T try to convert everyone into an ICT enthusiast – there will be those who are 'technophobes' and those who are resistant to change. They may need to be nurtured, their skills and enthusiasm growing organically as they are gradually influenced by the actions of others.

Finally, since learning platforms will become a very large part of the included and extended learning process then your platform should be at the centre of your development plan.

School ICT policy

A school's ICT policy will describe the school's approach to achieving the vision for ICT (over a specified period of time). It would cover all important aspects including: strategic management, teaching and learning (including extended learning opportunities), curriculum, assessment, professional development, resources and pupil outcomes.

It is the first step in communicating the aims to the whole school and should therefore be easily accessible to everyone. The first draft need only be an outline of intentions and will be reviewed and modified as part of the management cycle. The sections to be found in the policy could be:

Introduction
The introduction should outline what you want the policy to achieve:

- To ensure all staff understand and agree on the approach to using ICT.
- To assist planning.
- To explain the school's position to outsiders.
- To assist the governors in the allocation of funds.
- etc…

For example:

> This policy document sets out the school's aims, principles and strategies for the delivery of Information and Communication Technology. It will form the basis for the development of ICT in the school over the next five years…

It should define the meaning of ICT. For example:

> We interpret the term 'information and communication technology' to include …

Case study: An example development plan

A school has used a questionnaire, a number of observations and some informal discussions to audit the competence of staff in using ICT. The results reveal that:

- There is no formal process for identifying staff training needs – staff sometimes receive training if they request it or if a new resource is installed (e.g. an interactive whiteboard).

- There is no allocated budget specifically for ICT and staff suggest that ICT takes on a lower priority than other areas.

- Only a few staff feel comfortable with using common ICT resources and know when it is appropriate to use them in learning and teaching.

- Most staff feel that they are not best prepared for using ICT, they are unsure of the resources available for each subject area and they don't know how and when to use them.

- There doesn't appear to be anyone with responsibility for staff development in ICT.

- and so on …

Needless to say, this school has yet to achieve its ICT Mark!

Part of the vision for this school is that all staff will feel comfortable using a range of ICT resources to aid their teaching and to enhance children's learning. The ensuing CPD section of the development plan therefore includes the following:

What / How	Who	By when
Nominate someone to take responsibility for identifying staff development needs.	ICT leader	Now
Develop a simple procedure for identifying staff development needs.	The nominated person	End of current term
Add a section on ICT development into the ICT Handbook.	The nominated person	End of current term
Provide basic training for those who need it. A number of options are available including: in-house training (e.g. a devoted INSET day); team teaching/observation; external training course – cascaded to other members of staff; etc.	ICT coordinator, competent staff	Progressively and within 1 year
Familiarise staff with available ICT resources and how they can be used in each subject area.	ICT coordinator, subject leaders	End of current term

and so on …

The plan is not exhaustive and could of course be broken down into more detail if required.

and make clear the significance of ICT. For example:

> Information and communication technology (ICT) prepares pupils to participate in a rapidly changing world in which work and other activities are increasingly transformed by access to varied and developing technology. Pupils use ICT tools to find, explore, analyse, exchange and present information responsibly, creatively …

Vision statement
A summary of the school's ICT vision.

Managing ICT
Outline the duties of the ICT Management Team and other staff and stakeholders. See page 159 ('Team roles and respsonsibilities') for detail.

The remainder of the policy will cover the expectations for the curriculum, teaching and learning (including extended learning), assessment, staff development, resources, pupil outcomes, and management and administration.

Activity

If you wish to compare and evaluate existing school policies, you will find four on the Primary ICT website. There are plenty more to be found on the Internet.
Some of these are quite basic whilst others are far more comprehensive. They may give you some ideas about the composition of your own policy.

ICT handbook

The school policy outlines the principles behind the use of ICT in the school. Procedures, guidance, rules and other operational matters should be placed in a handbook. The handbook might include:

- role of the ICT team;
- duties of the ICT coordinator;
- duties of all those with specific responsibilities (see previous section);
- acceptable use of the Internet;
- data protection and security;
- health and safety.

Management cycle (evaluation)

And finally, each part of the ICT management process needs to be regularly monitored, evaluated and updated as required. Evidence needs to be collected to determine how effective the process is.

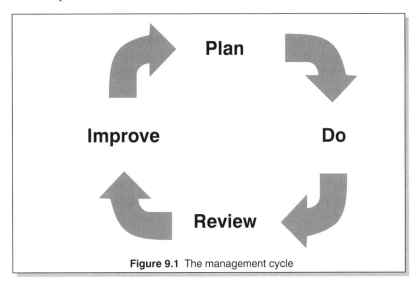

Figure 9.1 The management cycle

The periodicity of review will depend on a number of factors. Firstly, the rate of development of technology and its application to schools means that review must be carried out on a frequent basis. Secondly, there are many elements to the implementation of ICT and schools are unlikely to think of everything at the outset. Finally, the notion of short-, medium- and long-term planning has itself changed significantly over the last twenty years. What used to be 2 years, 5 years and 10 years is now more likely to be 6 months, 1 year and 2 years. It may also be that each element of ICT demands its own cycle. To begin with you might review some aspects on a termly basis until the cycle settles down.

ICT curriculum

> Pupils should be given opportunities to apply and develop their ICT capability through the use of ICT tools to support their learning in all subjects. At key stage 1, it is statutory to teach the use of ICT in the programmes of study for English, mathematics and science. Teachers should use their judgement to decide where it is appropriate to teach the use of ICT across these subjects at key stage 1. At other key stages, there are statutory requirements to use ICT in all statutory subjects, except PE.
>
> QCA (2008b)

The main justification for having an ICT curriculum is that it is a tool to aid teaching and learning and a set of key skills which permeate through many aspects of life. In order to meet the statutory requirements and to allow pupils to develop their ICT skills in interesting and challenging ways, the ICT curriculum needs to be well planned by implementing both discrete and cross-curricular opportunities which include a wide range of up to date software applications and other resources.

The balance between discrete and cross-curricular approaches will depend upon a number of factors including: the skills of all staff, ICT resources available, deployment of resources, current level of pupil skill etc. In general, curriculum planning should seek to achieve a balance between developing pupils' ICT skills and applying them to the learning that takes place in subjects.

The Becta Self Review Framework does not recommend any particular approach (although where ICT is taught as a discrete subject there is an assumption that ICT capability will be applied subsequently in a variety of contexts across the curriculum).

Discrete courses have their own schedule, aims and objectives and are therefore easier to plan and assess. Planning can be centralised. However, the danger of centralising discrete courses is that skills and knowledge may be divorced from application and the contexts chosen may be inauthentic or inappropriate owing to ICT teachers having insufficient depth of knowledge of other subjects. *This has perhaps been the case with key skills teaching in colleges.* For example, copying text from a book is an unsatisfactory way to develop word processing skills, whereas analytical writing in the context of history may be a more appropriate use.

It may be that some skills are taught in discrete ICT sessions, some are taught during other curriculum subjects whilst others are developed by pupils themselves (inside and outside school). Skills may need to be taught by subject teachers and some by ICT teachers.

Teachers themselves may need to acquire these skills themselves and a nominated staff member should identify needs and decide how these are best satisfied.

Skills may be split into a number of 'components':

- *Basic skills (routines)* – such as using a mouse or double clicking an icon;
- *Techniques* – such as adjusting margins on a page;
- *Processes* – such as developing a presentation for English, researching a project for geography or analysing the results of a survey in maths;
- *Higher order skills* – such as recognising when the use of ICT may be appropriate, planning how to approach a problem, deciding where to source information, testing a hypothesis, reflecting on the effectiveness of ICT in a task.

Each component is typically developed in a different way:

- *Basic skills* – are primarily learned through practice;
- *Techniques* – are developed slowly through trial and error, and copying others;
- *Processes and higher order skills* – are developed through examples, exploration, experience and reflection. The teacher's role may be one of support and guidance – taught sessions need not be overly elaborate.

A breakdown of the ICT curriculum, and how ICT can help pupils in other subjects, can be found on the QCA website at http://curriculum.qca.org.uk.

Learning and teaching

ICT can be used in a variety of ways to enhance both learning and teaching. It won't happen by accident – it needs to be planned. There should be a consistent approach to the use of ICT and this should be communicated in the school ICT Policy.

Once staff are familiar with the statutory requirements for using ICT across the curriculum, they are aware of the available resources, they have an appreciation of the uses to which ICT can be put, and they are competent users of ICT themselves, they will be in a position to decide when it is appropriate to use ICT and how best they can use it. In particular, teachers will readily identify when ICT is superior to more traditional methods.

There is no strict model – it will depend to some extent on the creativity and ingenuity of teachers and how they are able to share their practice with others. ICT should however permeate the learning environment and be seen to be used on a frequent basis.

The same will apply to pupils. Not only should they be able to use ICT resources in planned ways, they should also be increasingly able to decide when and how to make use of ICT to help themselves. After all, they will have their own expectations too. For example, when finding things out, Year 1 children will require guidance and direction in order to find information from books, CD-ROMs, the Internet etc. However, Year 6 children will be more independent and, to some extent, can decide for themselves how they will access information. In fact, these pupils may be able to independently select and use the most appropriate resources for a variety of tasks and explain why they have done so.

Not all pupils will be at the same level and each should expect to build upon previous experiences. This includes pupils with individual learning needs whether it be learning difficulties, physical impairment or gifted and talented.

The impact of using ICT should be measurable and should be part and parcel of the school's routine evaluation process. For example, it may be that the quality of some work is perceived to improve over a period of time, children are more motivated and involved (particularly those who might otherwise be disengaged or disruptive), the variety of learning activities expands, lessons are deemed more effective and interactive and, heaven forbid, children's attainment improves! The process will also identify weak areas which can be developed over time.

Responsibility for developing ICT in each subject area should be devolved to subject leaders (with advice from the ICT coordinator). Such development would be part of the overall development plan.

ICT will also play a pivotal role in the development of children with special educational needs – see Chapter 8 for more details.

Staff should make full use of ICT in their planning and recording. Word processors and other office applications can be used to create templates for schemes of work, lesson plans and so on. The school website and/or learning platform will provide ways to communicate with learners (e.g. timetables, learning activities, etc.) and to share ideas and materials with other staff. The school management information system (MIS) will provide a number of features for recording data and producing reports. These and more will provide a handy set of tools which are well worth investing in.

Assessment

Assessment can become a very broad and complex issue. For the purposes of this chapter however, it will be constrained to:

1. assessing the achievement of ICT skills;
2. making effective use of ICT during the assessment of all subjects.

Assessing ICT skills

One of the advantages of teaching ICT as a discrete subject is that it can easily be assessed in isolation from the rest of the curriculum – particularly when measuring attainment of basic skills and techniques.

However, let's assume that you have decided to 'fully' embed ICT into the curriculum. How then do you go about assessing it? Well, you could allow your pupils to assess themselves on basic skills and techniques (self- and peer assessment) leaving teachers to assess processes and higher order skills. The problem then is 'which teacher assesses what skill?'.

This requires coordination in order to produce an agreed assessment schema such that all teachers know what they are assessing and when. This will ensure that pupils are assessed consistently across the curriculum and over time. This is one of the key duties of the ICT coordinator (in cooperation with the assessment coordinator if you have one).

A moderation process should be implemented whereby assessment methods and results are checked for consistency (i.e. teachers are administering and grading their assessments in a comparable way and in accordance with any established procedures and standards). Benchmarking between departments and perhaps between schools is useful, adopting 'best practice' if deemed appropriate.

The idea of formative self- and peer assessment isn't new though often it isn't implemented in primary schools. It does have benefits because, as a result, pupils are able to gain an understanding of what constitutes good quality and, eventually, they will begin to develop their own criteria against which they are able to judge their own work and that of others. One way in which they can do this is to discuss their work in pairs or small groups.

Using ICT to support assessment

ICT can be an effective tool in the assessment process itself – both for the creation of assessment instruments and for the subsequent recording and processing of results. Here are some examples.

Reception class ICT assessment
MS Word (or Publisher) is used to create a simple self-assessment sheet. The parts of the teddy are labelled as follows:

- I am sensible when using the computer

- I can save my work

- I can print my work

- I can name the parts of a computer

- I can use a mouse

- I can write my name.

Each child has a printed copy and is allowed to colour in each part when they show that they can do what it says.

Figure 9.2 Teddy self assessment

Computer diary

Year 2 children keep computer diaries. The teacher has created a diary template for each pupil. It contains sections for them to type in:

- their task;

- who they worked with;

- what they did;

- how they feel about their work.

They use a new template each time they complete a new task.

When the task is complete, they save the diary to their own area of the school learning platform.

Their parents can view these.

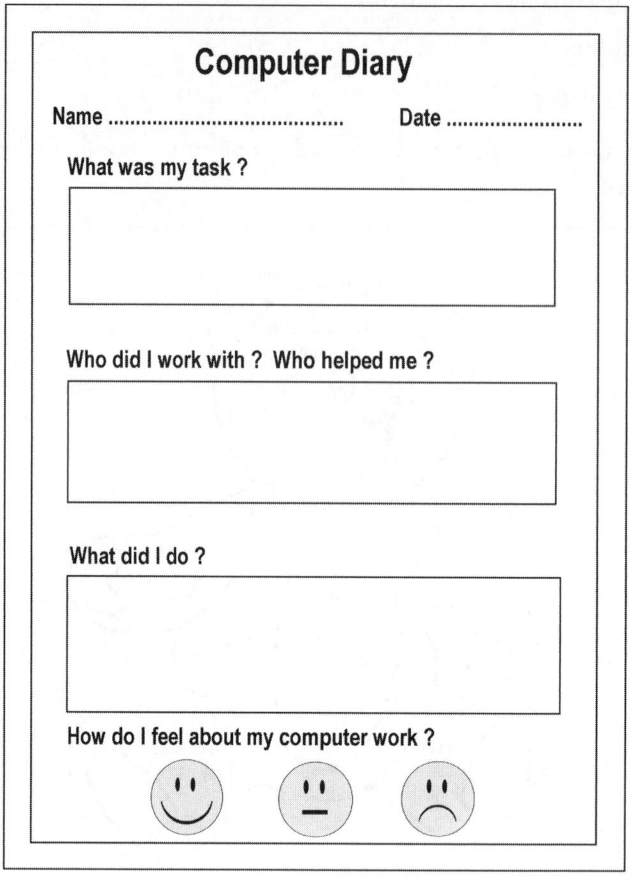

Figure 9.3 Computer diary

Profile

Year 3 children use a profile of ICT skills. They have created this themselves using a spreadsheet. For each skill they tick a box:

■   Green: I can do this

■   Amber: I can do this with help

■   Red: I can't do this yet.

	Yes I can	Partly	No I can't
I can cut and paste paragraphs			
I can insert tabs and indents			
I can use formatting features			
I can use tables			
I can crop images			
I can number and bullet			

Figure 9.4 Pupil profiile

Software with built-in assessment

Some software, including integrated learning systems (ILS), includes built-in assessment which offers formative feedback as pupils progress through the learning content. Other titles are designed specifically to assess components of the National Curriculum. For example, Rising Stars Mathematics and English are specific assessment programs to test children's attainment and are linked directly to the primary national strategy.

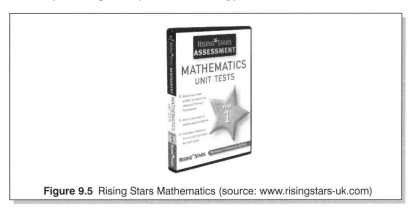

Figure 9.5 Rising Stars Mathematics (source: www.risingstars-uk.com)

Software for creating assessments

Free and commercial packages are available for teachers to design simple assessments. Hot Potatoes is a free package used for creating interactive exercises including multiple-choice, jumbled-sentence, short-answer, matching/ordering crossword and gap-fill.

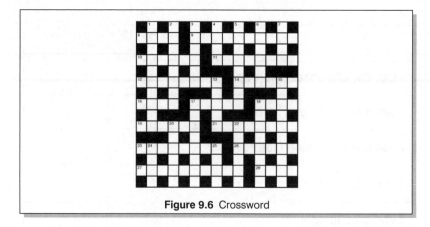

Figure 9.6 Crossword

Wimba Create (formerly Course Genie) easily converts MS Word documents into linked web-based learning content and assessments at the touch of a button. Questionmark Perception manages the whole process from creating assessments to delivery to grading to recording.

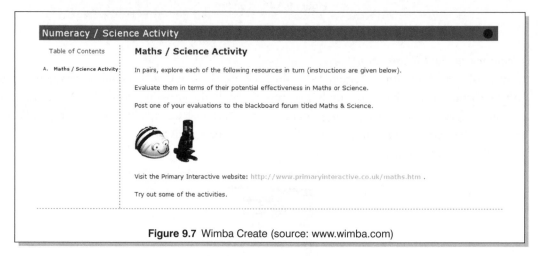

Figure 9.7 Wimba Create (source: www.wimba.com)

Learning platforms

Most learning platforms include their own set of content and assessment creation tools. Results can be managed, analysed and stored if the platform is connected to the school's MIS. Pupils can also use this medium to submit projects and assignments electronically and to store their work, making it accessible to teachers and parents.

E-portfolios

E-portfolios, blogs and wikis can be used as assessment tools (students can use these as records of their own achievement).

Interactive voting systems

Interactive voting systems actively involve pupils in quizzes, evaluations etc. in a fun and motivating way. They encourage full participation and can be used for formative and summative assessment. Feedback is instant and results can be stored and analysed. There are several offerings on the market.

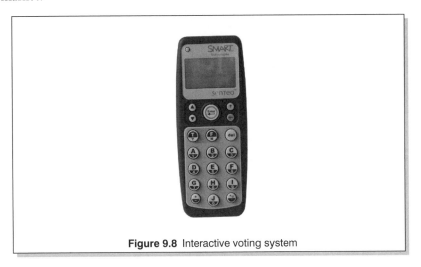

Figure 9.8 Interactive voting system

Computer-mediated communication (CMC)
CMC, in the form of discussion areas, can be used to perform collaborative constructive learning (CCL). Used widely in higher education, the claim is that collaborative learning can accomplish far more than individuals could hope to do on their own. This principle, if applied well, can be equally useful in the primary classroom where children often share and compare ideas following a variety of activities. With the advent of learning platforms, this has now become a serious option for children and is not only a means of learning, it is also a convenient method of assessment.

Recording achievement
There are several ways in which teachers and schools can record, manipulate, analyse, store, present and communicate assessment results in a way that paper based systems could never match. Contenders include: tabulated data in word processed documents, spreadsheets, simple database, specific assessment software and management information systems. In addition, work can now be handed in via the learning platform or email.

Continual professional development (CPD)

The right to CPD

Employees in all vocations have a right to expect opportunities to develop their knowledge and skills throughout their career. This is especially the case when related to technology which is advancing so quickly that it is difficult to keep pace. Not only are teachers having to come to terms with new resources and ICT initiatives, they also need to keep abreast of the accompanying changes in policy and pedagogy. For example, the recent government policy to introduce learning platforms into schools not only requires teachers to get to grips with the associated resources but also with the notion of teaching and learning online and how it differs from conventional classroom teaching. Staff need development so they can:

- improve their knowledge of teaching and learning – including the use of ICT (pedagogy);
- improve their knowledge of management and administration – including the use of ICT;
- keep pace with developments in ICT curriculum and legislation;
- work effectively in a teaching team;
- extend their subject knowledge of ICT;
- extend their technical skills and knowledge.

It is evident that the skills of teachers vary enormously between the 'enthusiasts' on one extreme and the 'technophobes' on the other. Many teachers feel intimidated by technically superior colleagues and shy away from ICT as a result. This is true despite the enormous amount of money spent on New Opportunities Fund (NOF) training between 2000 and 2003. Even with the best will in the world it is difficult to keep pace with change and it may be that we need to slow down and take better stock of what we already have in place before slavishly transiting from one phase of policy and from one generation of technology to the next. However, that doesn't mitigate schools from undertaking CPD.

So, when should CPD start? Well newly qualified teachers, as part of Initial Teacher Training (ITT) will have passed an ICT skills test and should have the ability to teach using ICT (TDA professional standards Q16 and Q17). They may also have used a range of ICT tools such as learning platforms, discussion forums, video conferencing and e-portfolios as a component part of their training. As a result, they are 'more likely to accept ICT as an integral part of their professional life' (Ofsted, 2002). This is only the starting point and, even for them, CPD should commence on their first day in school as a newly qualified teacher.

As a school, the first step is to delegate responsibility for CPD to a member of staff. In a small school this will likely be the ICT coordinator though it need not be so. The agreed duties should be documented and included in the ICT handbook alongside other ICT policies.

The CPD process, like any other, is cyclical and begins with an audit of both staff and whole-school needs. This will require an assessment of competence in using ICT and ability to incorporate it effectively into learning.

Activity

If you were responsible for CPD in your school, how would you go about auditing staff ICT needs?

If you've already carried out a 'resources' audit then you will know what resources you hold and what you are likely to hold in the short to medium term (in order to fulfil your vision). Using this inventory as a checklist you can use a questionnaire, forum or other suitable survey instrument to gather the information you need (perhaps an informal approach would be more acceptable to your colleagues). Split the survey questions into categories such as:

- computer basics (file management, loading software, etc.);
- common office applications (e.g. word processing, presentations, spreadsheets, database, email, Internet etc.);
- generic resources (e.g. IWB, digital camera, software toolkit, etc.);
- subject specific resources (e.g. maths software, floor robots, etc.);
- network;
- learning platform;
- understanding how these resources can be used in curriculum subjects. You might ask for examples of how they are being used and how frequently.

You will find plenty of sample audit forms on the Internet. Try the grids for learning listed in Appendix 2.

You should endeavour to keep the audit as simple as possible otherwise you may not get the response you require and the subsequent task of collating and analysing the data may become unmanageable. You can carry out the audit in phases, tackling the most important issues first.

The ICT coordinator will have additional responsibility for keeping abreast of developments in technology and updating staff.

Methods of CPD

Once the needs of staff are established you will want to find ways of satisfying them. Budgetary constraints will come into play here so try to identify the most cost-effective solutions.

Low-cost solutions include: self-reflection; mentoring; team teaching; observing colleagues (and inviting critique of your own performance); informal chats; discussion forums (face-to-face and CMC), INSET days; utilising the services of advanced skills teachers; liaison with other schools; and self help (there's plenty of help to be found: tutorials on the Internet, help menus within software packages, ICT books, etc.). Don't forget also that your own pupils are a source of knowledge – they often know more than the teacher about some aspects of ICT and this should be harnessed! Don't forget, discussion forums, sharing ideas and resources and perhaps online learning opportunities can all be facilitated via your learning platform.

Medium–cost solutions include: courses provided by local authorities; online learning (e.g. http://primaryict.org.uk); and cascaded training by individual teachers that have attended external courses, seminars, exhibitions (e.g. BETT), conferences, etc.

An incentive might be to sponsor staff for courses which lead to recognised qualifications such as the European Computer Driving Licence (ECDL) or New CLAIT.

Training in whatever form should be 'just in time'. This simply means that staff must be in a position to put their training to immediate use or they will quickly forget what they have learned.

Evaluating CPD

The quality and effectiveness of staff development should be measured to ensure that it is effective and good value for money. This can be done in a number of ways including:

- immediate reactive feedback from individual teachers to the ICT Coordinator (e.g. completion of an evaluation form);

- feedback from individual teachers to the ICT Coordinator once they have had sufficient opportunity to practice new skills;

- observation of subsequent lessons;

- perceived improvement in pupil achievement;

- interview during annual appraisals (which leads to setting future CPD targets).

Extended learning

Extended learning is about creating opportunities for pupils and their families outside normal school hours and/or away from the school itself (at home and in the community). It not only helps children on the wrong side of the digital divide but it also supports the notion that children in the twenty-first century should be able to learn whenever and wherever is best for them. If this in some way includes their parents then evidence suggests that they are likely to achieve better results (whilst helping some parents and families too).

Uses of extended learning

Extended learning should be used by all teachers, and with all pupils, for homework, revision, consolidation and voluntary additional work. It can also be used to provide opportunities for pupils who are absent through illness and those who are disengaged from mainstream learning.

Home school links allow the promotion of a number of e-assessment methods including online tests, e-portfolios and blogs. It is also possible for electronic submission of work.

Parents are able to take an active interest in their children's work and to access their children's records, reports and attendance. Indeed, parents themselves might be offered classes in ICT in order that they can better help their children.

Facilitating extended learning

Extended learning can be facilitated using a variety of media and methods including:

- school learning platform/website/VLE (including discussion boards);
- email;
- third-party websites (including those associated with Extended Schools);
- CD-ROMs;
- podcasts/vidcasts;
- radio;
- television;
- mobile phones;
- PDAs;
- making ICT resources/facilities available to families outside normal working hours (including breakfast clubs, after school clubs, loan of laptops/mobile devices and other initiatives);
- ICT facilities offered by the wider community (libraries, colleges etc.).

Involvement of governors may prove useful here because they will have interests and connections outside the school.

Impact on pupil outcomes

If the implementation of ICT is to be effective then it must improve teaching and, more importantly, have a significant impact on pupil's overall attainment, acquisition of skills and overall enjoyment of their learning experience. What's more, the impact must also be measurable.

The assessment process should measure year-on-year progress in terms of 'value added'. That is to say, each pupil, whatever their starting point, will show an improvement over time. This offers a significant advantage both to weaker (and disadvantaged) pupils and also to the gifted and talented because they are being measured in relative terms rather than against a norm.

This improvement is not only in academic achievement but also in motivation, attitude, behaviour, confidence, self-esteem, creative ability and learner independence. In particular, pupils will eventually have mastered the generic skills which apply to all subjects. Namely to:

- access, select and interpret information;
- recognise patterns, relationships and behaviours;
- model, predict and hypothesise;
- test reliability and accuracy;
- review and modify their work to improve the quality;
- communicate with others and present information;

- evaluate their work;

- improve efficiency;

- be creative and take risks; and

- gain confidence and independence.

(QCA, 2008c: 1)

Resources

Schools need to hold a good range of ICT resources to consistently support learning, teaching and administration. This means that resources must be both appropriate and accessible. A walk around audit of the school would show evidence of ICT in use in all classrooms, other learning spaces and offices. If you are doing this formally, the audit should record what you have and where it is located.

For each piece of hardware, determine how old it is, what warranties it carries and how much life you think it has left (this will in part be determined by the currency of its specification, i.e. is it still up to the job in terms of its speed of operation, storage capacity, whether it can support the latest generation of software, etc.). Look also at how hardware is networked and whether it is efficient.

For each software title you need to decide whether it is still giving you adequate support for the subject(s) it is used in and whether an upgrade or switch to an alternative title would be better.

Procedures are also necessary for the identification and procurement of resources which meet the current and future needs of the school. Deciding what to spend your money on is a difficult task – Chapter 10 discusses this in more detail.

Technical support

Adequate technical support will ensure that equipment is largely serviceable with procedures of preventative maintenance and timely repair in place.

It is important that schools can keep a high rate of operability of their technology with the minimum disruption to learning and teaching. Technical support will normally be provided on a contract basis, either via the local authority, link secondary school or commercial contract. Large schools may have a permanent, on-site, technician(s), but smaller schools will have to rely on either periodic visits (e.g. fortnightly half-day visit) or on an as required basis. For the latter, it would be prudent to train one or more members of staff in the basics of looking after ICT environments.

Before staff wade in too deep, do bear in mind that staff may cost more per hour than a technician!

The bottom line here will be cost. Consider tapping into your local authority if it has a service level agreement or share support with other local schools.

It is often the case that technical and pedagogical matters are kept distinctly separate, the technician is not interested in teaching and teachers don't want to be technicians. Whilst this is quite natural it is not healthy and you need to find ways of 'dovetailing' these two aspects together if you are to get the best out of your ICT system.

Whatever your decision you should have a procedure which deals with what to do when technology breaks down and the preventive maintenance to be carried out to minimise such eventualities. For more detail on technical support, refer to the Becta Framework for ICT Technical Support (FITS) available at www.becta.org.uk/tsas.

Self-Review Framework (SEF) software

Becta provide an online tool which helps schools to assess and improve their use of ICT and benchmark themselves against other schools. The tool was improved in July 2008; however, whilst it provides an overview of the criteria for improvement (and possible means of evidence), it is primarily a means of recording progress.

There are more comprehensive SEF software packages available from commercial providers. For example, the bluewave.SWIFT all in one school improvement system (www.bluewaveswift. co.uk).

Funding

Allocation of funding for ICT changes on a frequent basis. For this reason, this section simply reiterates the information provided by the now defunct curriculum online website. From 2008 onwards, the Harnessing Technology Grant is the main source of funding for ICT in schools. Funding is allocated to local authorities – details on how much each one is receiving can be found on TeacherNet at www.teachernet.gov.uk/management/resourcesfinanceandbuilding/capitalinvestment/allocations/statement.

Local authorities determine the basis on which to distribute the grant to eligible schools, and are also entitled to keep up to 25 per cent of their allocation centrally for collaborative purchasing on behalf of all schools.

The Harnessing Technology Grant is capital funding and can be spent on ICT-related products and services which are classified as capital expenditure. Digital curriculum resources can be bought using the Harnessing Technology Grant, but only where the terms and conditions under which these products are supplied mean that they can be regarded as capital purchases (for example, if the assets acquired will have a life longer than the financial year in which they were purchased). Schools wishing to use the Harnessing Technology Grant for digital curriculum content services which involve an annual subscription are advised to contact their local authority finance teams to obtain their expert view on whether this is a permitted use of capital funding or if revenue budgets should be used to pay for such services.

Schools are able to use other sources of funding in addition to the Harnessing Technology Grant to pay for technology-related products and services – these include Devolved Formula Capital and the School Development Grant (for revenue expenditure).

Further information about funding for ICT in schools can be found on the Becta website at http://schools.becta.org.uk.

E-safety

The Internet is creating new and exciting opportunities for children's learning and creativity. However, whilst there may be significant benefits, schools have a duty of care to safeguard children against the potential risks involved.

E-safety is therefore a major priority for schools. As schools' connectivity to the outside world steadily improves, and the number of sites and systems that can be accessed increases, so does the chance that children may encounter inappropriate materials, meet undesirable people and become subject to cyber-bullying or intimidation.

E-safety covers a number of issues but is essentially about staying safe whilst online and keeping personal information secure. It is an important element of 'digital citizenship' where pupils and teachers are proactive in preventing anti-social behaviour and helping those who might be affected by these issues.

What are the risks?

The risks are many and include the following:

- inappropriate content – which may be sexual, violent, racist, bigoted or simply unreliable;

- contact with undesirable people – via instant messaging, chat rooms, social networks and online games – can lead to predation and grooming;

- exposure to commerce – advertising, spam email, scams, phishing, pharming and bluejacking;

- culture – bullying, camera phones, blogging and moblogging;

- malicious software (malware) – viruses, worms, trojans, spyware and adware.

 Activity

If you are not familiar with all of the terminology used here then now might be a good time to do some research!

Such an array of risks can be very off-putting and it's all too easy to apply a blanket ban on the Internet. However, to do this would be to deny the many opportunities that the Internet can provide and that is surely the biggest danger of all!

Developing an e-safety policy

In their Safeguarding Children Online guide, Becta (2008i) identify four important elements of e-safety which need to be addressed: an infrastructure of whole-site awareness, responsibilities, policies and procedures; an effective range of technological tools; a comprehensive e-safety education programme; and a review process which continually monitors the effectiveness of e-safety. These points manifest themselves in a number of policies and procedures including:

- a senior management team member with responsibility for e-safety;

- involvement of the whole school (including pupils) and other interest groups (parents, governors, LEA, ISPs and RBCs);

- a secure network with appropriate levels of filtering and protection against malware;

- an acceptable use policy (AUP) governing the way in which ICT systems can be used;

- an education programme for pupils and staff (including initial teacher training), and guidelines for parents and guardians, to make them aware of potential risks and how to stay safe online;

- methods of reporting and dealing with incidents;

- links to information on e-safety;

- inclusion of e-safety in the general policy for safeguarding;

- regular monitoring and review (keeping abreast of contemporary issues in e-safety).

 Activity

To help you compile an e-safety policy, which includes acceptable use of the Internet and other ICT resources, you should read the two documents 'AUPs in Context' and 'Signposts to Safety'. Both are available on the Primary ICT website.

There are many sample policies and AUPs on the Internet. Checkout school websites, grids for learning and local authorities. You can easily tailor them to suit your own needs

E-safety audit tools

There are a number of free online tools that can help you with the adoption of good e-safety practice including:

- National Education Network (NEN) at www.nen.gov.uk/hot_topic.

- WMnet E-safety framework at www.wmnet.org.uk/21.cfm.

Useful Internet safety websites

You can't have too much advice on e-safety so here are a few useful links:

- Childnet International: www.childnet-int.org. Includes their '5 smart rules' plus links to other e-safety websites.

- Childnet knowITall: www.childnet-int.org/kia. Available also on CD-ROM.

- Kidsmart: www.kidsmart.org.uk.

- Get Safe Online: www.getsafeonline.org.

- Becta e-safety: http://schools.becta.org.uk. A range of e-safety advice.

- Grid Club Cybercafe: www.gridclub.com/cybercafe/teachers. An integral part of the Internet Proficiency Scheme developed to help teachers educate children on staying safe on the Internet.

- Smart Surfers: www.smartsurfers.co.uk. Critical skills for information searching and staying safe on the web.

- Parents Centre: www.parentscentre.gov.uk. Wide range of advice including Internet safety.

- Safetynet: http://lists.becta.org.uk/mailman/listinfo/safetynet. A mailing list for anyone who wants to discuss and share information about e-safety.

- Kent ICT: www.kented.org.uk/ngfl/ict/safety.htm. Lots of advice, sample documents, posters etc.

- CEOP : www.ceop.gov.uk. Child Exploitation and Online Protection Centre.

- Kent Community Network: www.e-safety.org.uk. Responsible Internet Use Guides & Internet Policy.

- LGfL: http://cms.lgfl.net/web/lgfl/safety. London Grid for Learning – e-safety.

- HGfL: www.thegrid.org.uk/eservices/safety. Hertfordshire Grid for Learning – e-safety.

- The new Council for Child Internet Safety.

Summary

In summary, here are the key things you need to do to successfully implement ICT in your school:

1. Establish the ICT team and define its task – led by a member of the senior management team and driven by an ICT coordinator.

2. Express your vision for ICT in general terms.

3. Agree roles and responsibilities – delegate to the extended team.

4. Carry out an audit – break it into chunks which cover the key elements – leadership, funding, resources, technical support, curriculum, learning and teaching, assessment, CPD, etc. Use prepared audit forms.

5. Draw up an ICT Development Plan to bridge the strategic gap. Split into two or more phases based on priorities and available funding.

6. Document your overall intentions (including the vision) in a school ICT policy – share it with everyone.

7. Create an ICT handbook with helpful guides, policies and procedures (including e-safety).

8. Put your plan into action – continually monitor and review.

The whole process could be achieved in two to three years.

If you wish to gain the Becta ICT Mark then you will need to subscribe to the Self-Review Framework – this can be part of your development plan and should be started during phase 1. You will find information at https://selfreview.becta.org.uk.

10

ICT resources

Choosing resources

Equipping schools with necessary ICT resources can be a very daunting prospect and, in the not too distant past, it was very much a hit and miss affair. Many software titles were not particularly suitable for a number of reasons, not least of which was that they did not closely match the learning objectives of the National Curriculum. Much has changed in the last five years. Software houses have become much more savvy. Many are 'in tune' with education and utilise the skills of teachers and other professionals in the design process. With careful evaluation (see the section on suppliers below) schools will find a plentiful and ever increasing supply of appropriate and cost-effective resources. In fact, there are now so many options to choose from it can be difficult to know where to begin!

The degree of control over the purchase of resources seems to vary widely between schools. Some are governed by the contracts formed by their local authority whilst others have complete freedom of choice. In fact, Becta (2008f) recommend that schools should not purchase their own resources but instead they should 'aggregate' purchasing using a larger group of schools or through the local authority (if they have such systems in place). This does potentially offer a discount and it also provides schools with reassurance when it comes to trickier matters such as network infrastructure and Internet connectivity. However, it may also mean that they don't get exactly what they want. There may therefore need to be a trade off between bulk buying and individual purchases. Assuming that you do have a say in the matter then how would you choose your core ICT resources? Here are some suggestions:

- Establish an all round staff awareness of the 'types' of resource available and their possible benefits. This is primarily the responsibility of the ICT coordinator. Remember – it isn't just about software, there are many other resources. Note that specific products and software titles should not be considered at this stage.

- Draw up a list of candidate resource types. Some resources will provide better value for money than others because of their versatility, i.e. resources which can be used across the curriculum, as a useful teaching aid and for administration and management. For example, interactive whiteboards, content free software, digital cameras and office applications. These items may perhaps be construed as more important than others. Again, don't worry about specific products yet.

- Draw up a shortlist – prioritising items in terms of their importance (e.g. essential, important, desirable). Items which serve more than one area (learning, teaching and administration) or more than one curriculum subject will be placed toward the top of the list.

- Now look at specific products and cost them. Revise the list to suit your budget. You can spread the cost over time and phase in resources in accordance with your ICT development plan. Don't forget that there are many free resources to be found including shared activities from resources banks (Teacher Resource Exchange, JISC collection for schools, the National Education Network and school websites) and open source software (see 'Open source software' below).

- Evaluate each item to assure its suitability (see the section on evaluating resources below).

Establishing awareness is a gradual process and can be done in a number of ways – exhibitions, training, team teaching, observations, liaison with other schools and leading by example. The ICT coordinator and subject leaders must be key to this process. Whatever you do, don't attempt to push staff if they are very resistant to the process – allow things to grow organically. Work on the enthusiasts and allow them to establish good practice. This will eventually spread (but don't expect miracles!).

Listing the 'types' of resource available can be done by the ICT management team though it would be best to include all your staff. They could each do this independently with a view to comparing results. That way you are less likely to miss anything important. If you have no idea of what's available then you can seek advice from your LEA and other schools in your area, scour the brochures and websites of the main retailers (see Appendix 3 for listings) or pay a visit to one of the large annual exhibitions, conferences or ILT showcases. The BETT exhibition (British Education and Training Technology) which takes place at Kensington Olympia in January each year is well worth a visit.

Here are many of the common resources used in schools.

2D/3D plotter	Cloze software	Digital book
A3 scanner	Computer	Digital camera
A4 scanner	Computer game	Digital effects unit
Assessment creation software	Concept keyboard	Digital microscope
Atlas/maps on CD	Concept mapping software	Digital notetaker
Audio CDs	Content free software	Digital pen
Augmentative communication aid	Content rich software	Digital recorder/player (mp3/mp4)
Automatic weather station	Control software	Digital video camera
Braille notetaker	Course authoring software	Document camera
Branching database	Data-logging system	Drawing packages (inc CAD)
Browser	Data projector (and loudspeakers)	DVD/CD writer
Calculator	Database	Dyscalculia software
CD-ROM	Desktop publishing software	Dyslexia software
Clipart	Dictionary software	Email program

Encyclopaedia software
E-book
E-portfolio
Ergonomic keyboard/mouse
Floor robot
Gaming console
Gifted and talented software
Global positioning system (GPS)
Graphic calculator
Graphics tablet
Handheld PC for blind pupils
Heart rate monitor
Image production and editing
Integrated learning system
Interactive voting system
Interactive whiteboard
Keyboard
Keyboard glove
Language software
Laptop computer
Large screen display
Learning platform
Microphone
Management information system (MIS)
Multimedia authoring software
Multi-sensory equipment
Musical keyboard

Netbook
Network (cable/wireless/hybrid)
Online resources
OCR software
Overlay keyboard
Painting/retouching software
Palmtop (PDA)
Pattern sequencing software
Phonics software
Photocopier
Play Station Portable (PSP)
Podcasting/vidcasting software
Presentation software
Printer
Programming software (logo/basic)
Programmable toy
Radio microphone/receiver
Reading pen
Reading ruler
Role play equipment
Rollerball mouse
Scanner
Screen reading software
Self-Review framework (SRF) software
Signing software
Simulation package
Social/life skills software

Software toolkit (suite of programs)
Sound production/editing software
Sound system
Specialist keyboards
Spreadsheet
Stopwatch/digital timer
Subscription website
Switch
Symbol software
Tablet PC
Talking word processor
Tape recorder
Television
Timing mat
Touch screen
Touch typing software
Turtle software
Video conferencing system
Video editing software
Visualiser
Virtual learning environment (VLE)
Voice output communication aid (VOCA)
Voice recognition software
Web authoring software
Webcam
Word processing software

The shortlist drawn from these resources, and the actual products chosen, will need to suit your particular needs and, above all, satisfy the school's vision for ICT. There should be a clear link between the purchase of resources and learning benefits for pupils. If your staff have a choice in the selection of resources then they will be more likely to use them. Don't forget also to consider free software (see section on open-source software below) and the possibility of designing some of your own activities before committing to spend money.

When you think you know which resources you want to buy you should take steps to evaluate them first.

This chapter does not recommend specific products because there are so many to choose from. It is better that schools familiarise themselves with the resources on offer and select resources which best match their own needs.

Evaluating resources

Evaluating resources before committing to buy is a sensible thing to do. It may seem tedious yet it could save you a good deal of money and lots of frustration too. If you buy something that's unsuitable you'll need to go through the whole process again!

The easiest approach to evaluation is to get someone else to do it for you. You might for example get a good recommendation from a colleague or consult with other schools to see if any of them are using your intended resources to good effect. They may be willing to loan resources to you or agree to share the cost of purchase whilst you jointly carry out trials (lending libraries may well loan software too).

Commercial suppliers will provide overviews of their products and, whilst they will have an obvious bias, you can still learn much about the product from them. They may be willing to provide you with evaluation copies of software, particularly if you become a regular customer. However, don't put all your eggs in one basket here, there are many suppliers and lots of products to choose from.

You should always pay a visit to the TEEM website (Teachers Evaluating Educational Multimedia) at www.teem.org.uk. They provide free access to a searchable database of resources which have been evaluated extensively by practising teachers. This will certainly help you to choose suitable software and CD-ROMs. They also provide a downloadable guide and other useful publications too. There are a number of other sites which provide evaluation including Schoolzone (www.schoolzone.co.uk).

Whatever else you do you should always perform your own evaluation if possible. Draw up a set of criteria which your resources must satisfy. There will be several general criteria and some which are peculiar to your own school.

Becta (2007f) offer good advice here. They have derived a set of quality principles which relate to the use of digital resources and they are divided into:

- Core pedagogic principles, which underpin effective learning and teaching, drawing from learning theory and commonly accepted best practice. They include: Match to the Curriculum, Inclusion and Access, Learner Engagement, Effective Learning, Assessment, Ease of Use and Innovation.

- Core design principles, covering issues such as resource design, accessibility and interoperability. They include: Good design, Robustness, Interaction, Quality of Assets, Accessibility, Interoperability, Effective Communication and Pre-Testing.

Activity

Link to the Primary ICT website and read the Becta documents titled 'Choosing Digital Resources' and 'Quality principle for digital learning resources'.
These are excellent documents which provide thorough and detailed guidance in choosing all types of digital resource.

There are some simple evaluation templates in Appendix 4 which you can modify to your own requirements if you wish.

Suppliers

Schools have a free choice from the many ICT suppliers (though Becta have published recommended frameworks for larger purchases). If you need help then this section may be of some use.

BETT

There are hundreds of suppliers of ICT resources to choose from and, if you've ever visited the BETT exhibition, you'll already have an idea who the big players are. For a full list of the exhibitors to their most recent show, visit www.bettshow.com.

BESA

BESA is a trade association (they currently sponsor BETT). They don't sell resources themselves but they provide information about their 300 member companies who provide ICT resources across the curriculum at all levels from early years upwards. BESA members adhere to a code of practice which ensures that they are reputable providers of quality products. To find members and products, visit BESA at www.besa.org.uk.

Becta Software for Educational Institutions

When schools make large purchases they are obliged to adhere to strict guidelines. With a view to saving schools the time and effort required to vet their potential suppliers, Becta have helped out by establishing a framework which validates suppliers. A new framework for software suppliers was launched in October 2008 (lasting for four years). It includes 12 companies: Academia, Civica Services, European Electronique, Insight Direct, Joskos Solutions, Pugh Computers, Ramesys (e-business services), RM plc, SCC, Sirius Corporation, Trustmarque Solutions and Viglen. The vendors offer proprietary and open source software including: operating systems; office productivity software; network and security programs; ERP and other software. Schools can source software and obtain online quotes, purchasing advice, technical support, training and licence management via the government OGCbuying.solutions site at http://online. ogcbuyingsolutions.gov.uk.

OGCbuying.solutions is a government agency providing a procurement service to the public sector to enable organisations to deliver improved value for money in their commercial activities.

Listings of ICT suppliers

Appendix 3 lists many of the regular suppliers. For fuller listings you can try the following:

- Teem: www.teem.org.uk
- Silver Surfers: www.silversurfers.net
- Where can I buy it: www.wherecanibuyit.co.uk

Managing resources

Total cost of ownership (TCO)

As with all other elements of management, the purchasing, review and updating of ICT resources should be part and parcel of the management cycle. You will need to keep a record of the costs of your current assets and those you intend purchasing in the future (in accordance with your ICT development plan). These costs will include the cost to acquire resources (including software licensing fees), running and maintenance costs (including technical support), Internet connection charges and consumables. This is referred to as the total cost of ownership (TCO) and it is something you will be required to do if you wish to obtain the Becta ICT Mark.

If you haven't already done so then you should carry out an audit to determine your current holdings and draw up an inventory. A spreadsheet would be ideal because you will need to perform some simple calculations. Becta provide a TCO tool specifically for this purpose.

Forecasting costs over a period of several years (known as long-term costing) will provide a good illustration of the future ICT position of the school. It will allow you to build in depreciation (in terms of cost, changes to the curriculum, and developments in technology) so that you can see when each of the resources will need to be replaced or upgraded. It will also give you some indication as to how meaningful your medium- and long-term development plans are.

Software licensing

Software licensing is quite simple but it can easily catch you out if you are not particularly careful and the penalties if you are prosecuted for being under-licensed can be quite harsh. In general terms you need to be licensed for each machine onto which your software title is installed. You can buy single, multiple or site licences. The licence will contain a set of rules governing the usage of the software. This is called the end use licence agreement (EULA). The EULA will vary from one manufacturer to another. Some will allow a backup copy of the CD-ROM to be made and some will allow software to be installed on staff machines in their office and/or at home without paying for additional licences. You need to read the EULA carefully. Store the licences safely and document the number of licences you hold and which of your machines the software is loaded on (this information could be part of your software inventory). You are allowed to uninstall from one machine and re-install onto another but ensure that you update your paperwork if you do. If you hold site licences then make sure you are adhering to the definition of site. It may be that your school has a hybrid network which serves more than one building and perhaps in more than one location. Make sure that you are covered. Site licensing is probably the safest bet but you may not need, or be able to afford, this option for all the titles you require.

Some software is paid for by annual subscription. You need to ensure that you renew your subscription each year. If your subscription is paid automatically (perhaps by your budget holder or bursar) then make sure that you still use it. If not, cancel the subscription and save yourself a pile of money.

Finally, an obvious statement perhaps but don't use illegal software – and if you happen to download what you believe to be free software then copy or print the copyright information and store it with your licensing records.

You may have placed the management of your ICT infrastructure in the hands of an ICT service provider, in which case licensing, and other issues will be their responsibility. If you wish to do this then Becta can provide you with a Framework for ICT Technical Support (FITS).

Resource guides

Resource guides were introduced in Chapter 6. They are useful documents to aid planning and they will help with the management process too because they are an extension to the resources inventory telling you where the resources are and how they can be used.

Open source software

There are many thousands of free software programs available for download. The term 'free' can be quite misleading. Some free packages may come with strings attached. For example, you are offered a basic package for free but need to spend money if you elect to buy the 'premium' version or if you wish to upgrade to the next version when it comes along. The only truly free software is 'open source' because it not only comes free of charge, it also gives you complete freedom to do with it what you wish.

What is open source software?

An open source software (OSS) program is a free package which allows its users not only to run the program but also to modify it and to redistribute copies without having to pay royalties to its developers (Wheeler, 2007). Such programs do not follow the commercial copyright law and, in fact, the principle of OSS has itself given rise to the term 'copyleft'.

For some time now we have become conditioned to using proprietary software, particularly the very familiar packages like MS Office. For many they provide a comfort zone – they have always used them (as does everyone else), there's plenty of training available and lots of books written about them. With many commercial packages you also buy into valuable support. Many large organisations, including schools, will automatically upgrade to the latest version of Microsoft (and other products) without a second thought and staff, particularly administrators, may be reluctant to make a change. But is it time to start thinking outside the box?

Why use open source software?

The most obvious answer to this question is 'because it's free' and, unlike other 'free' products, it comes with no strings attached. In addition you can access the source code. This means that, unlike commercial packages which allow you only to run the compiled code, you can get into the original instructions and make modifications in order to adapt the software to your own needs. The sceptic in most of us will naturally question why anyone would want to spend time developing programs in order to provide us with free software! Well that's a debate in itself and you may wish to research it in more detail yourself.

A good starting point would be Stallman (2009), who argues that software should not have owners, or Gonzalez–Barahona (2000) who discusses the advantages of OSS.

Suffice to say, however, that OSS software is on the rise and certainly here to stay. A very good example is MOODLE, a free OSS virtual learning environment which has been around for several years and is now used as the VLE of choice by many universities and colleges and has been chosen as a learning platform by a good number of schools too (for example, schools across Cumbria and Lancashire).

Obtaining a free software package is all well and good but this amounts to little unless it is comparable (or better) than its commercial counterparts. There are now many claims that, for some OSS packages, this is indeed the case and, whilst there are obviously many sceptics, here are some of the advantages together with answers to some of the concerns (adapted from Williams *et al.*, 2005)

Advantages

- **Lower software costs.** Open source solutions generally require no licensing fees. The logical extension is no maintenance fees. The only expenditures are for media, documentation and support, if required.

- **Simplified license management.** Obtain the software once and install it as many times and in as many locations as you need. There's no need to count, track, or monitor for license compliance.

- **Lower hardware costs.** In general, Linux and open source solutions are elegantly compact and portable, and as a result require less hardware power to accomplish the same tasks as on conventional servers (Windows, Solaris) or workstations. The result is you can get by with less expensive or older hardware.

- **Total cost of owenership.** Some schools argue that using OSS software brings down the total cost of ownership (TCO) for ICT, a claim which was supported by the Becta OSS in Schools Study in 2005.

- **Scaling/consolidation potential.** Again, Linux and open source applications and services can often scale considerably. Multiple options for load balancing, clustering, and open source applications, such as database and email, give organisations the ability to scale up for new growth or consolidate to do more with less.

- **Ample support.** Support is available for open source and is often superior to proprietary solutions. It is freely available and accessible through online communities via the Internet and conventional user groups. These communities can be an important part of the education process because they promote a sense of ownership and participation and tie in closely with the philosophy of social constructivism/social constructionism.

- **Escape vendor lock-in.** Frustration with vendor lock-in is a reality for all IT managers. In addition to ongoing license fees, there is lack of portability and the inability to customise software to meet specific needs. Open source exists as a declaration of freedom of choice.

- **Quality software.** Evidence and research indicate that open source software is good stuff. The peer review process and community standards, plus the fact that source code is out there for the world to see, tend to drive excellence in design and efficiency in coding. The freedom to modify source code results in more frequent updates.

- **Adaptability.** The code can be modified such that the program will do exactly what you want it to and will look exactly how you want it to look (the code can also be re-distributed and shared with the community which uses it).

- **Security.** OSS is less vulnerable to viruses because attacks are primarily aimed at large commercial companies (e.g. Microsoft).

Concerns

- **Open source isn't really free.** 'Free, as in a free puppy' is the adage meaning no up-front costs, but plenty (often unseen or unanticipated) afterward. However, implementation, administration, and support costs can be minimised and if you choose to pay for such services then, on balance, you are still likely to make significant savings.

- **There's no service and support.** Newer OSS packages may need time for support services to grow but for many OSS packages, support is equal to that available for proprietary software and is available for the same price or less.

- **Development resources are scarce.** Linux and open source resources are actually abundant; the developers can use the same tools, languages, and code management processes. In reality, the universe of developers is the largest of any segment. And, with the evolution of Mono (the open source equivalent to .NET), all of those Windows/.NET developers become an added development resource for Linux.

- ■ *Open source is not secure.* It might seem to be a simple deduction of logic to think that the code is available, so anyone can figure out how to break it. That's not quite true with the momentum of the community (especially Linux). Also, the modularity required for distributed development of Linux and open source also contributes to security with tight, function-specific, and isolated code segments.

- ■ *Training is not available.* This used to be true, but not anymore. Available Linux training, for example, has ballooned with certification courses coming from every major training vendor. Training businesses have grown around OSS software, particularly the longer established products such as MOODLE.

- ■ *All open source is a work-in-progress.* True for some, but not for all. Many of the available products are stable, secure, and well developed. Some open source offerings are still maturing, but they are nevertheless workable, and for the companies that use them (with access to source code), the software is good enough.

Even the European Commission has urged businesses and governments to use software based on open standards which should be adopted over proprietary ones. The European anti-trust commissioner argued that choosing open standards is a very smart business decision and that EU agencies must not rely on one vendor and must refuse to become locked into a particular technology (Fiveash, 2008).

There are already plenty of schools that are using (or trialling) OSS software and, in particular, Linux (operating system), Open Office (a complete suite of office packages), Firefox (web browser), Apache (web server), PHP (scripting language), MySQL (database) and several curriculum-based packages too. Indeed, with the newly agreed Microsoft licensing programme for schools, it is now possible to install Microsoft products on selected computers only without paying a site-wide 'all or nothing' subscription (Becta, 2008g). This removes vendor lock-in and frees up schools to trial other products. In addition, the Becta Schools Open Source Project will offer schools the option of choosing from a wide selection of operating systems and office software plus a range of support services, such as sourcing, installation, technical support and licence management. This is a positive move which addresses some of the previous criticism levied against Becta in as much as their lists of recommended proprietors were skewed in favour of commercial companies (Ballard, 2008).

Open Source Schools website

The Open Source *Schools* website (http://opensourceschools.org.uk) was formed in order to build a community of users (experienced and beginners) who can share information, ideas and experiences about OSS in schools via forums, information, articles and case studies. The aim is to keep you informed and help you decide whether open source software offers benefits for learning, teaching, engaging pupils and parents, managing information and resources, or school administration.

The site also presents reviews on OSS packages. Whilst the number of education content-specific software titles is relatively small, these will surely grow as the 'OSS movement' gains impetus.

Open source packages

This section outlines some of the open source software already available for free download. Many of these are tried and tested packages with a good reputation and adequate support.

Linux

Linux is an OSS operating system which is favoured over Windows by many IT enthusiasts. There are hundreds of versions (distributions) of Linux which can be freely downloaded from the Linux website at www.linux.org. If schools feel overawed by the number of distributions then they might choose one which is has been created in order to make it simple to use. Favourites include Xandros and Ubuntu which have both been used by some schools.

MySQL

If you have a website, VLE or learning platform then you may need a database to go with it. The MySQL® database has become the world's most popular open source database because of its consistent fast performance, high reliability and ease of use. Download it from www.mysql.com.

Other packages include PostgreSQL, MaxDB, Firebird and Ingres.

PHP

PHP is a widely-used general-purpose open source scripting language that is especially suited for web development and can be embedded into HTML. It is often used in conjunction with Linux, Apache and MySQL which together form the LAMP platform. Access it from www.php.net/downloads.php.

Other packages include Perl and Python.

Apache

The Apache HTTP Server is a robust, open implementation of an HTTP (web) server. The project is jointly managed by a group of volunteers located around the world, using the Internet and the Web to communicate, plan, and develop the server and its related documentation. This project is part of the Apache Software Foundation. Download it from www.apache.org.

Other packages include Aries, Tomcat and nginx.

Open Office

Open Office is the leading open-source office software suite for word processing, spreadsheets, presentations, graphics, databases and more. It is available in many languages and works on all common computers. It stores data in an international open standard format and can read and write files from other common office packages. Download it from www.openoffice.org.

The package is widely used by business and large organisations and has been installed by many schools (often in tandem with MS Office). Support and training is available from the Open Office community and commercially. Books have been written too.

Firefox

Firefox® is an award-winning OSS browser by Mozilla (who also developed the Thunderbird® email client). It will work for Windows, Linux and MacOSX operating systems and is claimed to be faster and more secure than any other browser. Installation and setup are very simple and straightforward and all settings from existing browsers will be imported into Firefox. Download it from www.mozilla.org.

Other browsers (Internet suites) include Seamonkey, Google Chrome and Flock.

KompoZer

KompoZer is a complete web authoring and editing package which incorporates the familiar features of a WYSIWYG tool (what you see is what you get) that are found in Adobe DreamWeaver and MS FrontPage. It's easy to use and therefore suitable for those that want to create quality web pages without having to master html and scripting languages. Download it from http://kompozer.net.

Other packages include Bluefish, Nvu, Quanta Plus and Cssed.

GIMP

GIMP is a versatile graphics manipulation package that will run on most platforms. Often lauded as the 'free Photoshop' it can be used as a simple paint program, an expert quality photo retouching program, an online batch processing system, a mass production image renderer, an image format converter and more. The advanced scripting interface allows everything from the simplest task to the most complex image manipulation procedures to be easily scripted. Download it from www.gimp.org.

Other packages include Inkscape, Blender, Dia and Paint.net.

Joomla

Joomla is a content management system which can be used to build websites whilst keeping track of all of its content including text, images, photos, music, video and documents. It includes RSS feeds, printable versions of pages, news flashes, blogs, polls, website searching and other features. Download it from www.joomla.org.

Other packages include Alfresco and Drupal.

MOODLE

MOODLE is a well-respected virtual learning environment which is widely used across the globe. It is a tool for creating online learning content for students and is perhaps the most familiar open source product around. Users will rightly claim that it is at least as good if not better than its commercial counterparts. It is the VLE of choice in many educational institutes and has recently been adopted by the Open University too. A number of schools have chosen it as their learning platform. It can be installed on an institute's web server, or hosted by a web hosting company. It is supported by a large community of users and by commercial 'partner' companies which have been formed around the product. Download it from http://moodle.org.

Other packages include Bodington and LAMS.

Xerte

Xerte is a suite of powerful tools for the rapid creation of interactive e-learning content. It is developed by Nottingham University and provides a visual, icon-based authoring environment that allows learning objects to be easily created. Xerte integrates text, graphics, animations, sounds and video, creating simple interactivity in an accessible interface. More complex structures and powerful components can be created by those who are able to write some code. Download it from www.nottingham.ac.uk/xerte.

Other packages include CourseLab and CourseBuilder.

TCExam

TCExam is an open source computer-based assessment (CBA) software system (also known as computer-based testing or e-exam) that enables educators and trainers to author, schedule, deliver and report on surveys, quizzes, tests and exams.

Other packages include Java Inquisition.

Audacity

Audacity is an easy-to-use audio editor and recorder for all operating systems. It is ideal for recording audio, editing and mixing sounds, converting tapes and records into digital recordings or CDs and producing podcasts. Download it from http://audacity.sourceforge.net.

Other packages include Podcast Generator, Juice and EasyPodast.

Mahara

Mahara is an open source e-portfolio system with a flexible display framework. Mahara, meaning 'think' or 'thought' in Te Reo Māori, is a user centred environment with a permissions framework that enables different views of an e-portfolio to be easily managed. Mahara also features a weblog, resume builder and social networking system, connecting users and creating online learner communities. Download it from http://mahara.org.

Other packages include PETAL, OSP, Moofolio and Klahowya.

Elgg

Elgg is an open source, flexible social networking engine, designed to run as a web-based application. It needs PHP, MySQL and Apache to run. Download it from: http://elgg.org.

Other packages include Pligg, NewsCloud, Mugshot, Drupal and AroundMe.

Scratch

Scratch is a new programming language for young people (ages 8 and up) that makes it easy to create their own interactive stories, animations, games, music, and art and share their creations on the web.

As they create and share Scratch projects, young people learn important mathematical and computational ideas, while also learning to think creatively, reason systematically, and work collaboratively. Download it from http://scratch.mit.edu.

Scratch is developed by the Lifelong Kindergarten Group at the MIT Media Lab. See http://scratch.mit.edu.

Other packages include Alice.

Scribus

Scribus is a powerful open source program that helps you create great looking documents of all kinds. Underneath the modern and user friendly interface, Scribus supports publishing features, such as CMYK colour, separations, ICC colour management and versatile PDF creation. Download it from: www.scribus.net.

Thunderbird

Thunderbird is a free, open source and cross-platform mail client for most operating systems including, but not limited to, Windows, Linux and Macintosh. It is based on the Mozilla codebase. It is a robust and easy to use client, similar to competing products like Outlook Express, but with some major advantages such as the best implementations of intelligent spam filters, a built-in spell checker, extension support and much more. Download it from www.mozilla.org.

Other packages include SquirrelMail and Egroupware.

Tuxpaint

Tux Paint is a free drawing program designed for young children (aged 3 and up). It has a simple, easy-to-use interface, fun sound effects, and an encouraging cartoon mascot who helps guide children as they use the program. It provides a blank canvas and a variety of drawing tools to help children to be creative. Download it from: www.tuxpaint.org.

Where to start with open source

To find out what some schools are doing with OSS, visit the Open Source Schools website at http://opensourceschools.org.uk.

Get hold of a copy of the OpenDisc (formerly known as OpenCD) CD-ROM from www.theopendisc.com. It's a collection of free OSS software that runs under Windows. The contents are updated on a regular basis.

For listings and reviews of software try the Centre for Learning and Performance Technologies (C4LPT) www.c4lpt.co.uk/Directory/index.html or the Hot Scripts website www.hotscripts.com.

A search on the Internet for open source software will provide all the information you need. You'll come across other free non-OSS software too and, whilst you should approach them with caution there are many useful products to be found.

Appendix 1
ICT journals

American Journal of Distance Education: www.ajde.com/index.htm

Association for Learning Technology Journal (ALT-J): www.alt.ac.uk/alt_j.html

Australian Journal of Educational Technology: www.ascilite.org.au/ajet/ajet.html

British Journal of Educational Technology: www.wiley.com/bw/journal.asp?ref=0007-1013&site=1

CIT Infobits: http://its.unc.edu/tl/infobits

Cambridge Journal of Education: www.educ.cam.ac.uk/research/cje

Computer Mediated Communication Magazine: www.december.com/cmc/mag

Computers and Education: www.elsevier.com/wps/find/journaldescription.cws_home/347/description#description

Contemporary Issues In Technology and Teacher Education: www.citejournal.org/vol2/iss4/toc.cfm

Distance Education Systemwide Interactive Electronic Newsletter: www.uwex.edu/disted/desien

Early Childhood Research Quarterly: www.sciencedirect.com/science/journal/08852006

Early Childhood Teacher Education: www.informaworld.com/smpp/title~content=t713872612

Early Education: www.early-education.org.uk

Early Years Educator: www.earlyyearseducator.co.uk

Education 3–13: www.tandf.co.uk/journals/titles/03004279.asp

Education and Information Technologies: www.springerlink.com/content/100163/

Education Otherwise: www.education-otherwise.org Alternatives to school education

Educational Computing & Technology: http://ect.downstate.edu

Educational Media International: www.ingentaconnect.com/content/routledg/remi

Educational Research: www.ingentaconnect.com/content/routledg/rere

Educational Review: www.tandf.co.uk/journals/carfax/00131911.html

Educational Technology Review: www.aace.org/pubs/aacej

E-Learning Today: http://purchasing.uk-plc.net

Electronic Journal of E-Learning (EJEL): www.ejel.org

The Information Society: www.indiana.edu/~tisj

Inside Learning Technologies: www.learningtechnologies.co.uk/magazine/articles.cfm

Interact: www.ltss.bris.ac.uk/interact/index.html

Interactions: www2.warwick.ac.uk/services/ldc

Interactive Multimedia Electronic Journal of Computer Enhanced Learning: http://imej.wfu.edu

International Journal of Early Years Education: www.tandf.co.uk/journals/carfax/09669760.html

International Journal of Education and Development using ICT: http://ijedict.dec.uwi.edu

International Journal on E-Learning (IJEL, formerly IJET): www.techknowlogia.org

International Journal of Technologies for the Advancement of Knowledge & Learning: www.techknowlogia. org

International Review of Research in Open & Distance Learning: www.irrodl.org/index.php/irrodl

JIME - Journal of Interactive Media in Education: www-jime.open.ac.uk/index.html

The Journal: www.thejournal.com

The Journal of Asynchronous Learning Networks: www.aln.org/publications/jaln/index.asp

Journal of Computer Assisted Learning www.jcal.info

Journal for Computing in Teacher Education (JCTE) access via http://journalseek.net

Journal of Distance Education: http://cade.athabascau.ca

Journal of Early Childhood Research http://ecr.sagepub.com

Journal of Educational Multimedia and Hypermedia (JEMH): www.aace.org/pubs/jemh/default. htm

Journal of Interactive Learning Research (JILR): www.aace.org/pubs/jilr/default.htm

Journal of Teacher Education: http://jte.sagepub.com

Journal of Online Learning & Teaching: http://jolt.merlot.org

Journal of Technology and Teacher Education: www.aace.org/pubs/jtate

Journal of Technology, Pedagogy and Teacher Education: www.tandf.co.uk/journals/titles/1475939X. asp

The Learning Technology: http://lttf.ieee.org/learn_tech

Literacy Today: www.literacytrust.org.uk/Pubs/literacytoday.html

Not school: www.inclusiontrust.org/notschool

Nursery Education: http://magazines.scholastic.co.uk

Nursery World: www.nurseryworld.co.uk

Practical Pre-School: www.practicalpreschool.com

Special Children: www.inclusive.co.uk/pubs/special.shtml

Teacher Development: www.informaworld.com/smpp/title~content=t716100723

Teaching with Technology Today: www.uwsa.edu/ttt/index.htm

Topics in Early Childhood Special Education: http://tec.sagepub.com

The Web Design Journal: http://thewebdesignjournal.com/

Web Developer's Journal: www.webdevelopersjournal.com/

Appendix 2
Useful ICT websites

This appendix offers some useful web links on a range of ICT issues. The listings have also been included on the Primary ICT website for easy hyperlinking. Be sure to look at the National Curriculum in action, DCSF and DfES Standards sites too.

There is no guarantee that any of these links will remain stable though you can usually find your way from the root of the site if the full path doesn't work.

Curriculum resources and activities

ARKive: www.arkive.org
At School: www.atschool.co.uk
Becta Music: www.mmiweb.org.uk/publications/webprimary/music.pdf
British Association of Advisers and Lecturers in P.E.: www.baalpe.org
BBC Bitesize: www.bbc.co.uk/schools/revisewise
BBC Languages: www.bbc.co.uk/languages
BBC Sport: http://news.bbc.co.uk/sport
BBC: www.bbc.co.uk/schools
BBC: www.bbc.co.uk/education. Maths and spelling games for children aged 4 to 8 years
BEAM: www.beam.co.uk. Free maths resources
Cbeebies: www.bbc.co.uk/cbeebies
Channel 4 Learning: www.4learning.co.uk/
Christianity for Children: http://atschool.eduweb.co.uk/carolrb/Christianity
Count On: www.counton.org
CrickWeb: www.crickweb.co.uk
D & T: www.thelighthouseforeducation.co.uk/designtechnology.htm
DfES Languages Website: www.dfes.gov.uk/languages
Dictionaries: www.dictionary.com, www.yourdictionary.com, www.pdictionary.com
Eco Schools: www.eco-schools.org.uk
E-How Sports and Fitness: www.ehow.com/guide_4-sports-fitness
English Resources: www.edit.legend.yorks.com/eng.html
Enrich: www.nrich.maths.org.uk
Free Resources: www.free-teaching-resources.co.uk/english.shtml

Funbrain: www.funbrain.com

Geo-Primary: www.sln.org.uk/geography/primary.htm

Geography Links: www.geographypages.co.uk/key12.htm

Good Night Stories: www.goodnightstories.com/read.htm

Grammar Card: www.grammarcard.com

Grid Club: www.gridclub.com

Grid Club: www.gridclub.com

History on the Net: www.historyonthenet.com

Holy days and festivals: www.bbc.co.uk/religion/tools/calendar

Hubbard's Cupboard: www.hubbardscupboard.org

ICT Activities: www.buzzin.net/ict/ictgeneral.htm

ICT Games: www.ictgames.com

Institute of Historical Research: www.history.ac.uk

It's Your Goal: www.itsyourgoal.com

Kent Early ICT: www.kented.org.uk/ngfl/earlyict

Knowledge Box www.knowledgebox.com/kbkids.htm

Learn: www.learn.co.uk

Learn ICT: www.learn-ict.org.uk/links/lnx_primary00.asp

Learn Spanish: www.studyspanish.com/travel

Learning Alive: www.eduweb.co.uk

Useful and interesting information for primary and secondary school pupils and their teachers.

Learnwise: www.learnwise.org.uk

Lingu@net Europa: www.linguanet-europa.org/plus/welcome.htm

MathsNet: www.mathsnet.net

MathSphere: www.mathsphere.co.uk

Maths Zone: www.mathszone.co.uk

Modern Foreign Languages Environment: www.ltscotland.org.uk/mfle/c4modernlanguages

My Primary: www.myprimary.co.uk

MyMaths www.mymaths.co.uk

Music-ITE: www.music-ite.org.uk/resources/primary-ite

NAAIDT (D&T): www.naaidt.org.uk/about/guidelines/ict.html

Naace Primary: http://primary.naace.co.uk/activities/index.htm

National Association for Pastoral Care in Education: www.napce.org.uk

Natural England: www.english-nature.org.uk/Science/nature_for_schools/primary.asp

Nuffield Primary History: www.primaryhistory.org

Numeracy Software: www.numeracysoftware.com

Numeracy World: www.numeracyworld.com

Planet Science: www.planet-science.com

Prescot School MFL Resources: www.prescot-school.knowsley.sch.uk/prescot-language/mfl-site/primarySchool/primarySchool.htm

Primary Design & Technology: www.primarydandt.org

Primary Games: www.primarygames.co.uk

Primary Geography: www.geography.org.uk/eyprimary/geographysubjectleaders/resourcesict

Primary Interactive: www.primaryinteractive.co.uk

Primary Resources: www.primaryresources.co.uk

Primary School Science: www.primaryschoolscience.com

Primary Stuff: www.primarystuff.co.uk

Primary Worksheets: www.primaryworksheets.co.uk

RE Exchange Service: http://re-xs.ucsm.ac.uk

Religion: www.ict.oxon-lea.gov.uk/weblinks/prire_main.html

REonline: www.reonline.org.uk

RE Today: www.retoday.org.uk

School Express: www.schoolexpress.com

School History: www.schoolhistory.co.uk/primaryindex.html

SchoolsNet: www.schoolsnet.com

School Train: www.schooltrain.info

School Zone: www.schoolzone.co.uk

Science Clips: www.bbc.co.uk/schools/scienceclips

Science Learning Centres: www.sciencelearningcentres.org.uk

Science made Simple: www.sciencemadesimple.com/index.html

Scratch programming: http://scratch.mit.edu/about

Sebastian Swan stories: www.sebastianswan.org.uk

Shapes of Time: www.shapesoftime.net

Sport England: www.sportengland.org

Teacher Resource Exchange (TRE): http://tre.ngfl.gov.uk

TeacherNet PSHE: www.teachernet.gov.uk/pshe

Teach ICT: www.teach-ict.com

Teaching and Learning Resources: www.teachingandlearningresources.co.uk/funscience.shtml

Teaching Ideas: www.teachingideas.co.uk

Teachingpets: www.teachingpets.co.uk

The Association for Teaching Citizenship: www.teachingcitizenship.org.uk

The Historical Association: www.history.org.uk/resources/resources.html

The Music Land: www.themusicland.co.uk

Time for citizenship: www.timeforcitizenship.org

Time to Teach: www.timetoteach.co.uk

Very Easy Guides: www.veryeasyguides.com/PRIMARY.htm

Video for schools: www.videoforschools.com

WBD: www.worldbookday.com/pages/content/index.asp?PageID=51

World E-Citizens: www.worldecitizens.net

World Religions: www.uri.org/kids/world.htm

Youth Sports Trust: www.youthsporttrust.org

School websites

Buckingham Primary: http://learning.bps.bucks.sch.uk/

Cavendish Primary School: www.cavendishprimary.com

Cloverlea Primary: www.cloverlea.org.uk/61.html

Coxhoe Primary: www.coxhoe.durham.sch.uk

Northwood Primary: www.northwood.org.uk

Northwood Primary: www.northwood.org.uk

Priory Woods: www.priorywoods.middlesbrough.sch.uk

Sir Robert Hitchams Primary: www.hitchams.suffolk.sch.uk

Snaith Primary: www.snaithprimary.eril.net

Woodlands Junior: www.woodlands-junior.kent.sch.uk

Information (including lead bodies)

Ask: www.ajkids.com. Search engine tailored to find child-friendly sites

Association for Citizenship Teaching: www.teachingcitizenship.org.uk

Awesome Library: www.awesomelibrary.org. Over 14,000 librarian-reviewed resources for kids

BBC Parents: www.bbc.co.uk/schools/parents

BESA (British Educational Suppliers Association) www.besa.org.uk

Becta: www.becta.org.uk

Collins Education: www.collinseducation.com

DSCF (formerly DfES): www.dfes.gov.uk

DfES Standards Site: www.standards.dfes.gov.uk

DirectGov: www.direct.gov.uk

For ICT Coordinators: www.ictcoordinator.co.uk

Futurelab: www.futurelab.org.uk

ICT in Education: www.ictineducation.org

Ictopus: www.ictopus.org.uk

ICT Teachers: www.icteachers.co.uk

ICTeachers: www.icteachers.co.uk/teachers/teachers_home.htm

Language Assistant: www.teachingenglish.org.uk/language-assistant

Learning & Teaching Scotland: www.ltscotland.org.uk

Literacy Trust: www.literacytrust.org.uk

Logo programming: http://mckoss.com/logo

My Primary: www.heinemann.co.uk/Primary/Primary.aspx

Naace: www.naace.org

NAPE: www.nape.org.uk

National Association for Primary Education Information available for birth to thirteen years

National Curriculum: http://curriculum.qca.org.uk

OFSTED: www.ofsted.gov.uk

Parent's Centre: www.parents.dfee.gov.uk

Primary ICT: www.primaryict.org.uk
Primary Teacher UK: www.primary-teacher-uk.co.uk
Qualifications and Curriculum Authority (QCA): www.qca.org.uk
Schemes of Work: www.standards.dfes.gov.uk/schemes
SchoolsNet: www.educate.org.uk
Schoolzone: www.schoolzone.co.uk
Talent ICT Training: http://ecs.lewisham.gov.uk/talent
TDA: www.tda.gov.uk
Teach Online: teachvu.vu.msu.edu/public
Teacher's T.V.: www.teachers.tv
TeacherNet: www.teachernet.gov.uk
Teaching Expertise: www.teachingexpertise.com/articles
Teaching Ideas: www.teachingideas.co.uk/ict/contents.htm
Teaching Times: www.teachingtimes.com
TEEM: www.teem.org.uk
The Association for ICT in Education: http://acitt.digitalbrain.com
The Educational Technology Site: www.ictineducation.org
Times Educational Supplement (TES): www.tes.co.uk
Virtual Teacher: www.virtual-teacher.co.uk

Subscription websites

At School: www.atschool.co.uk
Brain POP: www.brainpop.co.uk
Education City: www.educationcity.com
Espresso: www.espresso.co.uk
MyMaths: www.mymaths.co.uk
Oxford Reading Tree: www.oup.com
Primary Zone: www.primary-zone.com
Spark Island: www.sparkisland.com

Interactive whiteboards

Clasus: www.adaptedlearning.com
Hitachi: www.hitachi-education.com
Promethean: www.prometheanworld.com
RM: www.rm.com
SmartTech: www.smarttech.com

Interactive whiteboard resources:

http://cardiffschools.net/~roelmann/whiteboard/smart2.html

www.bgfl.org/bgfl/15.cfm
www.classtools.net
www.crickweb.co.uk
www.edu.dudley.gov.uk/whiteboard
www.easiteach.co.uk
www.active-maths.co.uk/whiteboard/index.html
www.we-learn.com/tz-primary-ict/2006IWBProject.shtml
www.ict.oxon-lea.gov.uk/whiteboards.html
www.interactive-resources.co.uk
www.iwb.org.uk
www.kented.org.uk/ngfl/ict/IWB/general_resources.htm
www.tameside.gov.uk/ttv/education/smart/tutorials
www.topmarks.co.uk/Interactive.aspx
www.wmnet.org.uk/14.cfm

Learning platforms

Assimilate: www.ramesys.com
DB Primary: www.getprimary.com
Digital Brain: http://corporate.digitalbrain.com
Frog Teacher: www.frogteacher.com
Talk 2 Learn: http://com.fronter.info
Kaleidos: www.learningplatform.rm.com
Knowledge Box: http://uk.knowledgebox.com
Kowari: www.kowari.co.uk/index.php
LearnWise: www.learnwise.org.uk/index.htm
MOODLE: http://moodle.org and http://moodle.com
Netmedia: http://website.netmediaeducation.com
Pearson: www.pearsonphoenix.com/
Skillspace: www.sercolearning.com
Studywiz: www.studywiz.com
TALMOS: www.talmos.net
UniServity: www.uniservity.com
Viglen: www.viglen.co.uk

Mobile learning

E-Learning Centre: www.e-learningcentre.co.uk/eclipse/Resources/mlearning.htm
M-Learning: www.m-learning.org/what/what-is-m-learning-.htm

Course authoring tools

Directory of e-learning tools: www.c4lpt.co.uk/Directory/Tools/authoring.html

Podcasting/vidcasting

Audacity: http://audacity.sourceforge.net
Creating Podcasts: www.freemarketingzone.com/rss/create-vodcasts.html
Podium: www.podiumpodcasting.com
Vidcaster: www.vidcaster.net

Social networking

Intuitive Media: www.intuitivemedia.com
Learning Landscape: www.ll4education.co.uk
School Together Now: www.schooltogethernow.com

Video conferencing

BGfL: www.bucksgfl.org.uk/mod/resource/view.php?id=2812
Global Gateway: www.globalgateway.org.uk/default.aspx?page=1607
Global Leap: www.global-leap.com
HGfL: www.thegrid.org.uk/learning/ict/technologies/videoconferencing/
Ja.net: www.webarchive.ja.net/community/schools/vc/
Northwood Primary: www.northwood.org.uk/videoconferencing.htm
SWGfL: www.swgfl.org.uk/services/vc.asp?page=vcstarted
Wakefield Internet Learning Domain: www.gowild.org.uk/CurriculumStandardsAndSupport/
    NationalStrategies/VideoConferencing/default.htm
WSGfL:http://wsgfl.westsussex.gov.uk/ccm/content/school-office/ict-for-children-
    --schools/broadband--isdn/video-conferencing/schools-video-conference-service.
    en?page=9

Regional broadband consortia

Cumbria and Lancashire Education Online (CLEO): www.cleo.net.uk
East of England Broadband Network (E2BN): www.e2bn.org
East Midlands Broadband Consortium (EMBC): www.embc.uk.com
London Grid for Learning (LGfL): http://cms.lgfl.net
North West Learning Grid (NWLG): www.nwlg.org
Northern Grid for Learning, Gateshead: www.portal.northerngrid.org
South East Grid for learning (SEGfL): www.segfl.org.uk
South West Grid for Learning (SWGfL): www.swgfl.org.uk

West Midlands net (Wmnet): www.wmnet.org.uk

Yorkshire and Humber Grid for Learning (YHGfL): www.yhgfl.net

Grids for learning

The National Grid for Learning (NGfL) and the NGfL Scotland, which were formed in 1997/98, have been discontinued since 2006. Their remit has now been subsumed into Becta, Learning & Teaching Scotland and NGfL Cymru. The following grids remain active.

Aberdeen: www.aberdeen-education.org.uk

Birmingham: www.bgfl.org/bgfl

Bridgend: www.bgfl.bridgend.gov.uk

Buckinghamshire: www.bucksgfl.org.uk

Cumbria: www.cumbriagridforlearning.org.uk

Ealing: www.egfl.org.uk

Edinburgh: http://egfl.net

Essex: www.e-gfl.org

Guernsey: www.education.gg

Hertfordshire: www.thegrid.org.uk

Hillingdon: www.hillingdongrid.org

Hull: www.hgfl.org.

Kent: www.kented.org.uk/ngfl

Lancashire: www.lancsngfl.ac.uk

London: http://cms.lgfl.net/web/lgfl/homepage

Middlesbrough: www.mgrid.org.uk

North West: www.nwlg.org

Northern: www.portal.northerngrid.org

Northumberland: http://ngfl.northumberland.gov.uk

South East: www.segfl.org.uk

South West: www.swgfl.org.uk

Thurrock: www.tgfl.org.uk

Torbay: http://tgfl.torbay.gov.uk

Walsall: www.walsallgfl.org.uk

West London: www.westlondongrid.co.uk

West Sussex: http://wsgfl.westsussex.gov.uk/ccm/portal

Yorkshire & Humber: www.yhgfl.net

Special educational needs

General

AbilityNet: www.abilitynet.co.uk. Charity providing advice on adaptive technology

Ace Centre: www.ace-centre.org.uk. Help and support for parents and carers

Adapted Learning: www.adaptedlearning.com. Free sharing of Boardmaker and other resources

Advisory Unit: www.advisory-unit.org.uk. Provides advice, training and technical support for pupils with a range of difficulties

ASBAH: www.asbah.org. Information about spina bifida

Better Living Through Technology: www.bltt.org. Promotes the use of technology to help people with a range of disabilities

British Dyslexia Association: www.bdadyslexia.org.uk

Claro Training: www.clarotraining.com. High quality training for people using educational and assistive software

Communication Matters: www.communicationmatters.org.uk. Charitable organisation concerned with augmentative and alternative communication

DCSF: www.dfes.gov.uk/sen

Equals: www.equals.co.uk. Promotes, shares and reflects best practice in learning and teaching through collaborative working with practitioners and professionals

First School Years: www.firstschoolyears.com/sen

Inclusion http://inclusion.ngfl.gov.uk. Resources to support individual learning needs

Inclusive Technology: www.inclusivetechnology.com. Useful site including free training materials, advice and suppliers of hardware/software

KidNeeds: www.kidneeds.com

Lewisham: http://ecs.lewisham.gov.uk/talent/pricor/sen.html

Literacy Trust: www.literacytrust.org. Literacy intervention for struggling readers

Makaton: www.makaton.org. Communication using signs and symbols

Mencap: www.mencap.org.uk. UK charity for people with a learning disability

Nasen: www.nasen.org.uk. The national association for special educational needs. Nasen is the leading organisation in the UK which aims to promote the education, training, advancement and development of all those with special and additional support needs

National Association for SEN: www.nasen.org.uk

NCTE: www.ncte.ie/SpecialNeedsICT. Advice and resources for teachers

Parents Centre: www.parentscentre.gov.uk/educationandlearning/specialneeds

SEN Bookshop: http://senbooks.co.uk

SEN Magazine: www.senmagazine.co.uk. The journal for special needs

SEN Teacher: www.senteacher.org. Free SEN teaching resources

Special needs and ICT: http://ecs.lewisham.gov.uk/talent/pricor/sen.html

Special needs ideas / resources: www.teachingideas.co.uk/more/specialneeds/contents.htm

TDA Behaviour 4 Learning: www.behaviour4learning.ac.uk

TeacherNet: www.teachernet.gov.uk/wholeschool/sen

Widgit: www.widgit.com

Communication

Afasic: www.afasic.org.uk. Unlocking speech and languages – range of services and information

I Can: www.ican.org.uk. Supports the development of speech, language and communication skills

The Call Centre: http://callcentre.education.ed.ac.uk. Expertise in technology for children who have speech, communication and/or writing difficulties

NHS: www.actwmids.nhs.uk. Access to communication and technology

Phonics for parents: www.phonics4parents.co.uk

Talking Point: www.talkingpoint.org.uk. All the stages of language development

Ebooks: www.ebooks.com. Books in electronic format

Project Gutenberg: www.gutenberg.org. Free e-books

Dyslexia

British Dyslexia Association: www.bdadyslexia.org.uk

Dyslexia: www.dyslexia.com/library/classroom.htm

Dyslexia Action www.dyslexiaaction.org.uk. Services and support for people with dyslexia and literacy difficulties

Dyslexic.com: www.dyslexic.com. Assistive technology website

Graded book list: www.dyslexia-inst.org.uk/graded.htm

Helen Arkell Dyslexia Centre: www.arkellcentre.org.uk. A registered charity helping those with dyslexia SLD

Institute of Child Education & Psychology: www.icepe.eu/dyslexia.html

Word finding difficulties: www.wordfinding.com

Autism

The National Autistic Society: www.nas.org.uk. Help, support and services for autistic individuals and families

AutismConnect: www.autismconnect.org

Behavioural, emotional and social development (BESD)

Adders: www.adders.org. Promotes awareness of ADD/ADHD

ADDinSchool: www.addinschool.com/elementary/socialskills.htm

ADDISS: www.adiss.co.uk. The National Attention Deficit Disorder Information and Support Service

Anti-Bullying Network: www.antibullying.net. Information for parents, pupils and others

Behaviour4Learning: www.behaviour4learning.ac.uk. Research & evidence base informing teacher education

Bullying UK: www.bullying.co.uk. Registered charity offering advice. Includes mobile phone bullying.

DCSF behaviour & attendance site: www.dcsf.gov.uk/behaviourandattendance

Improving Behaviour in Schools (DCSF): www.dcsf.gov.uk/ibis. Information on the DCSF's policies to promote inclusion and learning through positive behaviour.

LD Online: www.ldonline.org .The world's leading website on learning disability and ADHD

NAES: www.naes4besd.org. National Association of School Leaders within the Behavioural, Emotional and Social Difficulties sector (BESD) of Special Educational Needs.

National Behaviour and Attendance Exchange (NBAE):. www.teachernet.gov.uk/wholeschool/behaviour/exchange.The site aims to promote effective communication, provide mutual support and professional enhancement for all who work in the field of behaviour and attendance

National Programme for Specialist Leaders of Behaviour and Attendance (NPSL-BA): http://nationalstrategies.standards.dcsf.gov.uk/npslba.This site provides information for all those who work in the field of behaviour and attendance

Primary National Strategy: www.standards.dfes.gov.uk/primary.The key site for KS1 & KS2 resources and strategies

Social and Emotional Aspects of Learning (SEAL): www.bandapilot.org.uk.The SEAL resource provides a framework for promoting social, emotional and behavioural skills.

TeacherNet Behaviour and Attendance: www.teachernet.gov.uk. Highly focussed & useful materials on effective classroom and behaviour management.

Down's syndrome

Downsed: www.downsed.org/publishing/dsra/numicon. Down Syndrome Education International works around the world to improve education for young people with Down syndrome

Dyscalculia

About Dyscalculia: www.aboutdyscalculia.org

BBC Skillswise: www.bbc.co.uk/skillswise. For information, number fact sheets, work sheets, quizzes and games

Brain: www.brainhe.com/staff/types/dyscalculiatext.html

English as an additional language (EAL)

A4ESL: http://a4esl.org . For ESL activities

BGfL: www.bgfl.org . For lots of learning and teaching resources (go to Community Languages)

British Council – Learn English: www.learnenglish.org.uk . For help, advice and resources

DCSF: www.dcsf.gov.uk . For a range of publications titled 'Access and Engagement in …'. These cover how to teach children with EAL in all curriculum subjects

Discovery Educational Software: www.discoveryeducationalsoftware.co.uk. Free worksheets

English Club: www.englishclub.com/esl-games/index.htm. For ESL games

ESL Cyber Listening Lab: www.esl-lab.com. for EAL listening quizzes

Free Foto: www.freefoto.com/index.jsp. For a massive selection of photos covering general subject matter – free to use for educational purposes

ICT Testbed: www.evaluation.icttestbed.org.uk/learning/research/ primary/interest/eal . For research on EAL and the IWB

I love languages: www.ilovelanguages.com. For a guide to languages on the web

LangPix: www.langpix.com/categories/index.shtml. For many photos of everyday objects – free to use for educational purposes

Little Learner: www.littlelearner.eu/freebies.htm. For Polish and Romanian resources

NALDIC www.naldic.org.uk. National Association for Language development in the curriculum

NGfL Cymru: www.ngfl-cymru.org.uk/1-0-0-0_good_practice/gp-free-web-resources/gp-free-eal.htm. For 100s of free flash cards.

Primary Classroom Resources: www.primaryclassroomresources.co.uk. For general vocabulary support

Puzzles: sites such as www.teach-nology.com, www.puzzlemaker.com and www.bogglesworld. com . Allow you to enter word lists and create your own word searches, word puzzles, and worksheets

QCA: www.qca.org.uk/qca_7334.aspx. For guidance on teaching children with EAL

Sheffield College: weblearn.sheffcol.ac.uk/links/Basic_Education/ EAL/ more2.html. For a range of teacher and pupil resources

Teachers-Direct: www.teachers-direct.co.uk. For lots of SEN resources

Your Dictionary.com: www.yourdictionary.com/languages.html. For on-line dictionaries in 260 languages

Gifted and talented

BrightonOnline: (G&T) www.brightonline.org.uk. G&T resources

CSIE: www.csie.org.uk. Centre for Studies on Inclusive Education

Enrich: www.nrich.maths.org.uk/public/index.php. Problem-solving puzzles for gifted pupils

Mensa: www.mensa.org.uk/brightsparks. British Mensa Ltd (Junior Branch)

NACE www.nace.co.uk. National Association for Able Children in Education

NAGC: www.nagcbritain.org.uk. National Association for Gifted Children.

Simon Tatham: www.chiark.greenend.org.uk/~sgtatham/puzzles. Simon Tatham's portable puzzle collection

Teaching Expertise: www.gifted-and-talented.net. Enrichment activities for gifted and talented

YGT: http://ygt.dcsf.gov.uk/PrimaryPages/Library.aspx. Young, Gifted and Talented

Visual impairment:

RNIB: www.rnib.org.uk. Royal National Institute of Blind people

Sight & Sound: www.sightandsound.co.uk. Solutions for the visually impaired

Hearing impairment

BATOD: www.batod.org.uk. The British Association of Teachers of the Deaf

Dame Hannah & the Magic Carpet: www.damehannah.com. Dame Hannah Rogers Trust provides education, therapy, care and respite for children and young people with profound physical disabilities

Deaf Books – www.deafbooks.co.uk

Hearing Concern – www.hearingconcernlink.org

NDCS: www.ndcs.org.uk. National Deaf Children's Society

RNID – www.rnid.org.uk. Royal National Institute for Deaf People.

Appendix 3
ICT suppliers

SEN = Special educational needs, LP = Learning platform

2Simple www.2simple.com
　　Simple, powerful and creative software
4Mation www.4mation.co.uk
　　Motivating, fun and engaging educational software
Alphasmart (SEN) www.alphasmart.co.uk
　　Specialist notebooks and associated software
Aspex www.aspexsoftware.com
　　Educational software for home and school
Assimilate (LP) www.ramesys.com
　　Integrated IT solutions and managed services
Assistive Technology (SEN) www.assistive.co.uk
Assistiveware (SEN) www.assistiveware.com
　　Access and language products
AVP www.avp.co.uk
　　Supplier of educational resources to schools
Barry Bennett (SEN)
　　Specialist supplier for people with disabilities of all ages.
BESA www.besa.org.uk
　　British Educational Suppliers Association
BETT www.bettshow.com
　　Largest exhibitor of educational and training technology
Black Cat www.blackcatsoftware.com
　　Comprehensive suite of software packages
Blazie (SEN) www.blazie.co.uk
　　Access technology for blind and partially sighted people
Blissymbol Communications (SEN) www.blissymbols.co.uk
　　A system of meaning-based symbols for people with severe difficulties in speaking.
Blooming Kids (SEN) www.bloomingkids.com
　　Teaching software for children with special needs
Blue Hills (SEN) www.bluehills.co.uk
　　Management software for teachers and Local Authorities

Blue Moon (SEN) www.bluemooneducation.co.uk
Curriculum based children's software.
Bluewave Swift www.bluewaveswift.co.uk
The ultimate school improvement planning system
Cambridge Software House (SEN) www.cshsoft.com
Software that motivates and stimulates children of all ages and abilities
Churchill Toby (SEN) www.toby-churchill.com
Communication aids and environmental control
Clasus www.clasus.pt
Computers and interactive whiteboards
Commotion www.commotiongroup.co.uk
High quality educational resources
Cricksoft (SEN) www.cricksoft.com
Award winning educational software (inc. Clicker and ClozePro)
Data Harvest www.data-harvest.co.uk
Award-winning range of data logging and control systems (along with construction sets) for schools and colleges
DB Primary (LP) www.getprimary.com
Learning Platform aimed solely at the primary education sector bringing together the best in the latest learning platform and social network technologies.
DCP Microdevelopments www.dcpmicro.com
Datalogging and control (inc. LogIT)
Deaf Books (SEN) www.deafbooks.co.uk
Educational resources from DEAFSIGN – publishers of the LET'S SIGN Series of BSL materials for adults and children
Deltronics www.deltronics.co.uk
Computer control and datalogging interfaces
Digital Blue: www.digitalblue.org.uk
Cameras, microscopes and other resources
Digital Workshop www.digitalworkshop.co.uk
Multimedia authoring (Opus Pro)
Direct Educational Services www.des-uk-shop.com
Teaching resources for schools
Dolphin (SEN) www.dolphinuk.co.uk
Dedicated to improving the lives of people with vision and print impairments
Don Johnston (SEN) www.donjohnston.com
Technology to maximize the learning of pupils with physical, cognitive, or learning difficulties
Dynavox (SEN) www.dynavoxsys.com
Leading provider of augmentative and alternative communication (AAC) products and services
Economatics www.economatics-education.co.uk
Effective teaching resources across the curriculum

Education City www.educationcity.com/home/en
  Leading subscription website used by over 1.5 million pupils
Enabling Computers (SEN) www.enablingcomputers.com
  A full range of assistive technology suitable for pupils with special needs
Eric International www.ericint.u-net.com
  Books and software for literacy and numeracy
ESP www.espmusic.co.uk/about.html
  A range of music and computer resources
Espresso Education www.espresso.co.uk
  Subscription site offering a massive library of cross-curricular digital resources for use in the
  classroom at Foundation, Key Stage 1 and Key Stage 2
FineReader (SEN) http://finereader.abbyy.com
  Linguistic and artificial intelligence (AI) software
Fisher Marriot Software (SEN) www.fishermarriott.com
  StarSpell, StarFractions, StarStories and more
Flexible Software (SEN) www.flexible.co.uk
  Software programs for primary schools
Force 10 (SEN) www.forcetenco.co.uk
  Specialists in Sensory Loss & Hearing Loop systems
Freedom Scientific (SEN) www.freedomscientific.com
  Solutions for people with visual impairments (inc. JAWS)
Frog Teacher (LP) www.frogteacher.com
  Learning platform
Fronter (LP) http://webfronter.com/fronter3/info
  Learning platform
GL Assessment www.gl-assessment.co.uk
  A range of online assessments
Granada www.granada-learning.com
  The UK's leading provider of educational assessments, online school improvement resources
  and training
Griffin Education www.griffineducation.co.uk
  Supplier of scientific equipment to industry, educational and government
Hagger (SEN) www.hagger.co.uk
  A range of products for visual impairment
Halliday James Ltd (SEN) www.hallidayjames.com
  Cognitive and physical support for those with learning difficulties
Hitachi www.hitachi-education.com
  Interactive whiteboard and other products
Hope Education www.hope-education.co.uk
  Teaching resources for Pre-School, Primary and Secondary schools
Humanware (SEN) www.humanware.com
  Assistive technologies for visually impairment and learning difficulties
iANSYST (SEN) www.iansyst.co.uk
  Technology to help dyslexic people make the most of their abilities

I-Board www.iboard.co.uk

    Resources for interactive whiteboards

IEP Writer (SEN) www.iepwriter.co.uk/iep_writer.htm

    Software for producing Individual Education Plans

Immersive Education www.immersiveeducation.com/primary

    A number of resources including Kar2ouche

Inclusive (SEN) www.inclusive.co.uk

    Popular provider of some of the best special educational needs software

Indigo Learning www.indigolearning.com

    Educational software that is designed to inspire creativity

IntelliTools (SEN) www.intellitools.com

    Provides technology to help struggling students learn to their fullest potential

iTeddy www.iteddy.com

    The cuddly way to watch, learn and play

Kaleidos (LP) www.learningplatform.rm.com

    A learning platform that enables learners to access the resources and support they need, when they need them

Keen 2 Learn www.keen2learn.co.uk

    ICT resources for the whole curriculum

Key Notes www.keynoteseducation.com

    Resources for the whole curriculum

Key Tools (SEN) www.keytools.co.uk

    Helping people to use computers without risking their health

Knowledge Box www.knowledgebox.com/kbkids.htm

    A powerful digital learning system that delivers dynamic, effective, and engaging media to classrooms

Kowari (LP) www.kowari.co.uk/index.php

    An inviting and user friendly learning platform for young children

Kurtzweil (SEN) www.kurzweiledu.com

    Complete reading, writing, and study solutions

LD Online (SEN) www.ldonline.org

    The world's leading website on learning disability and ADHD

Leap Frog www.leapfrog.co.uk

    Innovative, technology-based educational products

Learn 2 Soar www.learn2soar.co.uk

    Helping children to soar to new heights of musical excellence

Lexion (SEN) www.lexion.co.uk

    A computer-based system for stimulating and training people with language related learning disorders, dyslexia, or aphasia

Liberator (SEN) www.liberator.co.uk

    A wide range of products, training and support for communication, inclusion and independence

Listening books (SEN) www.listening-books.org.uk

    The national listening library

Logotron www.logo.com
> A leading supplier of educational software to schools (in partnership with Rickitt Educational Media)

Lucid Research (SEN) www.lucid-research.com
> Software for SEN assessment and training

Maltron PDC (SEN) www.maltron.com
> Helping people to overcome disability and injury by enabling keyboard access to computers

Mayer-Johnson (SEN) www.mayer-johnson.com
> Enhancing learning and human expression for individuals with special needs through symbol-based products, training and services

Microlink Education (SEN) www.microlinkpceducation.com
> Technology and information to help with learning difficulties

Mike Ayres (SEN) www.mikeayresdesign.co.uk

MOODLE (LP) http://moodle.org   http://moodle.com
> Moodle is a free (open source) Course Management System (CMS), also known as a Learning Management System (LMS) or a Virtual Learning Environment (VLE) for creating effective online learning sites

Mouse Trial (SEN) www.mousetrial.com
> Fun animated online exercises to help kids with autism

My Reading Coach (SEN) www.mindcorp.ie
> Teaches struggling students to read. It is the only reading program that provides a virtual reading specialist and speech pathologist for every learner

Netmedia (LP) http://website.netmediaeducation.com
> A leading provider of Learning Platform and LA Portal, e-democracy and CPD applications and a Becta accredited 'Learning Platform Services Framework Supplier'

Netop www.netop.com
> Software solutions that enable swift, secure and seamless transfer of screens, sound and data between two or more computers

NVDA (SEN) www.nvda-project.org
> NonVisual Desktop Access (NVDA) is a free and open source screen reader for the Microsoft Windows operating system

OGCbuying.solutions http://online.ogcbuyingsolutions.gov.uk
> An Executive Agency of the Office of Government Commerce (OGC) providing a professional procurement service to the public sector to enable organisations to deliver improved value for money in their commercial activities (linked with Becta's new framework for software suppliers, launched in October 2008)

Optelec (SEN) www.optelec.co.uk
> Specialising in award-winning solutions for people with a visual impairment

Optima low vision services (SEN) www.optimalowvision.co.uk
> The premier distributor of low vision Aids in the UK

Orb Education www.orbeducation.co.uk
> A variety of digital teaching resources

Oxford Primary www.oup.com/uk/primary
> Literacy and Numeracy resources to help implement the National Literacy Framework

Oxford Reading Tree www.oup.com

Resources and subscription website.

Pearson Digital Learning www.pearsonschool.com

Technology products, solutions and support (inc. SuccessMaker)

Penfriend (SEN) www.penfriend.ltd.uk

A comprehensive literacy aid which can boost confidence and increase reading and writing skills across the age and ability range for those with dyslexia, physical disabilities, visual impairment and anyone learning another language

Philip Harris www.philipharris.co.uk

A large range of resources to make science lessons as engaging and productive as possible

Phrogram: http://phrogram.com

Programming for children

Possum (SEN) www.possum.co.uk

A range of products to enhance the independence and quality of life for people with special needs

Professional Vision Services www.professional-vision-services.co.uk

A range of visual aids

Promethean (IWB) www.prometheanworld.com

One of the leading interactive whiteboards plus associated resources

QED 2000 (SEN) www.qedltd.com

A large range of innovative products for people with special needs

Raising Horizons (SEN) www.raisinghorizons.com

Develops training materials to assist people with learning disabilities

Readplease (SEN) www.readplease.com

Award-winning text-to-speech software for Windows based operating systems

REM Rickett Educational Media (SEN) www.r-e-m.co.uk

A well established company offering resources and services

Resource (SEN) www.resourcekt.co.uk

Software resources across the curriculum and key stages

RM www.rm.com

Wide range of popular ICT resources plus the RM Classboard interactive whiteboard

Schoolzone www.schoolzone.co.uk/evaluations

Evaluation of educational multimedia

ScienceScope www.sciencescope.co.uk

Sensing and Datalogging for Science Education

ScreenReader (SEN) www.screenreader.co.uk

Assistive technology for blind, visually impaired and those who find reading a challenge

SEMERC www.semerc.com

Focusing on the use of ICT in SEN

Sensory Company (SEN) www.thesensorycompany.co.uk

A wide range of sensory products

Sensory Software (SEN) www.sensorysoftware.com

Creating software solutions to help disabled people do things that everyone else takes for granted.

Sensory Technology (SEN) www.senteq.co.uk
Design, manufacture, sales and installation of products and systems for the multi-sensory market

Serotec (SEN) www.serotek.com
Accessibility products that help those who are blind or low vision to get the most out of any computer.

Sherston Software www.sherston.com
The UK's leading provider of educational software for primary schools, with titles covering every part of the curriculum

Sight & Sound (SEN) www.sightandsound.co.uk
Solutions for the blind, visually impaired and those with reading difficulty

Silver Surfers www.silversurfers.net/education-schoolsoftware.html
Links to software suppliers

Sirius www.siriusit.co.uk
Provider of free and open source software services to schools

Skillspace (LP) www.sercolearning.com
Learning platform for schools

Smartkids www.smartkids2.co.uk/ukshop
Multi-sensory resources to engage children and encourage them to learn

Smarttech (IWB) www.smarttech.com
Producers of the Smartboard and related products

Software Express (SEN) www.softwareexpress.co.uk
Specialising in providing user-friendly software solutions

Soundbeam (SEN) www.soundbeam.co.uk
For special needs and music therapy

Soundlinks (SEN) www.soundlinks.com
Audio production, music Technology, and the use of speech and Braille in all aspects of work, study and leisure

SpaceKraft (SEN) www.spacekraft.co.uk
Wide range of multisensory equipment

Spark Space (SEN) www.spark-space.com
Idea mapping technology for education and business

Studywiz (LP) www.studywiz.com
Learning environment for schools

Synapse (SEN) www.synapseadaptive.com/edmark
Synapse provides integrated turn-key access solutions that empower individuals with disabilities

TAG (SEN) www.taglearning.com
Educational software for schools

TALMOS (LP) www.talmos.net
A highly scalable learning platform based on Microsoft SharePoint

Teachable www.teachable.net
Teaching resources

Teach IT Primary www.teachitprimary.co.uk
   Online library of learning resources
Techready (SEN) www.techready.co.uk
   Assistive technology products
Team Asperger's (SEN) www.ccoder.com/GainingFace
   Software to help people with Asperger's syndrome
Technology Teaching Systems (TTS) www.tts-shopping.com
   High quality educational resources for schools and parents across the UK
Teem www.teem.org.uk
   Teachers Evaluating Educational Multimedia
TextEase www.textease.com
   Innovative and creative software applications for education
TextHelp (SEN) www.texthelp.com
   Worldwide leader of literacy software solutions
The Keyboard Company (SEN) www.keyboardco.com
   Keyboard and mouse specialists in the UK
Thomson Software Solutions www.thomson-software-solutions.com
   Leading supplier of software for vision testing and screening in the UK
Tiny Hands (SEN) www.tiny-hands.co.uk
   A range of ergonomic computer peripherals and software designed to minimise RSI in
   children
Topologika www.topologika.co.uk
   Value-for-money educational computer software
UniServity (LP) www.uniservity.com
   A learning platform providing learners with social learning tools
Valiant Technology www.valiant-technology.com
   Educational products which help children to fulfil their potential
Viglen (LP) www.viglen.co.uk
   Total ICT teaching and learning solutions, from the supply of a single PC or notebook right
   through to the implementation of a local or wide area network
Visual Learning for Life (SEN)   www.skillsforlearning.net
   Stimulating visual perceptual skills
White Space (SEN) www.wordshark.co.uk
   Literacy and numeracy software especially suitable for dyslexics
Widgit (SEN) www.widgit.com
   Symbol based software
Worksheet Factory (SEN) www.worksheetfactory.com
   Printable Worksheets, Activities, and Tests for the Differentiated Classroom
Xavier Education Software (SEN) http://xavier.bangor.ac.uk/xavier
   Specialists in teaching aids for English language, early learning and dyslexia

Appendix 4
Evaluation sheets

Software evaluation sheet

Software Title: _____

Supplier: _____

Summary of resource: give a brief overview of how the resource works and the things it can do.

National Curriculum: what curriculum area/topic does it cover; can it help to satisfy the specific curriculum aims and objectives which you might include in your lesson plans?

Content: is information accurate and factual; is there any unnecessary cultural or moral bias; is the content acceptable in terms of the quantity and the balance of text, images and sound?

Currency: is it up to date; is it the most recent version available; when was it published?

Reading age: is vocabulary, structure and sentence length suitable for the intended age range; does it have a built-in dictionary; are there differentiated versions of text, is text supported with images or audio?

User interface: is it easy for the user to interact with the software; is it clear what to press or click; is there any on-screen help available; what is the quality of illustrations; can you alter colours and sizes of text or images?

Indexing: is there a menu or table of contents; is there an index; is it easy to navigate; is the program easy to enter and exit?

Presentation: is the information structured in a logical order; is it visually stimulating?

Facilities: is the software easy to install with clear instructions; are there print/save options; is there a bookmark facility; does the package keep records of a child's progress; are there any additional motivating features (e.g. hidden cues)?

Differentiation: are different levels/options available for use with children with different abilities; does the software automatically adjust to the level of the child or does an adult have to alter the settings; how easy is it to alter the settings; does it support SEN?

Assessment: Does it have built-in assessment instruments?

Diversity: Does it enable creativity, collaboration and flexibility; can it be used in more than one topic area?

Any other comments:

Hardware evaluation sheet

Hardware Title: _____

Supplier: _____

Summary of resource: give a brief overview of how the resource works and the things it can do.
National Curriculum: what curriculum area/topics does it potentially cover; can it help to satisfy the specific curriculum aims and objectives which you might include in some of your lesson plans?
Currency: is it the most up-to-date version; is it a contemporary resource?
Reading age: is vocabulary, structure and sentence length of supporting children's materials suitable for the intended age range/ability of the child?
User interface: is it easy for the user (teacher and children) to use the resource; are there any instructions; are these comprehensive?

Visual effect: does the appearance of the resource provide motivation/stimulation?

Differentiation: are different levels/options available for use with children with different abilities and SEN?

Assessment: does it have built-in assessment instruments?

Diversity: does it enable creativity, collaboration and flexibility; can it be used in more than one topic area?

Any other comments:

Website evaluation sheet

Name of website (include address) _____

Activity: _____

Summary of website: give a brief overview of what the website provides.

National Curriculum: what curriculum area/topic does it cover; can it help to satisfy the specific curriculum aims and objectives which you might include in your lesson plans?

Content: is information accurate and factual; is there any unnecessary cultural or moral bias; is the content acceptable in terms of the quantity and the balance of text, images and sound?

Currency: is it up to date; is it the most recent version available; when was it published?

Reading age: is vocabulary, structure and sentence length suitable for the intended age range; does it have a built-in dictionary; are there differentiated versions of text; is text supported with images or audio?

Differentiation: are different levels/options available for use with children with different abilities; does the software automatically adjust to the level of the child or does an adult have to alter the settings; how easy is it to alter the settings; does it support SEN?

Assessment: does it have built-in assessment instruments?

Indexing: is there a menu or table of contents; is it easy to navigate; are there useful hyperlinks?

Presentation: is the information structured in a logical order; is it visually stimulating; is good use made of web page layout; are frames used effectively?

Authority: reputation of publisher; author's identity, qualifications; source.

Stability: how often does web page content change; will the site still be there next week?

Any other comments

References

Armstrong, A. and Casement, C. (2002) *The Child and the Machine: How Computers Put Our Children's Education at Risk,* Roundhouse Publishing.

Ballard, M. (2008) 'Open source trumps Microsoft in UK schools' available on the Internet at www.theinquirer.net/inquirer/news/460/1035460/open-source-trumps-microsoft-uk [accessed 15/2/09].

Becta (2003) *Managing Special Needs: Recording and Reporting using ICT,* Publication No. 08/2003-04/043/a/PC/5K, Becta.

Becta (2004) 'What the research says about ICT and classroom organisation in schools' available on the Internet at www.becta.org.uk [accessed 22/11/08].

Becta (2007a) *Harnessing Technology Delivery Plan,* Becta.

Becta (2007b) 'Implementing a personal online learning space' available on the Internet at http://schools.becta.org.uk/index.php?section=lv&catcode=ss_lv_lp_03&rid=14413 [accessed 10/11/08].

Becta (2007c) 'Learning platform services framework supplier's available on the Internet at http://localauthorities.becta.org.uk/index.php?section=pf&catcode=ls_pict_06&rid=13139 [accessed 10/11/08].

Becta (2007d) 'Computer games in education project' available on the Internet at http://partners.becta.org.uk/index.php? section=rh&catcode=&rid=13588&pagenum=1&NextStart=1 [accessed 25/11/08].

Becta (2007e) 'Speech and language difficulties and ICT' available on the Internet at http://schools.becta.org.uk/index.php? section= tl&catcode=ss_tl_inc_ac_03&rid=1856 [accessed 14/12/08].

Becta (2007f) *Quality principles for digital learning resources,* Publication No. 03/DD07-07/201/MP/1.5k, Becta

Becta (2008a) 'What the research says about using ICT in Modern Foreign Languages' available on the Internet at http://partners.becta.org.uk/upload-dir/downloads/page_documents/research/wtrs_mfl.pdf [accessed 24/5/08].

Becta (2008b) 'The DCSF primary schools whiteboard expansion project' available on the Internet at http://schools.becta.org.uk/index.php?section=lv&catcode=ss_lv_saf_hs_03&offset=5&rows=5&orderby=1 [accessed 21/11/08].

Becta (2008c) 'Health and safety' available on the Internet at http://schools.becta.org.uk/index.php?section=lv&catcode=ss_lv_saf_hs_03&offset=5&rows=5&orderby=1 [accessed 01/11/08].

Becta (2008d) 'Infrastructure available' on the Internet at http://schools.becta.org.uk/index.php?section=re&catcode=ss_res_pro_bps_inf_04 [accessed 24/11/08].

Becta (2008e) 'What is the self-review framework? A guide for school leaders' available on the Internet at www.becta.org.uk/schools/selfreview [accessed 1/12/08].

Becta (2008f) 'How to purchase [ICT resources]' available on the Internet at http://schools.becta.org.uk/index.php?section=re&catcode= ss_res_ pro_bps_03 [accessed 28/1/09].

Becta (2008g) 'Microsoft software licensing 'available on the Internet at http://schools.becta.org.uk/index.php?section=re&catcode=ss_res_ pro_bps_sof_04&rid=15696 [accessed 14/2/09].

Becta (2008h) *Harnessing Technology Review 2008,* Publication 10/08-09/351/TT/15888/2k, Becta.

Becta (2008i) *Safeguarding Children Online,* Publication 01/DD07-08/150/BX/5k., Becta

Bhat, D. (2006) 'More than half of all 10-year-olds have own mobile', *The Times,* 19 Spetember 2006.

Biggs, J. (1999) *Teaching for Quality Learning at University,* Open University Press.

Boxer, S (2008) 'Video games: Lessons for a gaming generation' available on the Internet at www.telegraph.co.uk/scienceandtechnology/3357172/Video-games-Lessons-for-a-gaming-generation.html [accessed 15/11/08].

Brown-Martin, G. (2008) 'Home access – who benefits?' available from the Internet at www.handheldlearning.co.uk/content/view/57 [accessed 4/11/08].

Brunton, P. and Thornton, L. (2005) *Understanding the Reggio Approach,* David Fulton.

Cairns, G. (2008) 'Brain boxes: How digital technology can improve maths scores' available from the Internet at www.independent.co.uk/news/education/schools/brain-boxes-how-digital-technology-can-improve-maths-scores-993741.html [accessed 24/11/08].

Clements, R. and Fiorentina, L. (2004) *The Child's Right to Play,* Greenwood Press.

Cunliffe, D. and Elliot, G. (2003) *Multimedia Computing,* Learning Matters Ltd.

DCSF (2008a) 'The uses of a digital camera' available from the Internet at www.standards.dfes.gov.uk/primary/features/inclusion [accessed 12/4/08].

DCSF (2008b) 'Play' available from the Internet at www.dcsf.gov.uk/play [accessed 19/1/09].

DCSF (2008c) 'Special educational needs and disability' available from the Internet at www.teachernet.gov.uk/wholeschool/sen/[accessed 17/12/08].

DCSF (2008d) *What works in improving the educational achievement of gifted and talented pupils?,* DCSF-EPPI-04-08, DCSF.

DfES (2001) *Special Educational Needs Code of Practice,* DfES/581/2001, DfES.

DfES (2004) *Learning and Teaching using ICT: Example materials from foundation stage to Year 6,* CDROM box set, DfES 0315-2004 G, DfES.

DfES (2005) 'Learning platforms: primary' available from the Internet at http://publications.teachernet.gov.uk/eOrderingDownload/2101-2005.pdf [accessed 11/11/08].

DfES (2006) 'Independent review of the teaching of early reading' available from the Internet at www.thrass.co.uk/downloadsdocs13.htm [accessed 18/3/08].

DfES (2008) 'The Primary National Strategy' available from the Internet at www.standards. dfes.gov.uk/primary/[accessed 18/3/08].

DfES Standards (2008) 'Primary framework for literacy and mathematics' available from the Internet at www.standards.dfes.gov.uk/primaryframeworks [accessed 18/5/08].

Drake (2002) 'ICT in role play: Check it out!', *Nursery World*, 12 November 2002.

Education Business (2008) 'Mobile learners, not mobile learning' available from the Internet at www.educationbusinessuk.net/index.php?option=com_content&task=view&id=336&Itemid=10 [accessed 1/1/09].

ELSPA (2006) 'Unlimited learning: Computer and video games in the learning landscape' available from the Internet at www.elspa.com/assets/files/u/unlimitedlearningtheroleofcomputer andvideogamesint_344.pdf [accessed 25/11/08].

Garagouni-Areou, F. and Solomonidou, C. (2004). 'Towards the design of educational environments suitable to the needs of pupils with attention deficit hyperactivity disorder (ADHD) symptoms' in L. Cantoni and C. McLoughlin (eds), *Proceedings of World Conference on Educational Multimedia, Hypermedia and Telecommunications 2004* (pp. 4446-4451), AACE.

Garrison, D. R. and Anderson, T. (2003) *E-Learning in the 21st Century: A Framework for Research and Practice*. RoutledgeFalmer.

Gates, B. (2002) 'Keep taking the tablets', *The Guardian,* 26 September 2002.

Gonzalez-Barahona, J. (2000) 'Advantages of open source software' available from the Internet at http://eu.conecta.it/paper/Advantages_ open_source_soft.html and accompanying bibliography at http://eu.conecta.it/paper/Bibliography.html#stallman:why-software-not-owners:98 [accessed 14/2/09].

GTC (2006) 'To boldly go: Reaching out in Braintree' available from the Internet at www.gtce.org.uk/gtcpublications/gtcmagazine _summer2006/toboldlygo2/[accessed 1/11/08].

HGfL (2008) 'Visualisers' available from the Internet at www.thegrid.org.uk/learning/ict/technologies/visualiser/index.shtml [accessed 8/12/08].

Fiveash, K. (2008) 'Choose life, choose open standards' available from the Internet at www.theregister.co.uk/2008/09/23/becta_open_ source_schools_at_last [accessed 25/4/08].

Intuitive media (2009) 'Safe social learning networks for children' available from the Internet at www.intuitivemedia.com/ec.html [accessed 3/3/09].

Learning and Teaching Scotland (2008) 'Science lessons come alive' available from the Internet at www.ltscotland.org.uk/connected/articles/11/ictinpractice/theredplanet/ictandscience.asp [accessed 25/4/08].

Leask, M. and Meadows, J. (2000) *Teaching and Learning with ICT in the Primary School* Routledge Falmer.

LL4S (2009) 'E-safe social networking for schools' available from the Internet at www.ll4education.co.uk/[accessed 3/4/09].

Meadows, J. (2004) *Science and ICT in the Primary School,* David Fulton.

McLeish, J. (2008) 'Virtual boost for literacy skills' *Times Education Supplement,* 25 April 2008.

Milton, J. (2002) 'Languages, technology and learning' available on the internet at www. nestafuturelab.org/research/reviews/lang01.htm [accessed 25/5/08].

Montessori, M. (2007) *The Montessori Method,* BN Publishing.

National Autistic Society (2006) 'Computers: applications for people' with autism available from the Internet at www.nas.org.uk [accessed 29/12/08].

Nesta Futurelab (2004) 'Literature review in games and learning' available from the Internet at www.nestafuturelab.org/research/reviews/08_01.htm [accessed 13/03/06].

Next Generation Learning (2009) 'Learning platforms' available from the Internet at www. nextgenerationlearning.org.uk/en/Technology/Most-common-technologies/Learning-platforms-/[accessed 13/11/08].

NHS (2007) 'Autistic spectrum disorder' available from the Internet at www.nhs.uk/ Conditions/Autistic-spectrum-disorder/Pages/Introduction.aspx?url=Pages/What-is-it. aspx&r=1&rtitle=Autistic+ spectrum+disorder+-+Introduction [accessed 13/11/08].

Niace (2006) 'DigitalsStorytelling for EAL pupils' available from the Internet at http://archive. basic-skills.co.uk/sharingpractice/detail.php?SharingPracticeID=909846606 [accessed 20/1/09].

Nightingale, J. (2008) 'Alternative social networking: Overprotection or necessary control?' *The Guardian*, 6 May 2008.

Northwood (2008) 'Video conferencing' available on the Internet at www.northwood.org.uk [accessed 17/11/08].

OFSTED (2002)' ICT in schools: Effect of government initiatives' available on the Internet at www.ofsted.gov.uk/publications/docs/19.pdf [accessed 7/12/08].

OFSTED (2004) 'ICT in schools 2004: The impact of government initiatives five years on' available from the Internet at/www.ofsted.gov.uk/publications/index.cfm?fuseaction=pubs. displayfile&id =3652&type=pdf [accessed 25/11/08].

Passey, D., Rogers, C., Machell, J., and McHugh, G. (2004) 'The motivational effect of ICT on pupils: DfES Report No. RR523' available on the Internet at www.dfes.gov.uk/research/ data/uploadfiles/RR523new.pdf [accessed 1/11/08].

Pelgrum, W. .J. (2001) 'Obstacles to the integration of ICT in education: results from a worldwide educational assessment', *Computers and Education*, 37: 163-7).

Podium (2008) 'What is podcasting?' available on the Internet at www.podiumpodcasting. com/whatispodcasting/index.html [accessed 16/11/08].

Prashing, B. (2006) *Learning Styles in Action,* Network Continuum.

Prensky, M. (2005) 'What can you learn from a cell phone? Almost anything!' *Journal of Online Education* 1(5): 1.

QCA (2008a) 'National Curriculum for England' available from the Internet at http:// curriculum.qcda.gov.uk/key-stages-1-and-2/subjects/ict/keystage1/index.aspx?return=/ key-stages-1-and-2/subjects/index.aspx [accessed 11/11/08].

QCA (2008b) 'General teaching requirements: Use of ICT' available from the Internet at http://curriculum.qca.org.uk/key-stages-1-and-2/general-teaching-requirements/index. aspx [accessed 2/12/08].

QCA (2008c) 'ICT in subject teaching: Generic skills' available from the Internet at http://curriculum.qca.org.uk/key-stages-1-and-2/learning-across-the-curriculum/ictinsubjectteaching/ictinscience/index.aspx [accessed 9/12/08].

QCA (2008d) 'Identifying gifted pupils' available from the Internet at www.qca.org.uk/qca_2220.aspx [accessed 21/1/09].

QIA (2008) 'Mobile learning' available from the Internet at excellence.qia.org.uk/page.aspx?o=ferl.aclearn.page.id958 [accessed 31/10/08].

RNIB (2008) 'Using a computer without vision' available from the Internet at www.rnib.org.uk/xpedio/groups/public/documents/PublicWebsite/public_withoutvisinfosheet.hcsp [accessed 5/1/09].

Rose, J. (2008) 'The Independent Review of the Primary Curriculum' available from the Internet at http://publications.teachernet.gov.uk [accessed 23/2/09].

Rudd, A. and Tyldesley, A. (2006) *Literacy and ICT in the Primary School: A Creative Approach to English,* David Fulton.

Southwest Grid for Learning (2008) 'Learning platforms' available from the Internet at www.swgfl.org.uk/services/learning_platformshome.asp?page=schoolht_overview [accessed 11/11/08].

Sparrowhawk, A. and Heald, Y. (2007) *How to Use ICT to Support Children with Special Educational Needs,* LDA.

Stallman, R. (2009) 'Why software should not have owners' available from the Internet at www.gnu.org/philosophy/why-free.html [accessed 14/2/09].

TeacherNet (2008) 'Computer projectors — advice from the HSE' available from the Internet at www.teachernet.gov.uk [accessed 31/10/08].

TEEM (2008) '2 Simple Music Toolkit evaluation' available from the Internet at www.teem.org.uk/1823/classroom2471.html [accessed 19/5/08].

Vygotsky, L.S. (1978) *Mind in Society: Development of Psychological Processes,* Harvard University Press.

Wheeler, D. (2007) 'Why open source software' available from the Internet at www.dwheeler.com/oss_fs_why.html [accessed 11/2/09].

Williams, J., Clegg, P. and Dulaney, E. (2005) 'The advantages of adopting open source software' available from the Internet at www.informit.com/articles/article.aspx?p=376255 [accessed 14/2/09].

Wright, J. (2007) *The Primary ICT and E-Learning Co-ordinator's Manual,* Paul Chapman Publishing.

Index